GIVE A

GIRL

A KNIFE

ALSO BY AMY THIELEN

The New Midwestern Table

GIVE A GIRL A KNIFE

a memoir

AMY THIELEN

CLARKSON POTTER/PUBLISHERS
NEW YORK

Published in the United States by Clarkson Potter/Publishers, an imprint of the Crown
Publishing Group, a division of Penguin Random House LLC, New York.
crownpublishing.com
clarksonpotter.com

CLARKSON POTTER is a trademark and POTTER with colophon is a registered trademark
of Penguin Random House LLC.

Library of Congress Cataloging-in-Publication Data
Names: Thielen, Amy, author.
Title: Give a girl a knife : a memoir / Amy Thielen.
Description: First edition. | New York : Clarkson Potter/Publishers, 2017 |
Includes bibliographical references and index. | Description based on print version
record and CIP data provided by publisher; resource not viewed.
Identifiers: LCCN 2016054943 (print) | LCCN 2016044399 (ebook) |
ISBN 9780307954930 (ebook) | ISBN 9780307954909 (hardcover)
Subjects: LCSH: Thielen, Amy. | Cooks—New York (State)—New York—Biography. |
Cooking, American—Midwestern style.
Classification: LCC TX649.T46 (print) | LCC TX649.T46 A3 2017 (ebook) |
DDC 641.5092 [B]—dc23
LC record available at https://lccn.loc.gov/2016054943.

ISBN 978-0-307-95490-9
Ebook ISBN 978-0-307-95493-0

Printed in the United States of America

Book and cover design by Jen Wang

10 9 8 7 6 5 4 3 2 1

First Edition

For Aaron

CONTENTS

III

IV

PROLOGUE

"Everything takes five minutes."

This was the first decree of my line cooking career, and it made no sense.

My eyes flicked fearfully to the industrial clock hanging on the wall; I was too scared to look at it and too scared not to. On this night, my first working the hot line at Danube after three months' purgatory on the salad station, I knew that the chef was going to yell at me—but I didn't yet understand how the clock, its minute hand lurching toward the dinner hour, would be the one to kick my ass.

I'd shown up an hour early, but T1, one of two Austrian sous chefs named Thomas in our kitchen, was already prepping my station, presiding over three wide-bottomed pots on the steel flat-top stove, two filled with violently boiling water, the other with a hissing swarm of sliced shallots turning from gold to bronze. He stood in front of a cutting board popping the cores out of halved mature carrots with a long knife. Wedging the butt of his slicer into the faint line between flesh and core, he torqued for pressure and ejected each light orange center with a *pop*, leaving behind a smooth carrot canoe. This operation he performed without looking down, as if he were shelling peas.

As I hustled to set up my cutting board next to his, I asked him, in my not-very-Minnesota-nice blunt way that actually sort of works in professional kitchens, where speed is of the essence: "Don't some things take longer than that? Like making risotto?"

Ti held his knife loosely and dully replied, "Risotto isn't the only thing you're making," then pointed his blade toward the pots on the stove. As if to demonstrate the heroic number of tasks that he could fit into a mere five minutes, he hooked a spoon head into the handle of the pot of caramelizing shallots and jerked it to the cool edge of the stove, did the same to his sauteuse of red wine syrup, its center erupting magenta bubbles, and had already turned back to the industrial blender of parsley water, now jet-washing the canister in violent green, before he repeated: "Everything takes five minutes."

So apparently time was not time, and that subject was closed.

Before I knew it, while I'd been mincing shallots and herbs, Ti had stocked my vegetable entremet station and I slid—fully prepped but not in any way prepared—into my first dinner service on the hot line. We cooks on the meat side stood shoulder to shoulder like soldiers in formation, facing a mirror image of fish-side cooks across the hot double-sided flat-top. The Austrian chef de cuisine—Generalissimo Mario Lohninger, Chef David Bouley's chief henchman—assumed his position at the head of the flat-top, at the white-cloth-draped area known as the pass. There he stood waiting for finished plates to land for his inspection before handing them off to the food runners, who would steer them high overhead, like spaceships, to their proper tables. And then it was on.

Firing Table 16! Two cheese ravioli—one gröstl—and one skate! Followed by two venison—a dorade—and a squab!

The two cheese rav was me, as well as the garnish for the gröstl, the Austrian term for the mixed bag of leftovers Tyrolean grandmothers might fry up in a cast-iron pan for skiers returning home from the mountain, otherwise known as hash. Our gröstl was made with a lobster claw, a pad of seared foie gras, and some tissue-thin veal tortellini—you know, just some scraps from the kitchen. The cook to my left flung the lobster and the foie gras on a metal sizzle plate in my direction like a bartender slides a beer down the bar. I dropped a circle of red wine reduction on a white plate, topped it with the foie, the lobster, and then three veal tortellini. I crowned the lobster with a frothy head of milky green-pea foam, its bubbles rapidly winking shut one by one, and then turned around to whip up a small pot of corn sauce for my cheese ravioli.

"*Soigné!*" Mario snapped, calling for perfection in French—the universal language of European kitchens—tapping his finger on the rim of my ravioli plate. My eyes followed his finger. Five ravioli in a row, but the triangle points weren't lining up. One was upside down. I flipped it over.

"Oh, *bueno!*" he mocked in the kitchen Spanish he was picking up in New York. "Corn sauce, Ahmy! *On y va,*" he urged. "The skate is dying here for your *käise* ravioli."

As the chaos of the nighttime dinner kitchen mounted—the wall of sound increasing, the space between whirling cooks decreasing, the hot liquids seething, the cavalcade of tiny copper pots being chucked into the dirty bin in a crescendo of clunks—I located a weird stillness in myself. As the intensity tightened, the more my inner reverb began to hum.

Visually, it was a swarm. The portions were small, the tasting menus were long, and the plates were Technicolor. There was glowing red-beet-and-wine-soaked pasta. Neon-pink watermelon juice. Spinach puree the color of artificial turf. The night was an endless parade of bright sauces and shapes—blots and foamy peaks and swirled commas—accompanied by the fervent clacking of fine porcelain.

Before long, my vision became so nearsighted that I could barely see beyond the rim of the plate in front of me. The parts of dishes for which I was responsible began to look like familiar characters: floppy half-wilted leaves of spinach standing up on two legs before falling into corn sauce; tufts of horseradish cream swirling in cumulus patterns into rusty swaths of short rib jus; marble-size bone-marrow dumplings topped with fleecy tan beanies of buttery bread crumbs.

The cooks blindly moved copper pots around on the flat-top as smoothly as professional card sharks. Their movements looked at first to be haphazard but turned out to be as precise as animal instinct. Cooking here was all about caramelized edges and pooling juices and delicious pan-smudge and spoon-spit—that moment when you're plating and a final droplet of sauce falls at the last possible second onto an otherwise pristine plate, when the thing is so damned beautiful that the spoon itself looks to be drooling.

It was a mad world, but I got it. The food at the center of the plate was protected from the tumult of the kitchen—all its split-second saves and sharp words eddied at the perimeter, protecting the still eye of the storm. Remarkably, the two coexisted in a kind of harmony, like a steaming roast at the center of a moody family table. It kind of reminded me of home.

Very quickly I came to understand what Ti meant about the five minutes. Jobs like cleaning soft-shell crabs or trimming artichokes both took more than five minutes of any veteran cook's time, but the point was that proper hustling addled the brain, causing a thirteen-hour day to fly by like a six-hour one, and each thirty-minute block *to feel* like five minutes.

The kitchen operated on a bunch of these different clocks, only one of which corresponded to Greenwich Mean Time. The synchronized cooking of each dish for each table was coordinated by shouting out the minutes to plating. Once a table was fired (*"Fire Table 22!"*), the meat roast cook called out his requirement (*"Five away on the venison!"*) and we all counted down from there. *"Two on the squab!"* the guy to my left shouted. *"Two on the dorade!"* answered the fish cook. These minutes did not correspond to the exact ticking seconds but to a shared feeling of the same imaginary descending time line. Nightly, fights sprang up over the accuracy of a cook's minutes. (*"Serge, dude, your two is more like six!"*)

The point is, if you cook on the line for long, your personal time signature will change. It took about three months for my internal clock to flip over, but when it did, the time I spent cooking on the line slowed down and everything before and after sped up. My free time outside of work narrowed to a sliver—and even then, on the street or in the grocery store, I no longer just walked: I beelined, I took the turns tight, I dodged to the right, I foresaw the road ahead. Because once you've taught yourself to shave seconds off every task in order to be the most efficient, quickest cook you can be, it's hard to stop. Like saving precious moments of life, that's how essential it feels.

To me, time in the kitchen was like a loophole, a bubble, a cure. Once I found it, I crawled inside and told myself I never wanted to leave.

1

MY KITCHEN AFFLICTION

THE PLACE FROM WHICH I'D COME before cooking at Danube couldn't have been any more different if I'd imagined it—and sometimes I think I did.

To trace my journey to that kitchen in backward fashion, you have to climb up into a twelve-foot U-Haul truck with me and my boyfriend, Aaron, a truck whose broken-down starter requires us to park each night on a downward-facing slope that will flip-flop-flip-flop the starter to life each morning and keep us driving . . . up, down, and around the tight hills of upstate New York; then along the thick blacktop artery that clings to the southern coast of Canada, stopping periodically—without cutting the engine—to pick up foam clamshells of fried perch-and-chips in the finger of Michigan's Upper Peninsula; across the stubby swamplands of Minnesota through ghostly towns called Ball Club and Remer and Federal Dam on thinning two-lane blacktop; all the way to the dead-end, minimum-maintenance road that leads us back to the house Aaron built in the Two Inlets State Forest. This tall, one-room log cabin was best known to others for what it lacked—running water, electricity, all modern amenities—but was to us our scrappy home of the past three years. This humble place of origin, whose housekeeping hardships we generally ignored, gives you a pretty good idea why it never occurred to us to return a rental truck with a nonworking starter.

Aaron and I hadn't just driven a few thousand miles from northern Minnesota to Brooklyn; we'd also jumped forward a good hundred years. Our early life together was nothing if not a creative use of the time machine. At the house in the woods, we pumped water by hand from our own sand point well and hauled it into the kitchen in plastic jugs. We kept our meat cold on blocks of ice, lit oil lamps for light when the sun went down, and showered outside in the breeze. On the hill jutting out into a swollen creek, home to a crew of honking swans and a natural stand of wild rice that separated us from neighbors for miles, we basically lived on an island of the 1880s within a sea of the late 1990s. I liked to think of it as our own private epoch, but looking back, I'd say we pretty much lived in our heads.

I admit, when we first started dating—at ages twenty-four and twenty-one, respectively—and Aaron told me about his house I thought the whole enterprise sounded a little suspect. But that was before I came to understand his pragmatic optimism, his gift for turning flamboyant fantasies into realities that parade around the room as common sense.

Before we dated, I'd known of Aaron vaguely for years. He was my childhood friend Sarah's unusual older brother, one of our hometown's only ratty-haired punks, the sequin-caped lead singer of a glam rock band, and a sculptor. By the time I met him, he had graduated from art school in Minneapolis, was recently divorced from his high school sweetheart, and had moved back home to Park Rapids to build his house in the woods. He thought of himself as an old man and mockingly referred to himself as "retired"—a joke that hid a key shift of perspective. Going against the prevailing wind that nudged all artists toward backup plans, he reacted by throwing himself a retirement party and signing up for AARP. Making art would not be a secondary pursuit for him, but plan A.

And the new retiree was looking for a cheap retirement outpost. By building an off-the-grid house out in the country, he whittled his expenses down to nothing so that he could afford to work on artwork full-time.

That was the public story.

Privately, he also built the house because he was convinced that he was going to die. Only twenty-four years old but plagued with a bunch of mysterious physical symptoms (foggy thinking, odd blood tests, an unusual new tremor in his rib cage) he thought would kill him, he figured he'd better build the house he'd always dreamed of out on his family's hunting land.

Later we'd find out this wasn't just run-of-the-mill hypochondria talking, but instead the first bubble of a sedimentary anxiety—the artist's malaise—to burst to the surface. His sensitivity was largely spatial, ticklish to place. Sprawling big-box stores with thrumming fluorescent lights, suburban houses with overly wide hallways, and blinding expanses of Sheetrock—those were bad. But a small, low-lit house with high ceilings and lots of head space out in the middle of the woods felt right.

Fortunately, his health problems faded as his house rose up. Without any power tools—just a shovel, a cordless drill, his grandpa Annexstad's old Swede saw, and his own young back—he built his place right where his ten-year-old self had thought it should go: on a far hill overlooking the creek, miles away from the nearest electrical box, at the eighty-acre plot's most scenic, most inconvenient spot. When he was done, he dug out a garden and planted a few lilac bushes and thought of it in the future tense, as a homestead—in the evenings, a dreamer's somewhat lonely homestead.

Soon after, he got a girl to live back there with him, and that girl was me.

My decision to move to a rustic one-room house way out in the middle of the yawning forest was a puzzlement to my parents, my friends, and initially even to myself. Aaron's house lay only a precarious twenty miles away from Park Rapids, the hometown to which I'd never expected my postcollege self to return. As I drove past the green

Park Rapids sign POPULATION, 2,961, I saw my former isolation with clear eyes. My two-stoplight hometown was deep in lake country, four hours north of Minneapolis–St. Paul, and hours away from any town that might be considered a city. It was flush with nostalgia and pine trees but pretty short on great restaurants, bookstores, or cultural events—everything I'd come to love during my college years in Minneapolis. It wasn't exactly where I envisioned myself settling. I can track this trajectory shift back to a single moment, the coda to my Park Rapids childhood: When I turned sixteen, the winter my parents split up, I learned how to properly whip my car into a doughnut (what we called a "shitty") on the icy tundra of the empty nighttime grocery-store parking lot. My friends and I were good girls and didn't usually do such things, but we assiduously practiced our car twirls—speeding, whipping the wheel, and spinning wildly out of control—feeling the circadian swoop low in our bellies, as if by mastering it we could conquer our fears of moving out and moving on. When my family split and we left a few months later, it was as though I'd been interrupted midspin, leaving me for years afterward with an irrational surplus of feeling for my hometown. It was like a dumb phantom limb that wouldn't stop tingling.

Going almost home, to Aaron's house twenty miles north, felt close, but reassuringly out-of-bounds. It wasn't exactly a homecoming, but a do-over.

At the time I pinned my attraction to the place—in addition to the romance of shacking up with my new boyfriend in the woods—on our large garden and the chance to grow all our own food. As was typical of a late-1990s liberal-arts college graduate, especially one who had spent her senior year combing through farm women's journals for her thesis on outsider American lit, I was burning with desire to cook like the pioneers.

As I drove past my childhood split-level house in Park Rapids, the obsession felt incongruous. I'd grown up with a mother whose cooking was so outsized that she could have almost cut a window in her back door and gone commercial. She was a shopper, not a gardener, a woman who beat a five-block path to the Red Owl grocery store once a day and sometimes twice. Her caramels, her bacon-fried rice, and her Caesar salad (trademarked with a burning amount of garlic) made her a minor star in our neighborhood circle, and in our lives. But it was the area's rustic woodstove history, mixed with my grandma's memories of her farmhouse childhood, that gave me daydreams. Homemade sausage patties preserved under a thick frosting of white lard, horseradish-grinding sessions that drove everyone from the house in tears, long canning days that fogged the windows until they wept with steam, soaring homemade potato bread baked in twelve-loaf batches, four at a time. Installed now on a rough-board porch in the woods shelling a basket of peas from the garden, I had effectively driven myself two generations back in time to find the only things that my buttery, voluptuous, well-fed Midwestern childhood had lacked: baby greens and deprivation.

I wanted to cook like my Midwestern great-grandma had, with the feeling of scantness at my back. I wanted to pick a bowl of peas in the afternoon and bathe them in butter a few hours later to fully capture their fleeting sweetness. If I had refrigerated them (if I'd *had* refrigeration), their sugars would begin to turn to starch, like any old grocery-store pea. My cooking bug, which had begun innocently enough as a way to stave off the agony of writing papers throughout my college years, was growing into a serious habit. Or as Aaron described his own art practice: It was becoming an affliction.

In our kitchen, my turn-of-the-century farmhouse dream was distressingly accurate. At just four feet by six, it was my foxhole. Its compactness made it oddly convenient. A massive propane-powered 1940s Roper stove sat in the middle, its four burners set wide in an expanse of milky-white porcelain. Standing at the stove, I didn't have to move my feet to reach the sink or the shelves, and a quick pivot squared me to the large butcher-block counter to my left. The stove's two identical rust holes burned out on either side were the telltale signs of a lifetime spent firing double-wide boiling water-bath canners, so it had good genetics—but bad mechanics. To light the tiny oven, I had to turn on the gas, shove a lit match into the pilot peephole, lean back, and wait for the loud *whoof* of the burner plate erupting into flames.

Water was our daily preoccupation. Every morning Aaron heaved a full five-gallon spigoted water container onto the high counter over the double sink, under which we had positioned two five-gallon buckets. When I turned the spigot, the water ran into the sink and then down into a plastic bucket. When the bucket was empty, the echo of the water sounded loose and floppy; the echo sounded tighter—more nervous—when the water neared the top, as if to warn me that it was getting full. (Certain mistakes you make only once, and letting one of those drain buckets overflow is one of them.) To do the dishes, I filled a three-gallon kettle, heated it on the stove, poured the boiling water into the sink, and tempered it with the cold until I could submerge my hands, red and ringing, long enough to wash a pot. I liked it hot.

By my estimation, on a normal day, we used about three and a half gallons of water, and about five gallons when we had people over. I was surprised when visitors looked at this jury-rigged setup with lopsided grins because it seemed to me like a perfectly good system. With it in place I cooked everything we ate—breakfast, lunch, and dinner.

In the beginning, I picked all the green things from our garden, boiled them, soaked them in butter, and served them in a moat around a central chunk of meat—as my mother had fully equipped me to do. But soon I realized that unless I wanted to drive into town every other day for meat, I would have to cook differently. I'd have to focus on the vegetables from the garden.

At that single-slab counter, I learned how. In the mornings I fried eggs in butter with grassy, peppery rings of Hungarian wax pepper and steamed them until the yolks clouded over. I whisked aioli in a bowl perched on my belly to serve with the lone steamed artichoke we had coaxed to grow. I peeled buckets of apples we picked from an abandoned tree on an old homestead nearby and stewed them into coppery mounds of sauce. I simmered plum tomatoes with the sticky, resiny tufts of rosemary, then pummeled a lump of pasta dough, hooked a hand-cranked pasta machine to the butcher block, and painstakingly cut out long pappardelle. Underestimating how long this operation would take, I think we ate at ten that night, Aaron cramped with hunger, me with none at all. Sitting under a dark cloud, I picked moodily at the too-thin delicate noodles, which really would have been better with a cream sauce. I had so much to learn.

When word got out that a young lady was living back there in the woods with a rustic kitchen, older women—some of them virtual strangers—came bearing their abandoned preserving gear: stacked boxes of dusty pint jars, old dented water-bath canners, ancient pressure canners whose gaskets and dials and clamps made them look as intimidating as bombs. Following the fine print in the Ball jar canning book, I set out to assemble an old-time pantry, an arsenal of flavors that couldn't be found anywhere but here. Some were wild successes: chokecherry syrup that raced with tannins; crab-apple juice as tart as vinegar; fermented dilly beans as tingly as my grandma's brined dill pickles; wild-berry bachelor's jam embalmed in high-proof rum, instantly intoxicating. Other things—such as pickled eggplant (the texture of cotton balls) or wild Juneberry jam (which tasted only like its added sugar) or chowchow (just not into it)—felt like the waste of a good free jar.

FOR THREE YEARS we lived like Minnesota snowbirds: "up north" at the house outside Park Rapids for the six months of the gardening season and four hours south in Minneapolis for the winter months. To fund this routine we hoarded the income we made from our city jobs and coasted on it through our underemployed summers, during which we had no bills to pay. Aaron's summer days were filled with making sculptures and pumping water. Mine were taken up with cooking—at home and, eventually, three mornings a week at a diner on Main Street in Park Rapids, where I earned five dollars an hour, a paycheck that just about covered the gas it cost to get there.

At some point into our third summer in Two Inlets, after we'd gradually updated our situation to include a landline phone, a single solar panel, and a propane-powered fridge, I hit a plateau.

I remember sitting in our garden slowly thinning the baby kohlrabi we'd planted for a fall harvest. It was fine work, pinching out the crowd of extra stem follicles. The kohlrabi looked like a two-leaf clover, as did most of the sprouts, but I had learned to distinguish the baby brassica—the cabbages and broccolis and collards—as slightly duller than their shinier Swiss-chard-and-beet brethren. The kohlrabi sprouts were the opaquest of them all, their almost rubbery-looking leaves foretelling the waxy, long-armed globe that would eventually grow.

I worked so intently that the animals around me forgot I was there. The frog to my right made its way slowly through the beet tops, pausing mightily between each jump, as if making thoughtful moves on a chess board. A crow swooped in to land on our cucumber trellis, cawing and beating its heavy wings against the wood; the red-winged blackbird it was terrorizing replied with a scream from its fence perch. Two tweaky chipmunk rivals chased each other over the zucchini arms, the winner chattering in delight as it squeezed through a tiny hole in the fence. The sweet white wings of the blight-bearing cabbage moths fluttered around my legs.

I followed the chipmunks, pushing back the large furry zucchini leaves. Mine were not your typical Midwestern zucchini, the kind famous for its bonanza yields. I had paged through seed catalogs until I found an heirloom known for both its firmness and its flavor: Costata Romanesco. Leggy and overbearing, its vines walked all over the garden like they owned the place. This plant was miserly with its ribbed zucchini, but the ones that grew were tight and not a bit watery, with almost invisible seeds. I checked the one I'd been eyeing for two days, reached into the spiky vines, and snapped it off. I stripped ripe Romano beans hanging against the trellis until it looked like I'd gotten them all, then flipped my perspective and went around to the other side and found a bunch more hiding in the vines. I filled the basket with the rest of what needed picking—a couple of Hungarian wax peppers, a mound of fresh potatoes—and marched up the hill to the house.

With this motley assortment, I faced my big question of the day: how to make a memorable meal out of this mystery basket. My head filled with mental pictures from the cookbooks I'd gorged myself on the night before, I knew that great cooking began with the finest ingredients, and I certainly had those.

I dumped the dirty potatoes in the sink, rubbed the fine hair off the zucchini with a damp cloth, saved the peppers for breakfast, and put the beans to the side. I grabbed the two pork chops lying on the ice blocks in the fridge and rubbed them with dry spices as my mom did, planning to fry them in butter. With the zucchini, I wanted to make the dish I'd read about: a nest of julienned zucchini noodles dressed with garlic, pine nuts, and red pepper flakes, as al dente as a pile of pasta. For the potatoes I fell back on a family favorite: German potato salad.

I sliced the zucchini as thinly as I could and then cut the slices crosswise into strips—not as finely as in the cookbook illustration. I fired up a pan, the yellow propane flames surging up the sides, covered it with olive oil, and tipped open the very expensive jar of pine nuts I'd been saving. The nuts scuttled across my board. I bit into one and saw a pale white center; was that a core or a worm? Not exactly a hot item in Park Rapids, the pine nuts had sat on the shelf for who knows how long. I threw them into the pan anyway. I scurried to chop the garlic before the nuts burned, added it to the pan, walked half a step away to search for my jar of pepper flakes, and came back to find the garlic burning, I quickly dumped in the zucchini, stirred it up, and then turned around to the sink to scrub the potatoes. They came out of the ground in all sizes—some grenades, some gumballs.

While I cooked, the sun sank rapidly, as if someone were drowning it under the waterline of the horizon. I lit the two oil lamps in the kitchen and shoved all my dirty dishes behind a curtained cupboard.

We sat down to a caveman pork chop flanked by two hills: a sliding pile of bacon-slicked potatoes and a collapsed heap of zucchini noodles. My perfect zucchini, the ones that I'd babied from seed, slumped in an olive-green heap, slicked with burned garlic oil and studded with possibly wormy pine nuts. Why had I cooked it so early and let it sit? What a rookie mistake.

Aaron read my face. "What's wrong?" he asked. "This is fine!"

He nailed it. It was fine. No matter how pristine my raw materials were, I ended up with one thing: a fine plate of supper. It wasn't bad, but the composition was hardly artful. The flavors weren't roped together in any kind of meaningful, memorable way. *Individual notes don't a song make,* I thought and melted into my chair. My food obsession was growing at a disproportionate rate to my stalling skills, and every fresh trip to the garden followed by every night's disappointing dinner just made it worse. My cooking was starting to feel like blind groping: I could feel the shape of the thing I wanted to make, but I couldn't see it.

No question: Ours was a beautiful, simple life. I felt safe here, in our vegetable kingdom, in knowing that the asparagus and the rhubarb would return in the spring; that the chokecherries would come on the branch in early August and sugar would erase their woolly mouthfeel; that the wild rice growing on the creek—right in our front yard—would ripen around the time that summer came to a close. These things would continue to grow, with us or without us. The place wasn't going anywhere.

And I finally had to admit it: Neither was I.

Aaron was spending his evenings making art; he was on track. I was spending mine reading vintage cookbooks, filling the pages with scratchy marginalia, fishing around in the peach-colored lamplight for some motivation.

I found it, or a fraction of it, at my diner job. The weekend breakfast battle—so named because the horde of summer tourists could order anything on the six-page menu, from glorified hash browns to taco salads to hot beef sandwiches—ignited me. Hot in the middle of it, I opened the triangular points of a hot beef sandwich, nestled a big ball of mashed potatoes into its crotch juncture, poured a blanket of leather-colored gravy over every inch of it, right up to the plate rim just as the head cook told me to do, threw it up on the counter, banged the bell, and went on to the next thing. And the next. There was no time to pause or to think. The food at the diner wasn't the best (and certainly wasn't the worst), but remarkably, I loved that greasy, madcap world so much that it never occurred to me to question the tactical wisdom of returning to my rural hometown after college to become a short-order cook.

Gardening, canning, and dinner-making began to occupy so much of my waking brain that I thought I might as well try to get paid for it. Maybe it was time to merge my worlds—the heirloom vegetables and the hot grease of the diner griddle. Maybe the New York cooking school I'd spotted in the back pages of a food magazine could be my graduate school. Moving to the big city, with its fast pace and high cost of living, would surely cure my motivation problem.

Aaron was less enthusiastic about leaving the backwoods live/work space he'd built for himself but admitted that New York City—the center of the international art world—was probably where he needed to be. His best friend, Rob, also a sculptor, had already moved there from Minneapolis. And I seemed pretty hell-bent.

In September of 1999, after we put our garden to bed and harvested our wild rice, we made our own surprise chess move—a big frog's leap through the tall leaves—to Brooklyn.

————

WE PACKED AARON'S ART MATERIALS, all of my prized cookbooks and pots and pans, and the sixty-pound burlap bag of wild rice we hoped to sell, into a U-Haul and drove straight east until it came time to locate the studio apartment we had sublet on honking, congested Fulton Street in Brooklyn. The key the lease holder gave us in exchange for the three months' rent we'd given him a few weeks before, nearly all the money we had between us in the world, burned hotly in my hand. I just hoped it would open the door.

"Don't even say that," said Aaron, clutching the wheel as he navigated the map, his eyes scanning for house numbers amid the casual street bedlam that was Brooklyn.

Our dramatic move, from a log cabin in the woods to the hive of New York, was surprisingly painless, like riding a raft into a fast current. As soon as Aaron and I unpacked our few things—we used cardboard boxes in the closet for drawers, so that was pretty quick to set up—he called a friend of his from college and scored work with his art-handling crew at a museum. He started on Monday.

"That was easy," he said, setting down the phone, a bit suspicious of his instant job. Getting a show of his artwork would be another matter, especially without a proper, separate studio. I flopped down on the ratty couch, surveyed the one-room space, and, as is my nature, felt immediately at home. But given Aaron's sensitivity to fluorescent overhead lighting and wall-to-wall carpeting—actually, the dirty navy rug gave us both the heebie-jeebies—our apartment felt disarmingly foreign. His work-in-progress, the eight-foot slab of bowling-alley flooring he'd lugged in to carve, took up one of the four walls of our living space, and he started immediately to chink away at it in the evenings. As he reduced the surface into shapes, the wood chips flew, some of them landing squarely into my cardboard underwear drawer. (I sometimes found one later, as I walked to the subway, inside my panties.)

That same Monday, I started cooking school in Manhattan, the five months of which flew by more quickly, and less eventfully, than I had expected. I entered with wide eyes, hoping for a marinelike basic training with a bossy, brilliant French cuisinière, but instead found myself trudging through foundational European sauces with an unwieldy group of twenty. I was even more disappointed to find a fellow cookbook nut in my class whose grasp of culinary nerdery outmatched my own.

But the romance of cooking—the low buzz I felt inside when I inhaled my favorite cookbooks, Paula Wolfert describing a chanterelle-and-walnut tart in France or Madeleine Kamman on the momentous cabbage and duck tourtes of the Savoie; or even when my mom pulled the heavy aluminum pan of swirling brown butter away from the heat and then threw a pile of chopped scallions into it, sighed softly, and walked away, knowing that half of the scallions would frizzle to delicious brown bits and the rest would give her spaetzle a bright chivey flavor, just as they always did, time after time—the part of cooking that ignited my senses and my imagination at the same time, I did not find at culinary school.

Gradually, via the endless repetitions, as I stirred crème anglaise and prodded pork chops with my finger, I found the entrance to my tunnel vision. Down in the dark bottom of my obsession, as I watched a sauce reduce and thicken, the fine round pebbles swelling into loose, gaudy baubles, time hung in suspension—and it stayed that way, just as I liked it, good and frozen and undisturbed, for the entirety of my schooling and throughout my required school externship, at the restaurant we called the Danube.

2

SUGAR AND COLOR

HERE'S HOW MY BROTHERS, Bob and Marc, would eat their sugar cereal while watching cartoons on cold, housebound, midwinter Saturday mornings: They hoovered it up in one long inhalation, without using their lips. *Chwwhchchhwhech* . . . Liquid milk and bright pastel cereal bits flew into their mouths like dirt into a vacuum, their teeth clinking down on the empty spoon. *Chwhwchchwech* . . . I sat next to them slowly chewing my butter-logged bagel and wondered how they could manage to consume liquids such as soup normally but eat cereal like a couple of anteaters, and felt, just via my proximity, the perfect distillation of their joy of consumption. Immune in their happy bubble to all household responsibilities and family drama, they immersed themselves in the convergence of sugar and color, drawling out their pleasure in a trill of harmonic sucking.

That pretty much describes my first year of cooking professionally. I walked in the door of Danube and inhaled it in one long, knotty, seductive slurp. It was complete and total immersion. For once, I was not thinking about my *role* or *what I should be doing with my life*. I was just doing. I was moving—physically moving—and working far harder than I'd ever worked before. Eighty-hour weeks, and the hours flew by. By the time I'd finished my first month interning in a real kitchen in

Manhattan, I felt like I had finally activated the entirety of my DNA. Maybe I was a fair mixture of my parents after all: the workaholic businessman dad meets the sauce-simmering, stove-bound mom.

WHEN COOKING SCHOOL ENDED and it was time for me to find a restaurant to do my required six-week unpaid internship, I made a quick foot tour of the best fine-dining restaurants in the city—*why wouldn't you do your internship at the best restaurant possible?* I naively reasoned—and decided on the one with the most enticing dining room. I walked past the fragrant vestibule with its display of fresh apples into the dimly lit Bouley, Chef David Bouley's eponymous restaurant in Tribeca, and boldly asked the host if I could talk to the chef.

Looking back, it's easy to see that I had no idea where I was. Quite literally. When I told my friends at culinary school about where I hoped to intern, I rhymed Bouley with "duelie" instead of with "Vouvray." On my tongue, one of the city's greatest chefs sounded like a dual-wheeled truck charging through a mud run.

It happened that Galen Zamarra, chef de cuisine at Bouley, didn't need an intern and sent me to see Mario Lohninger, the Austrian-born chef de cuisine of their sister restaurant, who did.

Danube was Chef Bouley's ode to the decadent cooking of the Hapsburg Empire, complete with a dining room washed in gold metallic paint and ringed with gigantic Klimt reproductions. The menu promised both haute historical and contemporary Austrian, as well as truffles and foie gras and rare bottles of wine, everything necessary to lubricate the downtown financial-district boom economy.

Both of Bouley's restaurants were full-tilt fancy fine dining and considered to be among the very best in Manhattan. Yet everyone who worked there called it *the* Danube, a definite article slip that immediately put me at ease. Back home, people often tagged an extra *the* onto all their favorite haunts and restaurants. It was *the* Schwarzwald. *The* Park Drug. Our local grocery store, *the* Red Owl.

Tall and regal, but with a hipster's stubble and greasy curls, Mario interviewed me thoroughly, as if I were applying to join the ranks of the military, and then gave me a sweeping tour through the wine cellar stocked with Austrian Zweigelt and Grüner Veltliner and the storeroom shelves glowing with ruby lingonberries and green pumpkin-seed oil. On that first day he was overly polite with me. Decorous. Impervious to the turmoil swirling around him. With ramrod-straight posture, he led me through the downstairs belly of Danube's prep kitchen, stepping high over snaking vacuum tubes and puddles of water and flattened cardboard boxes. He strode past the prep cooks, who were calmly but deftly shelling fava beans and pounding out schnitzels and butchering fish, their eyes darting to me in small doses. I would soon know them as "the family"—Chef Bouley's tribe. This steadfast band of Dominican prep cooks—who might or might not actually have been related—sized up new recruits with a loose interest, like members of a crime family who don't want to get too attached before they know what'll happen to the new one. They outlasted all of us.

"Such a mess here today," Mario said politely, then turned around and shouted at the nearest porter, "Get this garbage out of here!" He shot me a look of mock outrage, as if this scene wasn't the normal state of affairs. But it was. Danube, which had been open for three months, was a madhouse. The place operated with the kind of working dysfunction particular to so many newly opened New York restaurants, but of a sorely under-organized brand all its own. The classic Austrian dishes on the menu—veal schnitzel; goulash made with beef cheeks; boiled beef, here called kavalierspitz—were upgraded to fine dining by giving each ingredient the high-end treatment. Bread crumbs for the schnitzel were made by hand, from dried baguettes. Vegetable and fruit juices—beet juice, pineapple juice, carrot juice—were extracted fresh every day for sauces. The cucumber salad was made twice a day, right before lunch and right before dinner. None of the filled pastas were made ahead, as they are in so many restaurants; here they were assembled in the prep kitchen during the service itself. "Two veal tortellini!" the waiter would shout down the steps, and three minutes later a prep cook would charge up the steps with eight tortellini, their plump veal tummies visible through the thin potato-and-duck-fat dough. The only organizational principle here was the old kitchen adage, "Make it happen." Bouley's perfectionistic standards strained like an overworked muscle against his trademark creative lawlessness. Where the system failed, talent and sheer adrenaline made it all work.

The restaurant was so new that it still had no organized family meal, the typical 3:30 afternoon dinner for the staff. The cooks, working fourteen-hour days, scavenged what they could, shoving bits of their extra mise en place—their prep, raw tuna scraps or cold short rib trim—into buns stolen from the baking rack. I began to see how food, the kind we were allowed to eat, was currency. I noted how crafty line cooks bribed the prep cooks: They'd slyly hand over copper pots filled with surplus pasta or buttery lobster trimmings to a member of the family, who would nod and hand over the quart of peeled favas the cook so desperately needed.

At first glance I assumed that the line cooks outranked the prep cooks, but I quickly learned that winning over the family was crucial to mastering any station upstairs. Until I learned to amass my own scrap-ammunition and to speak a few words of kitchen Spanish, my battleship sank farther every day. With hand signals and gestures, I begged the Spanish-speaking family to split my blanched English peas or to please juice two quarts of beet juice for me each morning. During my first month, they grudgingly did my bidding while laughing at me and sighing, "Mami, mami . . ." It was a term that struck me as offensive until a fellow line cook told me that it was the feminine equivalent of *dude*. All the guys were papis, all the women mamis. The female members of the family laughed and nicknamed me "Yo quiero." *I want*. It was the only thing I knew how to say.

———

I HAD VISITED NEW YORK A FEW TIMES before we moved there, but I hadn't bargained for the way it would smell on a daily basis. During my walk to and from work, I passed through shifting clouds of odors, some markedly sweeter than those at home (French bakeries) and some a whole lot fouler (rat piss, and lots of it). The atmosphere above the dirty sidewalks seemed to create a humid low-pressure environment, holding the scent fog down tight. Every once in a while a merciful gust of fishy sea air came in to flush the streets.

To my surprise, days spent plating tasting menus in one of New York City's finest food churches required an immunity to the vile underside of the city. Any restaurant job, whether at a diner or a four-star restaurant, puts you into contact with a tremendous volume of refuse, and that discard pile is not pretty. At the fanciest restaurants, the contrast between the backstage grit and the front-of-the house opulence is especially stark.

It was often past midnight when we plated the last tables, the hour at which the night porters arrived and began to tackle the mountain of dirty dishes with determined faces. One table was just beginning their six-course menu: after I filled a metal ring with four-star potato salad, laying down overlapping nickels of cooked potato and flakes of shaved black truffle in a tight fish-scale pattern, the food runner picked it up and lifted it up high to avoid the porter, who was balancing a large garbage bag on his shoulder, trudging toward the street. As the bag brushed past me, a sour rush of rancidity ran smack into the truffle's delirious damp perfume, giving me my first head-spinning lesson in the pungency of New York fine dining.

After a day spent handling such luxuries as fresh porcini mushrooms, top-flight bluefin tuna, and whole lobes of foie gras, I hit the street an hour later and walked a wide circle around the remnants of the night's crime scene: the garbage bags that leaked soft-shell crab spooge onto the sidewalk, the rats that skated through the juices, and the steaming tubs of grease topped with constellations of fried spittle.

The polarity underscored my own divide, which was just as wide. Even though I'd had exactly zero experience with fine dining, on either side of the swinging door, the ingredients I was handling at Danube felt somehow familiar. Here I found echoes of the German-American food my mom had made throughout my childhood: spaetzle fried in brown butter until the undersides bronzed. The spicy horseradish she served with beef roast, now grated fresh over barely cooked salmon, the white flakes falling like fat January snow. Crisp balls of pale green kohlrabi like the ones my dad ate like apples while watching the Vikings game on TV. Poppy seeds going into the grinder and coming out the other side a skein of crushed soil, smelling like dank fermented fruit—correctly ground "as fine as snuff," just as Grandma Dion said they should be. The place whipped up my sleeping childhood taste memories to a froth.

But of course the food was much, much fancier. Snobbish, some people back home in rural Minnesota might even say, the kind of reckless high-priced frippery they would take as an assault to their ground-beef thriftiness. That didn't register, though, because my mom had raised me to revere food. Food was beyond pretension. These Austrian plates were, in fact, the dreams of my Catholic mother, the perfect blend of her mixed French-Canadian and German lineages, the glitzy heights she'd always wanted for us. She harbored exactly these same illusions of grandeur when she served each one of her kids a rib eye and a full lobster tail with a sputtering candlelit butter dish for dipping. Compared with the piety of regular old Midwestern beef-and-potatoes, the food at Danube was positively papal.

If this was the Hapsburg Empire, Mario ruled the kingdom. He wasn't just intimidating; he was also Austrian. Cultured, snappish, and prone to brutal honesty, Mario had begun his cooking apprenticeship at the age of fourteen, and he didn't sugarcoat anything. When the young pastry sous chef came up with a new dessert for him to try—a fig wrapped in crumbly pastry—he inhaled it in three large fork-fuls and then pronounced it "Dumpf," crumbs falling from his mouth. I didn't need a translation to understand that one. Dull, lacking in acidity, no oomph, just like it sounded. *Dumpf* was pretty universal.

At around 10:30 each morning, I stiffened at Mario's arrival. He'd walk in and without a word to anyone reach into a nook and grab his hidden box of cereal, pour an overflowing amount into a porcelain con-sommé bowl, and bend down deeply to it, his limp locks of hair brush-ing the pass. Then he'd wipe his stubbled chin, clap his hands, narrow his eyes, and start prowling the line for vulnerable-looking cooks.

Not only was Mario one of the most technically precise chefs I've ever known, but his palate was savage in its accuracy; he frequently called out cooks for the slightest of deviations in the simplest of things. "This chestnut puree was made with milk and chicken stock, eh? It should be half milk, half veg stock." As if to make a show of this supe-riority, the depth of his passion, when he tasted one of our sauces he didn't just dip the tip of a finger or a spoon into it as other chefs did; he locked eyes with the cook and swiped two fingers through it repeat-edly, lasciviously, slurping up full tablespoons while taking the mea-sure of both the sauce and the cook's character at the same time. He lapped up precious mise en place like a Great Dane. Those of us who often slid into service with just enough of this or that sauce feared Mario's two-fingered taste.

When I first began on the canapé station, Mario paired me up with Nick, a guy with sweet eyes, a ripping-sharp knife, and severe cramp-ing of the central nervous system. He was wound as tight as a pulley cord, taut with trying to get it all done. He'd be skating along, gliding through tasks with smooth movements, diving in and out of the reach-in fridge, until a moment of indecision paralyzed him. Faced with the problem of what to do with batons of foie gras that were graying at the ends from oxidation, he visibly shook, crumpled up the parchment, and tossed it—foie gras, which rivaled gold for the price per pound—in the trash.

I was no better. I left my crap all over the place: half-built beet terrines abandoned while I ran upstairs to take a pan of quince out of the oven; a cluster of herbs and garlic for a sachet left on the corner of a shelf while I searched for where I'd set the cheesecloth; my notebook, just four inches long, full of precious scribbled formulas, I lost and recaptured daily. Until the day that it fell into the evil hands of the sneering Austrian pastry chef, who wouldn't give it back.

He stopped icing a Sacher torte to launch a screed in my direction: "This is the third time this week you've left your *stupid little notebook* in my pastry room! You don't deserve to keep it!"

A middle-aged crank trained in the rigorous art of Austrian pastry, he had no tolerance for me. We scrapped as if on a middle-school playground, him holding the notebook high above his head, me lurching for it. And then I did my signature counter leap, one knee on the counter (turns out I can spring up suddenly like a cat), snatched the notebook, and stomped to the locker room. Huffing, I ejected all the shit from my locker in one bear-paw heave.

"Did you learn your lesson?" asked Harrison, the meat cook.

I stared at him, unable to speak. Did I?

Harrison kicked his locker shut. "You learned that the pastry chef is a major asshole. That's a good lesson."

BY THE END OF THE SECOND EIGHTY-HOUR WEEK, I was exhausted. That night I'd made 189 orders of potato chips threaded with sardines, and just as many portions of octopus-pineapple salad and cured mahi with beet-fennel slaw. Blitzed with fatigue, I stood in the bright basement prep kitchen completing my last task of the evening, making a sachet to drop into the overnight braised oxtail, wetting a clump of cheesecloth and slowly fanning out its damp corners as if smoothing open petals to press a flower. With my dad's baby face and my mom's small stature, I looked more like a self-serious twelve-year-old than a cook in a professional brigade. My hair was pinned back from my face with a bunch of barrettes and I was basically wearing oversize pajamas: loose black pants, black comfort shoes, and a size 44 chef's coat, which was at least four sizes too big. The chef coat assortment at Bouley was always mostly extra-larges, making me look like I was playing dress-up. (The smaller guys nabbed all the 36s and 38s, took them home, and washed them themselves, but I didn't know that yet.)

The coat situation pointed to the obvious gender gap in Danube's kitchen, and throughout much of fine dining at the time. All women cooks dealt with it differently. Some of these lone females fought back by excelling in aggressive sexual innuendo—by talking even dirtier than the boys. I combatted my ladyness by stomping out of my sweaty pants in the coed locker room and letting everyone have their fill of my saggy briefs and graying sports bra as much as they liked—in other words, by pushing my femininity all the way to the way-back. I'd spent my college years stalking patriarchal dominance in literature, but when I found myself immersed in a testosterone world, I no longer cared for the social argument. I didn't want to talk my way into this kitchen; I wanted to prove myself on their battleground, through my cooking. Most of these boys, I thought, were completely unaware of the feminine roots of their culinary art. I doubted they could imagine what strength and skill it took to assemble a proper pantry arsenal back in the old days, but I could, and I knew the work had been much the same.

Never much of a girlie girl anyway, I figured there would be time later for pedicures. As it was, my toenails were broken and stained purple from rubbing against my black socks, as anyone looking on could see: the locker-room situation at the Danube spelled out the ratio of the gender dynamic. There was only one. An open box of cornstarch always sat next to the sink, free for anyone who needed to powder his balls. (Key to preventing crotch bite, you know.)

After cutting off the plastic-wrap belt I used to hold up my chef pants and openly changing into my street clothes, I trudged up the steps, slipping the thick strap of my messenger bag over my head. If

Aaron ever hinted that he was jealous of my boy-filled workplace he never let on—and needn't have, either. The only thought on my mind was getting home to him. I hoped that he'd still be awake and would want to sit up with me. I wanted to unwind amid the wood shavings from his carvings and the long panoramic photos of home he'd pinned up on the walls, a sort of shrine to our rural life back in Minnesota: our rock-garden flower beds, the trees draped in fog on Indian Creek, his fading 1973 Buick Centurion that was still parked in our yard. All I really wanted was for him to open a bottle of wine in that amazing way he did, by unscrewing the cork with a cordless drill running backward—*rrr-wrrrrrr*—and to conserve my evaporating energy long enough to bring it to bed.

If he was already asleep, I would crawl in next to him and nestle close, my hair smelling deeply of fried sardines, not yet realizing that my exit routine desperately needed to include a shower.

I also didn't yet recognize the hunger paradox particular to line cooks, the strange phenomenon that occurs the moment your feet touch the pavement, when your appetite surges back like a demon after a dinner service full of glorious tastes that have temporarily suppressed it. I thought of myself with multiple stomachs, a ruminant, albeit with two chambers instead of four—one stomach for flavors and the other for bulk. The flavor side turned out to be desire itself, which had been satiated; the food side, the actual fuel tank, began to ping hollowly every night around 12:30. And so before going home I hit the Pakistani cab stand on Church Street, where the middle-aged ladies dumped my choice of meat, two vegetables, rice or naan, and double cilantro sauce onto the plate with the same ennui as had the lunch ladies of my childhood—although the spicy, full-flavored food these women scooped was as powerful as kryptonite in comparison.

MY FAMILY CONSIDERED MY INTERNSHIP A GREAT COUP. My mom fretted over my hours while encouraging me to put the recipes she'd taught me on the menu—as if I were a contributor. Grandma Dion, my mom's mom, wrote to me in loopy cursive asking me how I liked working at "the café." Aaron knew exactly where I was, and was happy for me, but he was also somewhat fearful of my unbridled enthusiasm: what devotions to this city it might inspire, what long-term commitments would keep us from returning to our house that summer to grow our garden. To my car-dealer dad I simply reported the numbers.

"It's all six-day weeks, Dad, thirteen to fourteen hours a day."

"Wonderful!" he boomed. He worked a long six-day week himself, so this was not considered excessive.

"Actually, Dad," I corrected, "it was eighty-seven hours last week."

"Even more wonderful!"

As the fifth week of my internship slid into its final one, Mario teased me as he watched me herky-jerkily dice some potatoes with my heavy German culinary-school-issued knife. "Ahmy," he said, gesturing with the blade of his sharp Japanese slicer. "When you going to get a real knife?" The entire kitchen staff was obsessed with a Japanese knife shop within walking distance of the restaurant called Korin. Cooks on their day off regularly stopped by to show off their new knife candy, injecting a spot of cheer to our long days.

Mario had given me no hope that my tenure there would be anything but temporary. But for some reason I found myself boldly saying, "I'll get a new knife when you start giving me a paycheck."

It was true. I couldn't afford one.

He looked at me through eyes slitted for seeing a distance.

"Okay. You start for real on canapé on Monday. By yourself."

I knew the honeymoon was over. My marriage to the fine-dining brigade—which at times felt more like admission to an unfriendly harem—was about to begin.

I WENT TO KORIN and bought a very good Japanese carbon knife, soft and easy to sharpen on a water stone. It's still the one I use most often, its brand forgotten, its dark charcoal blade swirled with a hot wind of orange rust.

The guys set about teaching me how to take care of it. Nick ran his knife frantically on the sharpening stone, like an adolescent taking matters of need into his own hands. Kazu did it slower, and taught me to sharpen the first side more than the second and to feel the roll of the burr on the underside before gently whisking it off against the stone. All of them gauged sharpness by reverently slicing against the grain of their arm hairs.

Not every cook in the kitchen was so neurotic about keeping their edges razor-sharp. Yugi, the young fish cook (nicknamed Eugene by the Americans), smiled and shrugged with Japanese modesty, saying, "My knife is sharp enough." The Austrians were of the same mind. The other Austrian sous chef named Thomas, whom we called T2, used a heavy German cook's knife, never sharpened it, and could cut a butternut squash into precise matchsticks in about three minutes, his knife powered not by a razor edge but by intention and sheer confidence. T1 constantly ran his long Japanese slicer against a honing steel, never on the stone, and could do the same.

I might have learned how to sharpen my knife, and how to cut a sheaf of chives into paper-thin rings, but I was still greener than a fern. And everyone knew it.

"J. Lo is in the bar! Her ass is on a barstool!" the guys hooted, and they could not believe that in the year 2000, at the height of her rise, I did not know who she was. Jennifer Lopez I might have faintly heard of, but not this bootylicious "J. Lo." I had literally just spent much of the last three years in the woods, deprived of media.

In a lot of ways, my innocence saved me. If I had known exactly where I was or who I was knocking shoulders with, I would have been too freaked out to work, because this kitchen was stocked with the highest density of cooks who would go on to cook famously than any other kitchen I'd ever work in again. Gabriel would own three restaurants on Nantucket and appear regularly in food magazines. Harrison would helm a cultish small place in the East Village. Cesar would open

Brooklyn's first Michelin three-star restaurant. King would own a bunch of notable Filipino restaurants. Einat would open a couple of Israeli spots in the city and write a cookbook. Galen, next door at Bouley, would launch multiple restaurants of his own, and Bill, the Bouley pastry chef, would eventually become pastry chef at the White House. There was not a slouch in the bunch. It turned out to be a beautiful thing, that naïveté, because it gave me a blind courage. I've been dealing with the sad aftereffects of its erosion ever since.

I was twenty-four years old, ancient for a European cook, but average for Danube, an experienced kitchen. The head fish guy was in his midthirties and the meat guy was maybe pushing forty, and yet the three Austrians liked to point out how *old* we were. To their point, our knees were aging fast, scaling the steps between the upstairs serving kitchen and the downstairs prep kitchen at least fifty times a day.

In cook years, however, I was still a babe in the woods. After eventually moving up from canapés to garde-manger, even my salads were off, and Mario was not afraid to point it out.

"What are you doing, *beating up* my salad?" he scoffed, throwing the contents of my mixing bowl into the trash. He started with new greens, squirted them with vinaigrette, and tumbled them with his hands, as one might wash a delicate bra, and then lifted them in an airy heap onto the plate.

"Never break their ribs," he said softly, guilting me as effectively as if I'd been breaking their bones.

We felt someone standing behind us and turned around.

"My dad is here!" Mario beamed, formally introducing us. "He is making us the goulash today."

His father, who had come all the way from Mario's hometown in rural Austria, smiled widely (for he didn't speak much English), and motioned for the canister of hot paprika on the shelf above my head.

He took the paprika and sprinted away. Small and quick. *That's odd,* I thought, *he seems too young to be Mario's father.*

"Um, Chef, can I ask? How old are you?"

"Twenty-four," Mario said, leaning over into my sink. He slurped up water with his hand, rubbed it all over his face, and casually wiped himself down with a brown C-fold towel as if mopping off from a shower. I thought for a second that he was going to dig out his ears with it.

"You and I are the same age?" I asked. I was shocked. He was so young and so . . . *good.*

"Yes," he said, narrowing his eyes and smiling. *"We are the same age."* He dropped the smile, tilted his head, and searched my face.

"Ahmy, you are so old." Meaning so old to be working garde-manger, the cold appetizer station.

In any normal narrative, I might easily have spent nine months on that cold station. But as the fairy tale goes, someone quit. I remember that his name was Joel. He was a petite, quiet-spoken, sandy-haired guy, struggling on the line, sliding roughly around the station in an untucked uniform every night. Before that evening's service Mario clapped his hands above his head and called us in for circle time. With theatrical formality he announced, "Everyone, Joel is leaving us. To become a *food writer,"* he said with a predatory smile. "His last day will be tomorrow. We wish him the best of luck in his future career." This grandiose crew meeting was as effective as a snicker, as we never congregated to discuss someone's leave-taking and certainly not for an early-out. In cases like Joel's, the guy would usually just shove the contents of his locker into a white takeout bag after service and call the night his last. Joel, with a blanched face, nodded and blinked at the floor.

Mario came up to me and laid an arm around my shoulders. "You should come and eat in the dining room tomorrow night." Did he mean I should go there for dinner? We couldn't afford that. He felt the hesitation in my back.

"No, you and your boyfriend come to dinner on me. Taste the dishes. Come tomorrow." He said it politely, but I understood; it was painfully obvious that I needed contextualizing, that I needed to eat this food in order to learn how to cook it. It also meant that I would be taking Joel's place as meat entremetier on the hot line.

I was thrilled with the chance to bring Aaron into my world. We both dressed up—him in a suit, me forsaking my grungy sports bra for a real one and my clunky work shoes for heels. We walked into the dining room and were struck with instant, simultaneous fear. The lighting was womblike. There was a tiny door behind the bar that led to the kitchen and servers passed through it swiftly, letting out just flickering slivers of its harsh fluorescent light and none of its hot energy. In the dining room, the head servers—called captains—tracked around smoothly as if on rails. The bubbles in the champagne cocktail that Stefan the bartender handed me rolled up serenely on invisible filaments from the bottom to the top. I was shaking with the formality of it, uncomfortable being on the other side of the swinging door. Aaron looked similarly shivery.

The first glass of wine helped. My glass would be my crutch. First came the amuse-bouches, just as I had been making them: the crispy sardine in potato chips, the sweet-and-sour octopus salad, the little cup of spiced squash soup. They all tasted so much better in the dining room than they did in the kitchen. The second I finished my wine to accompany the first course, Didier the head captain was there to refill my glass. I didn't realize that with a wine pairing, it was wise to pace yourself. Eric, another captain, smiled broadly.

"I recognize this smell," Aaron said, eating the sardine, "from your hair after work."

He looked around the room, at the gilded rafters, the glittering Klimt reproductions, the plush velvet banquettes, the grandmotherly fringed lamps. "This place is totally crazy," he said, absorbing every facet of the room's excesses with growing admiration, "over the top . . ." I knew he was thinking of performance and decadence, of David Bowie, of glam rock. The reason he had worn a glittery cape when performing with his band, Aaron America, had everything in common with this dining room. "They got the lighting right, though." They had. It was soft and luscious, like the food, like my rapidly evaporating sobriety.

I let my head drop low over the new course and inhaled, rather dramatically. The monkfish with artichokes and black trumpet mushrooms, which had seemed to me the least exciting dish we made, surprised me the most. It expressed something dark: hidden corners and sweet earth and a weird candle-burning spice . . . that pinch of *réglisse*, or licorice root powder. In the kitchen I had tasted the sauce alone, droplets from the tip of my spoon, but never with the roasted fish itself. Knit together into one forkful, the monkfish was a soother in a tasting menu of dynamic courses, a low-buzzing romantic dish.

The captains hovered around our table, spoiling us, circling back to make conversation as I sunk into a loose state of drunkenness. Eric came over and dropped some complaint about Didier, and then Didier came back to pour more wine and bitch about Eric, and then before I knew it they were standing over us, whispering hotly, quietly fighting in the relative cover behind our corner table. I leaned back and smiled at Aaron, my eyes lost inside my high pink cheeks. I belonged. We belonged. My nerves fully unwound, I reached to grab his hand to punctuate whatever it was we were talking about . . . when my delicious Zweigelt, my chokecherry and plum and moss forest-floor wine, spilled in a moat around his pink lamb chops. The captains broke their huddle and Eric immediately laid a calm hand on Aaron's plate.

"Let us replate this for you, Aaron."

"Nah!" I bleated, not wanting to be a bother to my fellow cooks in the kitchen. "He'll just eat it like that." Aaron glared at me. He didn't want to eat it like that. That's when everyone, including me, knew that I was completely toasted. This was not so bright. The next day I was coming in early, to train with Ti on the hot line.

———

THOMAS KAHL, the first of our two sous chefs named Thomas to arrive from Austria, had a shaved bald head and wore heavy combat boots and an expression of disdain. He bounced ever so slightly at rest, like a lion ready to pounce, which suggested to me that he'd experienced some serious kitchen combat and had exited it triumphant.

For his first week he hustled around the kitchen muttering a single word: "Bullshit." Later on his English would kick in, but in the beginning the hot, uncovered braised beef cheeks steaming on the lower shelf of the walk-in were bullshit. The dregs of Dijon mustard in the jar next to the newly opened one were bullshit. My bloody cutting board, smeared with the guts of so many badly butchered sardines, was really bullshit.

When Thomas Myer arrived, with a more sensitive demeanor, wearing loafers, his plaid pants tucked into his socks, smacking of the rural Michelin-starred auberge he'd just come from, we called the first Thomas T1 and him T2 (and sometimes Terminator 1 and 2). They both regularly pulled sixteen-hour shifts, keeping long hours on the bullshit patrol. Both Thomases and Mario spoke devoutly of their former kitchens in Europe, mostly of the restaurant they had all worked at together, Chef Hans Haas's Tantris in Munich, which led the charge in Europe for contemporary Austrian cuisine. They spoke of Hans Haas with deep-bass-note reverence, much like the Jedi. *Tan-tris.* I imagined a shadowy dining room draped in black.

I knew that the Austrians clearly thought that we Americans all pretty much sucked, so I was curious as to why the newbie me had been plucked from the garde-manger and chosen to work the entremet. I asked T1, "Why me instead of one of the other guys?"

"None of you are that good, but your mom made the spaetzle, right?"

I blushed, caught gushing about my mother's home cooking to this international crew. "Yeah, and noodles."

"In brown butter, I know," he said. "But let's go, hey. Big list today."

I crouched in front of the low-boy refrigerators below the station, expecting to see a menagerie of station prep but finding nothing but a quart of picked parsley leaves and a tub of plum jam. I fell back on my heels. Joel had left me nothing?

Ti smiled at me from above, tapping his knife on the board, keeping his beat.

"I threw it all in the garbagio. No fucking bueno." This phrase was his new "bullshit," more fitting to the Spanish patois of our kitchen. He motioned for me to grab an empty bus tub and hurtled down the stairs to the vegetable walk-in refrigerator.

In the cool walk-in he started loading down the tub: twelve endive, a vanilla bean, fourteen carrots, a bunch of celery, a bunch of chives, some thyme, rosemary, a handful of fresh bay leaves—"the Turkish bay leaves, like this," he grabbed the fatter ones, "not the California ones, too much perfume"—two celeriac roots, a head of red cabbage, a few anchovies, ten lemons. "You get the micro greens. Just for garnish. Kohlrabi and beet only." I reached up on tiptoe and opened the plastic lid to a dizzying array of plug trays of baby spouts. Kohlrabi, I knew that one. And there was the red-stemmed beet. Cool. I scooped them into two corners of a metal prep container.

He handed me another and gestured to a plastic tub in the corner. "Fill this with crème fraîche."

As I was scooping up the white goo, he said, "Hey, Amy," kicking off a routine that he would repeat every chance he got for the rest of my time there. "We need horseradish, too." I turned around to find Ti waiting with an enormous rough-skinned horseradish root hanging from his fly, its rhizome top forked into two knobs. Horseradish schlong: so infantile and yet so absurdly apt I had to crack a smile. His head nodded with silent laughter. Real sexism in the kitchen I would later learn to recognize—it was a lot more underhanded and more insidious—but this obvious shit I found amusing.

Back upstairs, I tried to shake the image out of my head and get down to business.

"Let's start with the purees," he said. The vegetable purees, the backbone of the meat garnish station, were the down pillows of the plate. I dragged a rondeau to a hot spot on the wide steel flat-top, lobbed in a chunk of butter, and hastily rustled together the heap of flat parsnip coins between my hands.

"No, no, wait. You salt the vegetable first on the cutting board, so it can start to sweat." He misted fine sea salt over the parsnips and muddled them with his hands. Almost instantly a mist of perspiration beaded up on each slice. "Now when you cook them in the butter, they'll taste more like themselves." He tapped his spoon on the metal piano—the outer ledge of the stovetop's apron—and continued: "Use a lot of fat. Cook them all the way soft. If you add the stock now, when the vegetable is half-done, you're not making a puree, you're making soup."

It seemed I did everything wrong. I oversalted everything that shrank upon contact with heat: mushrooms, spinach. He made a sour face and wordlessly threw the entire pan into the dish tub. I cooked the schnitzel too slow and it came out looking soggy. "Limp, like an old man." I cooked it too hot so that its crust puffed properly into a toffee-colored balloon, but it wore bedsores of blackness on its bottom. He threw those out, too. Mostly, though, I was just too slow.

I reserved most of my attention for the more glamorous things I'd never seen before: foie gras cooked medium, fleshy pink at the center like liver putty; cherries braised in balsamic; endive cooked into a marmalade; wild mushroom confit; truffle sauce made with a quart of reduced veal stock, a bottle of fine Madeira, and a fifty-dollar jar of truffle pieces. I babied the truffle sauce, ignoring my potato stock boiling away on the flat-top.

"Hey." He nodded toward the stock, which was going berserk. "Not so bueno."

I quickly whipped my pot to the cool side of the stove, where its violent bubbles sputtered out.

His voice sharpened. "You know, this is not about the truf-fles and the *fwaah*," he said with a forced American accent. "Good cooking is *potatoes and onions*."

Danube's kitchen didn't look like one that ran on potatoes and onions. From what I could tell, it looked to be pretty well fueled by the foie, the engorged liver of a force-fed duck; we went through so much of it. But while flurries of truffles rained down on shiny butter-poached lobster claws, I saw that Ti was right. Many sauces relied on the potato stock for their base: an emerald-green chive sauce to accompany pan-seared scallops, a honey-colored horseradish sauce for beef.

The potato stock was a deceptively simple concoction, made by sweating onions, garlic, and sliced raw potatoes in butter, deglazing with white wine, and simmering everything in chicken stock until the potatoes were tender. Pushing it through a sieve yielded a soupy blond puree. It tasted a lot like my mother's potato soup without the bacon. But the brilliance of this stuff belied its humble origins. It gave conceptual sauces a country backbone, pulled them from the clouds back to the terra firma. Banyuls vinegar and green pumpkin-seed oil were new to me, but potatoes and onions, these things I understood.

IT WOULD BE WEEKS ON THE HOT LINE before I had a real conversation with Chef Bouley himself, the ghostly, swift-moving presence responsible for this machine. I soon learned that his unpredictability was the hallmark of the Bouley kitchen. To his cooks, it was the unfortunate consequence of his insane creativity. All night long Bouley cooked personally, off menu, shuttling between his side-by-side restaurant kitchens, for countless VIPs—friends, celebrities, known gourmands. He'd show up at 6:00 P.M. in the middle of the first seating rush toting a case of Concord grapes, throw it on someone's cutting board, and say, "I want you to clean these and steep them in the lobster-port sauce," totally kinking the cook's flow. Or he'd drop a box of scallops in the shell onto the cold app station and say, "Shuck them, save the coral roe, sauté it, and put it in small dice under the ceviche," forcing that cook to wedge himself onto the hot line to find space on the flat-top dining service. This put all the cooks on edge and constantly in the weeds—but it kept Bouley's own improvisational inner demon on track. Even without the last-minute arrivals, not a single night went by without Bouley throwing a wedge into the gears of dinner service. I thought this was how all kitchens were.

I didn't know what to expect of a chef with one three-star and one four-star New York City restaurant, but I suppose it was something more distantly managerial: I didn't expect him to cook the fish or plate the food himself. Or to wear formal dress shirts and cuff links beneath his chef coat, like he was playing 007, a Bond masquerading as a chef. Or to talk to me.

"You've got the orange powder over here?" he whispered steamily in my ear.

I quickly dropped the piece of schnitzel I was breading back into its crumb bath and started flipping through my tiny ring-bound note-book as his impatience mounted. Orange powder?

"She doesn't have the orange powder?" he said to Mario. "Where in the hell is my orange powder? It was in a little foam cup . . ." And he started to ransack my station.

I'd come to learn that the orange powder—made by grinding can-died, dehydrated orange peel to a dust—was one of the many extra things I was expected to have on my station for these moments when Bouley decided to come in and go rogue, which was nightly. In addition to the regular printed menu, he had a running list of dishes that he was constantly changing, working on, reinventing.

He'd tell the fish cook, "Give me the garnish we did for the axis for that guy." (Axis being the kind of Texas venison we used.)

"Which was that, Chef? The lobster beet setup?" Reduced beet juice, red wine, and truffles.

"No, no." Bouley sighed, basting sturgeon with foaming, browning butter. He threw his spoon into the metal spoon bin. "Go ask Shea, he'll know." Meaning the dish he did next door at Bouley. Meaning that the cook should leave his station, walk outside, go into the kitchen next door at Bouley, and ask Shea, the meat cook, for the "axis setup Chef did for the guy." Shea, deeply weeded in service himself, would just laugh and send the cook back with a saucepot of celery puree, sautéed wood ear mushrooms, and a pot of mushroom réglisse sauce. Most of the time he guessed right.

As Bouley cooked and plated, you could see him juggling proportion and generosity: what was just enough, what was just a hair too much, what degree of excess would sink the diner into a kind of delirium. Trained in cutting-edge kitchens in France in the late 1970s, he absorbed his mentor Roger Vergé's preference for light vegetable-based sauces over the old-school meat reductions and then took it one step further; his culinary mind tripped on the sauces. Some of them seemed to have been devised by plumbing the depths of the color itself. The mango-curry-saffron mixed far-flung flavors, but tasted like a totally natural fusing of the elements that make yellow. Ocean herbal sauce—composed of three herb oils as well as fennel, celery, and garlic purees—mined the color green. His sauces were so vivid they were almost libidinous—virile and romantic at the same time, like him. One look at his plates identified the guy whose eyes conquested all female passersby to be the same one who had also personally picked out the dining room's gaudy tasseled velvet pillows.

His food was precise, but not so tight that it blocked out artistry. There was a looseness, a drunken glee for cooking that was very pronounced here. A Bouley consommé wore a technically incorrect shimmer of fat on top, as thin as gold leaf, which effectively lubricated the happiness going down. It was the industry norm to gently shake off the juices that erupted when you cut into a filet of medium-rare meat, so as not to dilute the sauce, but when the meat cook did this, Bouley shot him a look and said quietly, "I want that venison juice." The cook complied, his eyes transfixed to the translucent bloody dome that grew by the second on the venison's cut edge, threatening to flow a river through his pale celeriac puree. It made little sense until you just accepted the fact that juice was juice. Cooking was about sensation, about carnality, and Chef was certainly no prude.

This kind of cooking required real knowledge—cooks who could hit the outer edge of perfection, who trusted themselves enough to color right *on top* of the lines, not inside them. When the service was bumpy and we weren't hitting it, Bouley slipped down the line and whispered hotly into the space between me and the meat guy, "Don't give me what I ask for. Give me what I *want*."

"What the hell did he say?" my comrade hissed, but I just shook my head. There was no time to answer. Hot plates were hitting the steel piano. Bouley threw his cautions as effectively as a ventriloquist, shooting whispers across the line. He had a way of mumbling a criticism so that it hit its intended recipient right in the basket. The one I often caught was "The potatoes are too loose." He was right, of course. They were supposed to flop softly, but mine looked like they were melting. When I looked up, Bouley was onto the next thing, gently pinching one of six plated langoustines on the pass. He hesitated for a minute and then punched his thumb through the ivory flesh. And the next one. He angrily crammed all six langoustines into a rough ball and started stacking the brittle porcelain Bernardaud plates, one on top of the other, making it sound like a stack of poker chips. The captain who was waiting for the course moaned and steered his head out the door.

"Come on, people," Bouley muttered sarcastically. "Oh, let's just hurry up and make shit."

The entire weight of the diner's experience hung in the balance as the long minutes ticked off to the table's refire and replate.

One day, during a calmer lunch service, Bouley stood on the fish line cooking halibut and started talking to the cook nearest his elbow about the fish, who happened to be me.

"You guys need to cook the halibut more slowly, give the fibers a chance to unwind. Halibut's a tight fish," he murmured. "You want to slowly bring out its natural sugars." Never did he press his spatula on top of the fish to suture it to the pan and improve its browning, as the regular fish cook did. No, he laid three flat fingers on its bulging middle to urge it to settle down—more like the way a mother rubs a sleepy kid's back. He looked up to see who was listening and took in my girlish barrettes holding back my bangs, my intent expression, my smooth, glistening pane of bleached-white indoor skin, and gave me a rakish smile, because he could spot the latent female in anyone.

"What's your name?"

"Amy," I said, "not Ah-my."

He laughed. "Where are you from?"

I hesitantly said, "Rural Minnesota," knowing that the mere mention of my home state conjures up its own brand of wholesome hickness from which I couldn't hide.

"What do your parents do?"

"My dad's a car dealer. My mom's a teacher." I wondered, *Why is he asking me this?* "When we were younger, she stayed at home with us. She cooked a lot."

"Uh-huh," he said, tasting a sauce. "What did you go to college for?"

I never said I went to college. "English," I said. "American literature."

"And what is it you want to do?" he said, setting the fish on a tuft of parsnip puree.

When I grow up? He doesn't assume I want to be a cook? "I want to cook, Chef!"

He wiped the edge of the plate with a damp cloth, looked me in the eye, and smiled crookedly. "Are you sure?"

I nodded. Oh god, I was in for it.

He grabbed a large metal prep spoon and said, "You know, back when I was starting to cook, we didn't use small spoons for plating. We used these big catering spoons." I marveled at the absurdity of this. We often plated with the tiniest spoons we could find; my uniform's breast pocket concealed two espresso spoons I'd cribbed from the coffee station that very day. He dipped the wide spoon bill into his small pot of ocean herbal broth and ladled it deftly onto the plate, then picked up a miniature corona of sautéed squid legs by the tip and gently dropped it into place.

He threw his arm around my shoulders and then tightened it around my neck in a friendly choke hold, and squeezed my opposite shoulder with a masseur's precision. I stiffened, not because it felt flirtatious, but because it felt possessive. "Amy, can you run downstairs and get me two toes of garlic. And a bunch of chevrille." (He had his own culinary language: toes for cloves, chevrille for chervil.)

"Oui, Chef." I sped off. Holy crap, this was not a job. Bouley wanted to know who the hell you were, if you had any taste, any culture, any education, a good family. Basically, he wanted to know what the fuck you were doing in his kitchen and if you were worth his time to teach you. Cooking wasn't just a job; it was a life—what looked to all outsiders, including my own boyfriend, like a pretty terrible life. It was, as Aaron feared, a real affliction. And possibly, a dysfunctional relationship.

Initially, I mistakenly thought that my attraction to this job was due to my reunion with the browned butter and ground poppy seeds and spaetzle of my youth, but the truth was, it was something greater than the flavors of my childhood that drew me to the Danube. It was more about the way the two captains sprang into a fistfight with each other the second they bridged the marble threshold into the kitchen, bursting into fire behind closed doors. It was the way the throbbing, merengue-blaring downstairs prep kitchen brushed up against the silent, methodical upstairs service kitchen, matching each other in intensity. The way an imperfect crew functioned perfectly, channeling all their hopes and wishes and ambitions into the center of the plate, letting their liquid emotions fall off the sides, the food always beaming in the eye of the storm. It was the simultaneous agonies and thrills of the job. It was the unrelenting syncopation of the merengue and of the clacking plates. It was the threshold itself.

I knew I'd found my people. Crossing lines, jumping the boundaries between rural and urban, high-flung and low-down, garbage juice and black truffle juice, felt right to me. Fancy and shitty, that was to be my loop. Cooking, I'd found, contained the multitude I sought. It was the kind of work that spanned worlds, that could knit the two sides of a hungry, home-seeking, dramatic sort of person back together.

In no time at all, I had entered the belly of the ship. I was a convert, to all of it, and would cook on the line in fine-dining kitchens in Manhattan for the next seven years.

Give or take a gardening summer or two back home.

A FEW MONTHS LATER, on April 5 to be exact—I will never forget the day—I was setting up my station for lunch when I got a call on the kitchen phone.

Aaron was on the other end, and I could hardly make out what he was trying to tell me. Finally I understood that his brother Matt's three-passenger plane had gone down. Matt hadn't made it.

It took me a minute to make the jerky progression from imagining his brother as hurt to gone; the brain struggles with moves like that. I repeated what he said to the guys around me and the sous chefs began yelling at me to go, go, go!, and suddenly I was throwing the gray messenger bag over my shoulder and flagging down a cab to Brooklyn.

Back in our apartment in Fort Greene, tears were spraying from Aaron. I had never seen him cry. We huddled on the couch, our limbs curled into a knot, and through my hand on his back I felt him heave and deflate, his body trying to process the news like a spider struggling to take in something big. I pictured his sister, Sarah, my child-hood friend, in her Peace Corps apartment in a small town in Latvia; her return would take days. I could see his parents in their gold-wallpapered kitchen in Park Rapids, our hometown. I knew Aaron was probably thinking of the last time we had seen Matt, kind of a long time ago, in the kitchen of the khaki-colored house in the suburbs he shared with his wife, Evon. He had made us a chicken hotdish, she an apple crisp for dessert. I closed my eyes and felt frozen, as if the min-utes kept ticking but went off the rails, setting us on an alternate course. I repeated "I'm so sorry" until I felt the empty bottom in this phrase and there was nothing left to say. We sank into the couch, David the renter's horrible dirty couch. My exhausted body released its tension hold and our breathing found its deep together pattern. I wanted to lose consciousness, to make this news go away.

"Are you *falling asleep*?"

"No!" I jumped. I knew, given how much I'd let the insanity of my working life warp my perspective, that I could say nothing in my defense. I reeled in the entire length of my failings, the long rope of my shitty girlfriendness, and gathered it all up against my belly. It was true, what Aaron's eyes were saying: I don't understand—because Matt was only thirty-one years old and this was surreal. I don't understand—because I have not lost a brother. I don't understand—because I am a terrible girlfriend who had not paid my boyfriend two minutes of attention since I started this job. It hit me bleakly that if it weren't for Danube, we would be at that very moment packing up the car and driving to Minnesota.

Oddly, Aaron already had plans to drive back to Minnesota with his friend Rob the following day to set up his show at an art center in Min-neapolis. The evening hours seeped away nearly silently as we got him ready to go.

The next day at work Mario was sympathetic. "I hear you need to go to a funeral?"

Yes. I explained that I needed at least five days off because it would take me a day to get there, then a day for the wake, a day for the funeral, a day to be with Aaron, and a day to come back. I might as well take the week, I said. I could tell he was puzzled and that he wouldn't take off that much time to bury his own grandmother.

"There's no direct flight to my town," I told him. "It's really small. Like a village." I was breathless. "I'm going to take a plane to Minneapolis and then a much *smaller* plane" —my hands swerved in the air— "to a small town north of mine, and then drive an hour south." By the time I finished my long-winded description he was waving me off and telling me to give my boyfriend his condolences. He gave me three days.

Two days later I was set to leave from JFK airport at 3:00 P.M. This also turned out to be the day that Hans Haas, everyone's favorite Austrian mentor, came for a visit. It bears noting that when chefs "visit" each other they do not hang out and catch up in the traditional sense. Sometimes the visiting chef will sit down to a tasting menu in the dining room, but generally, if they're close, the visiting chef simply suits up in his work duds and joins the kitchen. They commune by working.

So it was that when I came in that morning Hans Haas was down in the basement, breaking down salmon. One fish after another, swiftly, wordlessly. He was doing the mise en place for the slow-cooked salmon with Styrian *wurzelgemüse* (*wurzelgemüse:* overstuffed German for julienned vegetables), the menu dish that Mario and Bouley had copped from his Tantris menu in apparent tribute.

Chef Bouley had heard that I was leaving early, before dinner service, and had been looking for me. "Amy," he said, grabbing me by the wrist and pulling me next door, where he was in the weeds with one of his own projects, the last-minute production of hundreds of glutinous rice cups for a large party of Thai dignitaries. (I had just finished making a batch of German potato salad to go underneath the sturgeon for an offsite catering gig for President Clinton; was it possible that both of these events, in addition to Hans Haas's dinner, were on the same day? Yes, in New York, it was.) Bouley pushed me in front of three cast-iron pans with golf-ball-size round divots in them, the kind I'd seen used to make Danish *aebleskivers,* those little pancake spheres. I started out pouring lightly sweetened glutinous rice batter into the twenty-four holes, all of which promptly stuck—until I learned to work the cups by swabbing each one with clarified butter. As the rice batter cooked, I topped each one with a spoonful of sweet coconut pudding and then rode my offset spat around the brown cooked-lace edge to tugboat them out of the divots. Twelve, twenty-four, forty-eight rice cakes stacked up on a paper-lined half-sheet pan. Bouley dropped lightly hot-smoked cubes of sea trout on top and garnished each with a thatch of miniature basil sprouts. It was a thrilling canapé, one I wish I'd written down. Sixteen more, twenty-four after that. I didn't look up for hours. Then a glance at the clock on the wall revealed that it was time for me to go, but I hesitated: I'd customized this job so much that it was hard to abandon it. But I was going to be late for my flight. So I handed my spatula to the guy standing nearest to me on the line and took off running, leaving behind a jagged opening that missed me for about thirty seconds before sucking firmly shut and going on just fine without me. I realized then that my bond to this kitchen might have felt strong but was in fact impermanent; I needed it more than it needed me.

The plane I took from Minneapolis to Bemidji turned out to be a prop plane. As it started its approach to land, like a piece of paper wavering to the ground, I quaked with mounting anxiety. This plane was way too small.

It seemed like all of Park Rapids attended the funeral, which passed by in a dirge of minor pipe-organ chords. I held tight to Aaron, but he was in another world. He and his family grieved the way you do when the universe steals away your firstborn child, your tall, ambitious, golden-haired thirty-one-year-old son, your admired older brother—down through their toes and into the glacial bedrock.

Members of Aaron's family sat at a table and shuffled old pictures like decks of cards. I couldn't leave, and yet my ticket tugged, insistent. How much do I regret not pushing Mario for four days or more? Deeply.

Aaron stayed back home with his family. When Matt died, along with him went the other half of Aaron's childhood imagination, the commitment to fantasy and play that fueled so much of his work. He told me it would be for a few weeks, but I knew it might be longer.

I returned to Brooklyn, and to Danube, whose challenges no longer seemed so amusing. I floundered my first day back on the line, Mario shouting at me while I tried to stopper my weepiness and plate the schnitzel with some sense of precision. The many jocular details of my day, formerly organized in situ for retelling to Aaron, didn't seem to matter. They weren't so funny anymore.

In Brooklyn without Aaron, I realized how much our fields of vision differed and how much I had been relying on his to supplement mine. He was more panoramic, more long-sighted; he saw our New York stint as temporary, a time to build the skills we'd need when we eventually returned home to live out our days in the woods and ply our crafts. My view was more near-sighted: I saw a flood of shapes and colors, a world of vivid, moving plates. I saw my shoes, sturdy and flour-dusted against the tile floor. But outside of work my mind continued to churn with the sights of the kitchen and I didn't see much but the clouds; I could hardly cross a street safely without him there to pull me back to the curb.

That level of spaciness works when you have someone by your side looking out for you, but now, alone, I am forced to pay more attention. New York, chameleon city, with streets that can look like gold when you're up, looks darker now, as if it had recently flooded and the mud just receded. Stranger exchanges on the street that usually fade off into the din sound bright and ominous, dangerously emotional. After work, I stop at the Pakistani cab stand, and when I get home I sit in our grungy window well overlooking Fulton Street and methodically eat all of my chicken korma, all of my green-velvet palak paneer, and all of my spicy chickpeas.

The constant stream of trucks on Fulton Street honk at one another as rudely as the swans do back home on the creek in front of our house. One bleats, another answers. Like migratory birds inhabiting the same old familiar waterway, they're all just verbalizing to make conversation, blaring to communicate their gripes, their wishes, and their warnings—but these here in the city with a greater sense of urgency and way more out of tune.

3

HOME COOKING

FOR A MONTH OR SO AFTER HIS BROTHER DIED, Aaron was okay. Devastated, but functional. He walked around the city in his usual patterns until one day the buried panic, which he thought he'd stuffed down a hole, rose up again. Like an emotional autoimmune disorder, his central nervous system began to attack itself, leaving him terrified to leave our apartment alone, terrified to drive in Brooklyn, terrified to take the subway by himself. For every plan, he had to consult his anxious mind for permission. Given the isolation he was living in, he might as well have been back in our house in the middle of the woods. He said very little about this, to me or anyone, and using his natural gift for persuasion, he found friends to accompany him where he needed to go. The one he really needed was me. And I was still working about eighty hours a week. I had no idea the terror I left him with each morning when I went to work, but late at night as I turned my key in the lock of our apartment door, I sometimes heard him singing his own songs at stage volume, his mournful voice seeping out of the cracks of the door like smoke from a fire. The full measure of my guilt over this, for so loving my job at Danube while Aaron suffered at home, came later.

Six months in and working the lunchtime meat entremet, I arrived in the kitchen early every day, second only to Michael on the meat roast station. He was cheerful and seemed to be in control of all the sauces on his list, rare for that position. Each morning I copped a new breakfast treat for us from the rack in the next-door Bouley prep kitchen—Seba, the French-African baker, just smiled and looked away. Michael and I agreed that the light, coarse-sugar-topped savory brioche buns were better than the pastries, especially when they were warm and the butter seemed to perspire right through the dough; the few meager pebbles of sugar on top were sweetness enough.

Then one day Chef Bouley called me into his office. Wearing a slim-cut pair of wool pants, a stiff French-cuffed shirt, and a cabled sweater, he possessed all the calm of a bolt of lightning at rest. Without looking up from his work, he asked me if I'd like to work on his cookbook. I was to stop working the meat entremet and start to shadow every cook at Danube, write down each station's recipes, and hand them over to Melissa Clark, the book's coauthor.

Bouley was sitting with steel-rod posture in an office chair in the center of a tornado of clutter, an office so full of papers and white shipping boxes that it looked black and white, and I admired this surrounding shitstorm—just as I did the serious avalanche of unpaid parking tickets that fell from his glove compartment on our last catering job—because the disorder seemed to me a sign of his brilliance. I also have a disordered mind—although he didn't know that. He thought that because I was a young, nerdy, clean-cut girl, I must surely also be disciplined and efficient, and that I would be the perfect person to help him whip his long-overdue cookbook into shape.

I was intrigued. *Recipes! Cookbook!* It was an opportunity so perfect I couldn't have dreamed it up. But I was so loving my current groove that I said without thinking, "But what about working entremet? I want to be a line cook."

He finally looked up at me over his red-framed reading glasses. "What? Why do you want to be a line cook? You can always do that."

He dismissed me. He barely knew me, but he knew my type. Of course I'd do it.

Mario called a group huddle to announce my new position, which I suffered through, feeling both precocious and like a deserter. Then he grabbed Harrison, who was working fish roast, T2, and me and ceremoniously carried a tureen of the soup he'd been making all morning down to the plush private dining room near the wine cellar. With florid Austrian gravitas, Mario ladled it out for each of us.

"Goulash soup!" he informed us, and handed each of us a Christofle spoon. "This is the soup of the Tyrol, where I am from." He tipped his wineglass, filled with sparkling water, into the air.

"To Ahmy's success on the cookbook!" he said, and winked. By this point I knew to be suspicious of his Austrian formality routine, and this one was turned on full jets. Mario slipped out to grab a napkin, and Harrison, thinking about the stacks of preservice work he'd left behind on his station, quickly spooned the goulash soup into his mouth, then leaned over and hissed, "This is so fucking weird." And it was. But I would soon know why: Mario was anticipating the cookbook process ahead and he wanted me on his side.

Quickly, I saw the issue: There were no recipes written down. Few fine-dining kitchens have a full set of typed-up recipes, but the Danube kitchen was positively negligent. It appeared to exist prelanguage. All I had to go on were the line cooks' scribbled notes, which showed no quantities but included lots of arrows to show the passage of time: "brown butter —› shallot —› celery root —› sweat out all the way —› white wine, reduce —› fill up with half-milk/half-veg stock." The cooks' recipes were as reliable as a game of telephone; that is, slightly more corrupted each time someone new took over the station. We ran fully on taste memory, which, among this tribe, was pretty finely tuned. And I soon discovered that taste memory was, in fact, more precise than a printed recipe. The act of translating an oral tradition to a written one would be both a corruption of everyone's artistry and a record of their collected genius all at once.

Embarking on what became a kind of culinary graduate school, I worked alongside each cook and recorded the separate parts of every dish in long, painstaking recipe form. Being a novice, I made a lot of mistakes. Mario and Bouley tasted every one of them.

I spent most of my time chasing one or the other of them across Duane Street as they hustled between the two restaurants and the office, toting small pots of parsnip puree, apple-horseradish sauce, or veal ravioli. Each individual component might have been an education for me, but divorced from their completed dishes, they stood out in odd isolation. Working on the meat station one day, I brought a small portion of beef cheek goulash, Danube's signature dish, to the office for Bouley's approval.

"How is it?" he asked, pulling a cleanish plate out from under a mountain of papers. I reluctantly handed him a fork, suddenly insecure.

"I wouldn't make a meal out of it."

"Mmmhhf," he agreed, chewing. "There's way too much vinegar. Next time, more pickle juice at the end to acidify, less vinegar in the beginning. Vinegar cooks out harshly." This, I never forgot.

The cooking details I absorbed from Bouley and Mario stacked up so thick and so high I couldn't access them until much later, but I did know one thing: I was seriously lucky to have this job. Unfortunately, however, without the military structure of line cooking, with no impending service, no real schedule, and no one charting my progress, and as befitting an undisciplined twenty-four-year-old coming off eighty-plus-hour weeks, I started coming in late. And then even later.

It didn't seem to matter. It felt almost as if the chefs avoided me with my incessant foisting of small pots. I chased down Bouley at the entrance to Danube, trying to get him to approve my latest recipe, mushroom goulash with leek dumplings, made under T2's guidance. It was a homey, stewy thing built on shallots, garlic, paprika, two kinds of chanterelles, black trumpet mushrooms, and crème fraîche, then garnished with a plush little leek dumpling, its browned face shiny with butter. T2 made it Austrian-housewife style, by vigorously beating eggs and smashed butter-fried croutons into a lump of room-temperature butter. The emulsion was surprisingly tricky. T2 perspired lightly as he whipped it, muttering, "My mother made it like this. . . . I don't know how you'll make it a recipe, it's really by feel." I presented it to Bouley with two forks. We both dug in to taste.

"See, this is so straightforward," he said. "So pure. So rustic. So good!"

He then launched into a tangent, as he was prone to doing—passionate descriptions tripped by the sight of whatever was right in front of him. He rarely said a thing directly, but always made you feel like you were entering midstream into some sort of ongoing narrative he was writing about the senses. He talked about the sweetness of the onions his grandma cooked in the ashes left after a wood fire; the softness of fresh homemade vinegar in comparison to the harsh commercial "battery acid" we used in this country; the intoxicating aroma of thousands of Frenchwomen passing by him in a crowded ballroom in some fancy château, every one of them smelling like a different exotic animal in her own perfume, yet somehow it's not overwhelming, each one is really distinct, just a delicious parade of woman scent. . . .

"This book really needs to be about home cooking." He interrupted his daydream and looked at me directly. "Home cooking is different. It comes from the heart, not the head. It's not refined in the way that we're refining it here. Home cooking is simple. Every single part of the whole, every ingredient, needs to taste perfectly delicious. You can't catch up to that later. Everything in this book should be stripped to its basic elements. That's where home cooking is really powerful."

What? I thought. *Now he's changing the book from whole recipes to separate components?*

And then suddenly he was walking away with my pot. "And tell Mario let's leave out the crème fraîche, make this in larger batches at the beginning of service so it can sit, and garnish it with the cream à la minute."

Back in the kitchen, Mario swished this suggestion away. He leaned in close to me conspiratorially and said, "Ahmy. We are not going to do a home-cooking book here. Don't make things simpler. It should be like a European book. A chef's book. Don't take away. If anything, *add*."

So it continued with Bouley whispering in one ear, Mario in the other, and Melissa the coauthor sighing and saying she'd need to make the recipes more home-cook friendly.

That's what I tried to do, but it was so much easier just to reproduce the restaurant dishes. For instance, it's easier to slavishly replicate Foie-Gras-Stuffed Squab with Parsley Puree and Schupfnudeln—even if it did take me a full day to make all the components—than it is to trim it of its cheffiness. How should one conjure up the original Austrian grandmotherly inspiration for such a dish? Did Grandma have access to foie gras? How about the Vitamix blender required to make grass-green parsley puree? Did she have one of those? Mario said yes, yes, of course.

But then something turned over in me, and I knew that Bouley was right: good home cooking, the kind that's both rustic and sophisticated, is so much harder to pin down. It reminded me of those days spent in my nineteenth-century-like garden-based kitchen back home, my struggles to elevate a freshly dug perfect potato. On the surface, complexity looked difficult, but in truth, simplicity was a lot harder to pull off.

When the time came for the cookbook photo shoot, Mario told me he needed me for the duration and then proceeded to speak urgently in German to T2 and the Austrian photographer (yet another Thomas) all day long, shutting me out of the conversation. I got it. I was lucky to be on the project: I was just supposed to help cook. We shot all of the food photos in the dark, raw-industrial lower level of the Mohawk building across the street, where creatures scurried in the corners. But taking away the sound, the sights were life-changing. There were no food-styling tricks at play on this shoot: no tweezers, no blowtorches used to make congealed cheese melt, no pots of hot water vaporizing behind the scrim. The minute we finished cooking in the kitchen, we ran across Duane Street with pots covering the pots, and pans covering the pans (because there's no such thing as a lid in a restaurant kitchen), keeping everything hot. The steam was real. Everything was plated just as lovingly as it was for the guests, everything looked as ravishing as it did in the kitchen, and everything was delicious. Once a shot was called (*"Fertig!"*) we broke down the set and scooped the contents on the plates into our mouths with our hands, because we had no forks in the Mohawk. Striped bass stuffed with paprika-bacon-wine-kraut, cabbage rolls filled with foie-gras-stuffed dates, an entire suckling pig, the pan juices scooped up with shards of crispy skin. I promptly gained five pounds. Not a good move, because soon I was going to France with my mom, just the two of us, to eat. And also to locate the origins of her French-Canadian father's people. But mostly to eat.

To put the haute cuisine in which I found myself immersed into some kind of perspective, let me submit to you the rural Midwestern cuisine of my youth.

There were ice cream buckets, lots of them, and they rarely contained ice cream. In the summertime, women walked in the door with the handles of swinging buckets hooked over their arms like purses. If the potluck party was at our house, they stacked these buckets, two high, in our downstairs refrigerator. The labels promised Kemps French vanilla, Edy's Grand rocky road, Blue Bunny butter brickle, but when you pried open the lids with a dry, cracking sound, the contents under the bluish plastic were always a surprise. You might find yellow potato salad, Italian macaroni salad, fruit-and-marshmallow Jell-O salad, or that wrong (but oh, so right) crushed-ramen-mock-crab-almond salad. Or maybe you'd find a pile of cold chocolate-chip cookies (which, in retrospect, did not even require refrigeration; however, if you ever want to refrigerate an entire batch of cookies, you should do it in an empty gallon ice cream bucket).

Later I would roll my eyes at the buckets, because I couldn't see these milky, repurposed, plastic gallon containers for what they really were: a symbol of the whole community's eating, a marker of generosity and thrift at the same time. In any other place, these ideas of abundance and frugality would sit at odds with each other, but in the Midwest of my youth they were bosom buddies, as tight as tongue and groove. The irony is this: Many of the traditional Midwestern favorites require a lot of time and effort to make but no one would ever want to say so. A neighbor lady might make potato salad by the gallon, spending an hour dicing potatoes into baby-bite-size cubes, but then, with consummate modesty, as if to say "No big deal," she would carry it around in some junky, old reused plastic tub. If people sometimes wonder why Midwestern food hasn't gotten the respect it deserves, I want to say that it's not the food, which is generally quite good; it's the shitty, self-deprecating plastic storage vessels.

There were also lots of plastic Tupperware containers with yellow and orange tops whose bright button centers looked exactly like childhood drawings of crayon-colored suns with radiating rays. Light aluminum nine-by-thirteen pans with plastic lids. Rinsed-out glass mayonnaise jars, none of which were ever thrown away. Some of the dearer salads, such as the mock crab and the clam dip, were ritually made in smaller batches and went into empty Cool Whip containers—that is, if you were a Cool Whip family. Which we were not.

No, Karen Dion's taste defied the local inconspicuous consumption. She was in the habit of whipping real bona fide heavy cream for our topping pouf. And in general, going against the grain of the town's collective thrift, she liked fancy things. Following her lead, we were all vulnerable to the charms of the tiny newfangled Häagen-Dazs pints. Just one of them was enough for my brothers and me if we ate our ice cream as she did, in a teacup, topped with a spray of broken pecans and a thick spoonful of Mrs. Richardson's butterscotch caramel, the cold ice cream turning the caramel into thick, chewy clods. It was possibly some remnant of her French-Canadian father's side that caused my mom's penchant for all things "petit" in a supersized Midwestern world, but despite that, sometimes my mom bought ice cream by the gallon, once in a while anyway, just so she could have the buckets. They were that requisite.

She was no snob, though. At the store, honest ingredients like chuck roasts and fresh ginger shared her cart with bags of miniature candy bars, cans of mushroom soup, and Lipton onion soup mix—the addition she insisted made her pulled-beef sandwiches better than everyone else's. (When I later found her beef recipe on the back of the packet, I was disappointed, but nothing could take away from the fact that that onion soup mix, with its telltale rattlesnake shake and its burned-sugar-and-soy tang, possessed the power to reach through the decades and jolt all my dead memories alive.)

She bought canned black olives, too, which at the time were considered—I'll say it—a little bit exotic. In our town, those fat black O's were everywhere: on top of chili, in Mexican Chicken Bake, mixed with slices of pepperoni and cubes of Swiss cheese in Pizza Enchiladas, and, of course, on pizza. Mexican, Italian, or even Asian, black olives were the diplomats of our diet, serving as foreign ambassadors from everywhere else. They ruled what our hometown grocery store called the "Ethnic Aisle."

That we were card-carrying members of this Midwestern culinary world and yet two steps different was a feeling that lay dormant in me for years.

It was a distinction I remember noticing while accompanying my mom on her daily shop at the local Red Owl. She ran her finger over the tight plastic covering the top half of a chuck roast, sighing, showing me how this one didn't have any of the proper marbling and wouldn't get really tender. "This part, the deckle, is too damn lean," she said, forcefully whacking the bell on the counter to see if she could score a better roast "from the back"—a bold position for a woman of her era, standing as she was beneath a poster advertising lean pork as "The Other White Meat." Accompanying my mother at the meat counter, I always got the sense that some mysterious saboteur was stockpiling the good stuff, thick-cut pork chops of rosy dark meat and heavy jumbo-cut Boston butt pork roasts with thick caps of fat, behind the swinging doors.

MY MOM IS IN NEW YORK two days before we leave for France, making dinner for me and Aaron and all of our expat Minnesotan friends, and she is not afraid to cook for Mario. She's making her specialty— slow-roasted pork with spaetzle and gravy—known in our family as "the meal."

"Did you ask him?" Her lips slide into a wicked smile.

"No."

"Well, then maybe Bouley wants to come for the meal. Did you ask *him*?"

"Mom, neither one of them can take a day off to come out here to eat pork roast and spaetzle." Even though I think that her spaetzle, crowned with brown butter and possessing a soulful chew, is actually better than the photogenic, puffy ones we serve daily at Danube.

"And gravy!" she says.

"And gravy. I mean, I'm sure they'd be flattered, but they won't do that."

I admire her nerve. I would never dare to cook them a home-cooked meal from my grubby apartment kitchen. When we turn down the lights after dinner, roach feelers wave out from the crack between the counter and the sink and mice peep out of my burners on their haunches to have a look at what's going on. I can't bear to ask them over.

At this point, my mom is about seven years divorced from my dad and largely recovered from it. Single and thinner, she has lost her trademark perm, and she is ready to go looking for her roots, the homeland of her long-ago-departed French-Canadian father. All of my coworkers at Danube expect my trip to France to include some kitchen stints (called stages) at three-star Michelin restaurants, but no—we plan to eat in them. Our first Michelin stop will be Pierre Gagnaire in Paris, our second Michel Bras in Laguiole, deep in the Auvergne countryside. On this trip, neither one of us gets to play queen cook in the kitchen; we will both be submissive eaters, absorbing our family's French lineage through the plates.

Actually, I wish I had asked Bouley and Mario for dinner, because "the meal" is, as always, quite impressive. Her pork, specifically, is a marvel. Hours of slow, low-temperature baking turn the meat inside to pure plush—as soft as angel food cake—and its outside into a cage of golden, holy crisp. The fat slowly leaks out of the roast's carapace, leaving behind vacancies, like the comb in a beehive. This effect cannot be achieved if the cook continually opens the oven to peek and poke at the roast, allowing the pent-up humors to fly out the door. No, honeycombing happens only to the faithful.

I'd tried to make her crispy roasted pork a couple of times back at our house in Two Inlets, but it always came out tough; I blamed the first failure on the local-pastured pork roast, the second on our leaky 1940s Roper oven. When I tried making it in my Brooklyn kitchen, with a store-bought Boston butt roast and the same plain, cheap, air-locked oven my mother had at home, it still refused to collapse for me the way it did for her. Long-cooked pork went properly slack for me at work, but this one defied me. I cursed myself and then thought that I was not entirely sure that she has really given me the real recipe. Maybe it's not three and a half hours, but more like five. Maybe the temperature is lower, below her stated 325 degrees. When it comes to recipes and the women in my family, you can't trust them to hand over the truth. You'd think after having watched her make it all those years I would have absorbed her technique through the skin, but some meals, they're like pets. They have an unshakable loyalty to their owners.

And for the first time, I am slightly sheepish about one facet of "the meal," a thing she does that marks us with our small-town origins: the cheese sauce.

Like all of her sauces, she prizes this one for its thinness and the way it cloaks the steamed broccoli and runs so nicely into the meat, but still, it's just block American cheese melted in milk. I loved it as a child, for the way the bland yellow cheese ran down my throat, but now I think: It's so processed. And—what's the deal?—she doesn't even put any butter in it. She puts butter in everything.

The tensions in this kitchen run high.

"Move a little slower!" she says tightly. She hates the way I lob the sauté pan from one hand to the other as I make the browned Brussels sprouts, my sole contribution to this meal. It's macho, I suppose. Some of that testosterone-rich swagger has rubbed off on me. Also, totally irritating to her, I cook over such high heat that flames dance under the pan.

"Amy," she says with shock, "fire is *shooting* up the sides!"

"Mom! The Brussels sprouts need to *brown* or they'll taste *steamed*." What can I say? I'm a newly minted line cook. I live to sear.

What my mom sees in me is a pace of working that seems frantic, a speed that disgraces the memory of my great-grandma, my grandma Dion, and herself. That I am her only daughter but have not inherited their smooth, almost vehicular way of moving in the kitchen is a shame. She purses her mouth in disapproval.

We are like flipped-screen images of each other. On the surface I look to be frenetically juggling three things, but on the inside I'm as calm as a cat; her outward movements are as smooth as a ball in the air, but I can feel in my head, as constant as a metronome, the insistent beat of her inner fretting. When I'm cooking with her, I enter a weird kitchen void. I am caught between the worlds of home cooking and professional cooking, of my past and my present, like a panicky bug trapped in the space between the window and the screen.

I know that the emotion below the iceberg is the fact that I'm not trying to replicate her best dishes, as a good daughter should. She thinks I only want to cook like Bouley, like Mario. I don't think it occurs to her that I'm trying to cook in my own style, to fashion my own repertoire that will take influence from all of the great cooks I've known, including, obviously, her. But I can't figure out a way to explain this without offending her, so I say nothing.

We are both perfectionists, but with different motives: I like to invent a dish, resolve all its problems, and then I don't feel the need to make it again. She has a tried-and-true arsenal of about twenty block-buster meals. It's an age-old battle, really, between improvisation and repetition.

Silently, we fuel a standoff that pits professional cooking against home cooking in the unfairest of ways. She seems to take no interest in what I'm learning to cook firsthand from the best chefs in New York City, asks me no questions about it, and never wants me to make anything. To her, I am turning my back on our food, on our family.

Neither of us is wrong.

Essentially, we take sides that neither of us really believes in. It will be at least another five years before she allows me to contribute a dish of my own to her Thanksgiving table. It will be just as long before I give her the full measure of props she deserves.

As we sit down at the table, even after our plates are loaded her eyes stay on me, and when her chewing slows, her food sitting in her mouth like marbles, I know she's trying to hold herself back from saying something and I know what it will be. "Oh, honey, your plate looks dry." By this she means that my plush mound of soft meat is under-sauced, vulnerable, open to the air—the worst of all plate offenses. "Can someone pass Amy the cheese sauce?" Even though I don't think it needs it, I dutifully comply.

———

MOM AND I arrived in Paris in the morning, but not our morning.

I walked down to the grocery store and bought the most beautiful strawberries (looking unwashed, as they should be), little pots of whole-milk yogurt, and two croissants, and brought them back to our room. We ate our breakfast on our little balcony overlooking a side street in the Marais, the fourth arrondissement, and then I wanted to take a nap—but she'd have none of it. Having just finished the cookbook shoot and not slept while crossing the ocean, I was eager, in my heavy fatigue, to luxuriate in the cool sheets and give in to being prone for a while. And this was just the first of the trip's repeating battles: I wanted to sleep in and then careen around the city in regular noncomfortable shoes without a plan. I wanted to pretend that I lived there, that I was just going to the corner café to get a glass of wine after work and watch the locals come and go, the women with their lace-encrusted bras that they dared to let show through their blouses, the men in their shiny shoes and slim-cut pants. She wanted to query the desk people at the tourist bureau for their recommendations, to ask the waitress, "What's good here?" I wanted to order unfamiliar things, take indirect routes, and make my own mistakes. My mother wanted to eat croque monsieurs and tour-book us to a crisp.

As I look back on it, she had only flagged the requisite museums and cathedrals, perfectly amazing places I otherwise would have wanted to see, but I railed against her devotion to what I privately called her "demonic day-planner." It was unreasonable, it was the tired part of me talking, and it was our generational gap, to be sure, and if I could gently seat-kick my younger self from fifteen years in the future I would.

Our first Michelin-three-starred stop was Restaurant Pierre Gagnaire, which the gracious reservationist from Bouley had called to reserve for me. Its formality was paralyzing, in the way that the fanciest restaurants in the world feel simultaneously welcoming and terrifying. I recall the first time that Aaron and I ate at Danube, and how spooked we were. By this time, it should have felt old hat, but this was *Paris*.

The parade of dishes was epic—delicate, precise, and manic with flavor. I struggled to unpack the various components and then just gave myself over to the dazzling artistry: the three kinds of protein used in so many of the courses; the *pétoncles* I'd just eaten that the slim French culinary dictionary I was sitting on translated as "barnacles." With each course I grew ever more aware of the invisible hands of the cooks on my plate, and more impressed by the complexities at work. With its wild juxtapositions, this place had more to do with Aaron's world, with conceptual art, than anything else.

This realization both rattled and soothed me at the same time; the extraordinary house wine we were drinking helped settle me down. As we ate, and ate, my belly swelling into a smooth rock, I prided myself on my growing stamina to put away a long tasting menu. My mom and I made small talk about our plans, voicing an occasional "ooooh" over the food but not dissecting it. On the sixth course, a crisp translucent disk of sweet-and-sour eggplant set on a pad of yellow sauce, my mother finally made a comment.

"This part, this yellow sauce, is too tart for me," she said, surprised. Once she said it, I knew she was right. The yellow pepper sauce, infused with a bizarre amount of acidity, had slipped right by me. Embarrassed, I realized that the showmanship had blinded me. My enthusiasm for the industry had snowplowed my palate.

When the chef came out to greet the tables, tall and regal with long silver-blond California-beach-bum hair, I was totally star-struck. Meanwhile, my mom was struck with the bill.

"I knew it would be expensive, but four hundred dollars for lunch! My god, it's only our second day."

We promptly ordered two mint-green chartreuse digestifs, to ensure that we got our money's worth.

———

Trips to France were not littered throughout my childhood; in fact, I had never before been out of the country. But taking her daughter to her departed father's fatherland to taste its delicacies was on my mom's bucket list, and if she hadn't been paying for everything, I wouldn't have been there. Before we left she had told me, "I'll pick up some prepaid calling cards for us both."

The only one I wanted to call was Aaron. We'd rarely been apart in four years, and even less so since Matt's death, and had never gone a day without talking, but I figured, Okay, maybe we could handle touching base just every other day, or every third.

But my mom kept a tight rein on the calling cards.

"Why do you need to talk to him? Let him miss you a little bit," she said, mumbling something about making the heart grow fonder as she walked away. I held off until the fifth day when I grabbed the card from her wallet and folded myself into a phone booth. I reassured him that I was okay and that we were somewhere in the Savoie region. It was clear who held the purse strings on this trip.

We had good times, though, on our way to our second Michelin-starred meal. We dipped south to visit my mom's cousins who had retired to a farmhouse outside of Marseille. We went to the touristy village of Châteauneuf-du-Pape and bought six bottles of the delicate red wine, the boxes for which we passed back and forth filled with Christmas gifts for years to come. My five years of strictly B-minus high school and college French grudgingly came back to me, and I was able to navigate the rural roads, get us into hotels, and even snag a recipe for apricot confiture from my cousin's neighbor. If it had to do with food, I could muddle through.

My mother, not so much. It was clear that the simple French phrases she'd crammed on the airplane hadn't stuck when she walked into a restaurant and brightly declared *"Merci!"* in greeting. *It's* bonjour, *Mom*, bonjour! It quickly became the running gag we pulled out whenever we needed to break intergenerational tension.

Over the food, all our sharp edges fell off. We both loved the buckwheat galettes, the frisée salads with duck gizzard confit and walnut-oil vinaigrette, and the pâté en croûte, even the supermarket kind, and somehow managed to cram three full meals of these, our new favorites, and more into each day. Sitting on a sunlit terrace in Provence, in front of a milky half-orb of fresh chèvre with niçoise olives and oven-dried tomatoes, we finally had to agree to disagree.

"How can you not like this goat cheese?" I asked. "It's almost impossible." The curd was so fresh the milk trickled out when I broke it, and the signature flavor of the goat milk laid down low in the background. But the woman who had introduced her kids to stinky blue cheese, dripping rare beef, and fresh coconut—whose tastes always pushed back against our small town's collective conservatism—was sticking to it.

"Sorry, I just don't like it. I've never liked goat cheese."

She turned away and I couldn't persuade her to enjoy the only good goat cheese she'd never have. In her I saw my own food prejudices reflected—although I count among her favorites some things I now dislike: raw green bell peppers, undercooked green beans, and, yes, even our family's beloved American cheese. I vowed someday to strike them all down.

We made our pilgrimage to Normandy, to the small town of Mortagne-au-Perche from which her Dion ancestors had migrated so long ago, and scaled a tiny turret inside a historical museum devoted to the horde of North American tourists tracing their roots to Canada. Jean Guyon (Dion) arrived in what became Montreal in the seventeenth century, making ours one of the first French families to settle in Canada. On the walls hung grainy black-and-white photos of the short, round, dark-haired men and women who had immigrated to Montreal. That round belly, which occasioned the men to belt their pants around the middle like an equator, I recognize as belonging to my grandfather and his father before him. Had my mom's dad lived long enough, he would certainly have grown the same midsection magnificence. Yes, these were our people. We were French, but more specifically, we were *les Canadiens. Voyageurs.* Northern people, going back many generations.

My mom asked the director of the museum the question that visitors must have asked, oh, just a few times a day: Could we be related to Céline Dion, the singer? Of the ten CDs my mom owned, Céline Dion's was the one she liked to play at top volume in her sporty sedan, the operatic high notes booming out the moon-roof blowhole.

Oh, yes, very probably, most certainly yes, the director said, nodding vigorously. My mom's face glowed with a rapturous inner light.

"Je t'aime Céline Dion!" she boomed, getting it mostly right.

Our mission here was done.

ON THE SECOND DAY of the trek toward Laguiole, a dot of a town smack in the middle of the map of France, the road began to narrow and wind around the hills even more tightly than the day before. My mom was starting to sigh about this ever-lengthening side trip and even I was beginning to think, *This had better be mind-blowingly good.* I hadn't been keeping track, but it seemed that she had already spent a ridiculous amount of money. We nearly drove right by the innocuous sign: MICHEL BRAS was printed in light type on a whiteboard, announcing the entrance to a thin black asphalt trail. Looking up, I could see the restaurant, a glass-walled building perched on the hill, as flat as the horizon itself.

This is the working French countryside, where men in dusty overalls drink beer (not wine) in the *tabac* in the morning. We had just stopped at one, looking to buy some water, which cracked up the crowd standing at the bar. Their big cheeks shook and one of the guys walked around the bar to get me an empty container, indicating that I should fill it with tap water. I couldn't make out anything he said but *"l'eau,"* so the bartender translated. "Best water you'll ever drink, he's saying, comes from right here." I felt sheepish, as if I had just walked into the Two Inlets Country Store back home and asked the crew sitting at the horseshoe bar where I could buy some nice imported New Zealand venison. They would have laughed and the owner would have slipped into his apartment in the back, grabbed a white package from his deep freezer, lobbed it to me, and said, "Take some of mine! We have plenty." It occurred to me that we'd been driving for days, straight into the midwestern heart of France, a place where common sense ruled.

Any rural posturing stopped at the door of Michel Bras. The building was striking and yet unobtrusive, a contemporary jetty cantilevered gracefully out from the tallest plateau. It had a helipad on its roof.

They seated us in front of the enormous picture window that seemed to slice off one side of the restaurant, looking out onto a grassy meadow stuck with little daisies. One of them was in a vase on the table next to a dish of yellow butter and a bowl of homemade crackers as brittle as old paper. All of the butter in France was richer than any I've ever known, but this one tasted of sunburned grass and of time left to sit out and absorb the local humors and moods. Real cultured butter tastes like culture.

Every dish seemed to have a clarity to it, a message: "This is the spring day we took a picnic on the hill." "This is a gray day's supper in front of an open fire." "This is the melt and the high water and the first green chives." "This makes up for the week of relentless freaking winds."

The cooking at Michel Bras wrestled with place in a way that I'd never known possible, somehow conveying the range of emotions that belonged to those who live all their lives in one spot and see their childhood refracted through the lens of their adulthood. *This is the middle of nowhere and the center of the universe.* It contained the hometown struggle set against the backdrop of the landscape. I had been wrong: The local pride did not end at the entrance to Bras; this was where it bloomed open.

The fourth course was a flat puddle of fawn-colored sauce encircled with a fairy ring of mushrooms, small ones I'd never seen before. I ate it slowly, looking for the fireworks I'd found in everything we'd had up to that point, but couldn't find them. My mom seemed to read my mind.

"See, I love this one. Everything doesn't have to change you. Sometimes things can just taste of what they are."

And that's what mothers are for, to remind their children of the simple things, of their particular, unspectacular, indelible histories.

"Oh, look at that." She nodded toward the table next to ours, where an older woman in a long skirt, not dressed as a waiter or a cook, was ladling a creamy puree high into the air from a copper pot, stretching it like taffy. It was *aligot,* a regional specialty, smooth ivory potatoes stringy with masses of local tomme fraîche de l'Aubrac cheese. The waiter assisted her, scooping out pillows of the potatoes and making quenelles of them with two spoons. "I think the chef has his mother making the potatoes!"

Indeed, he did.

The family devotion to this hill in the middle of France was palpable. And a gust of bittersweet homesickness for my own small house in the hill in the middle of nowhere arrived with the dessert.

THE THING ABOUT ME and my mom is that even though our mother-daughter issues hum below the surface of our cooking lives, they always rise up through the food channels. No matter how sore the conflict, when the dust settles we will always return to take our places on either side of the stove to produce heroic quantities of food—whether laughing or fighting or both. We are mother and daughter, but, above all, we are two cooks in a kitchen.

That summer after the trip to France, we reunited to make the food for my brother Bob's firstborn's baptismal party. How we could return from an eating tour like that (a gastronaut's blowout by anyone's standards), and come to stand in my mother's apartment kitchen in

St. Paul, stirring a vat of diced chicken and canned water chestnuts glued together with murky, industrial, carrageenan-rich canned "soup," the essential fixative in the Midwestern hotdish, is a total puzzler. And yet, when faced with the prospect of feeding fifty people a hot lunch, my mom reached into her recipe box, and into her past, and pulled out a card for Macy's Hot Chicken Salad—known to all Minnesotans as chicken hotdish. Now, before it has dawned on her how bleak it sounds compared to what we've just lovingly gorged ourselves on in Grandpa Dion's old country, we are already too far into it to turn back.

So here we are. I have pinned my knee into a yellow-flowered vinyl chair for leverage, because dragging a spoon through this quantity of chicken-chunk mixture is as hard as rowing a boat into the wind. I am amazed by the sounds coming out of it. *Pleef!*, it gasses, making the very same sound your sweaty lower back does when it disengages from a hot vinyl seatback. Like an elementary-school kid, I burst out laughing and say, "What did this thing eat?"

"It's got indigestion!" she says.

My mom picks off a floater of chicken and lobs it into her mouth for a taste, and I think back to the way Michel Bras's mother plucked at her potato puree to check its spring: Both of them make the same semi-agreeable "eh" kind of face.

But now my mom is crushing bags of crispy kettle chips and then raking them over the surface of the hotdish so that they will brown into an even gold crown across the top, and I have to admit, it is impossible not to pinch off a chip, its bottom soaked in a salty, sticky, implausibly delicious cream. What we are making is one gigantic, addictive dip.

The glorious junkiness of this thing does not elude me. For once, it is wonderfully comic. Mom and I are both hooting, noses up, then pitching forward, flimsy stems in a rollicking wind. Her famous hoot has been reduced to a whistling high C.

"Heeee!" she wheezes, hardly audible. "It's no French chicken fricassee!"

She pulls down the low oven door and squats, reaching into the oven to take it out, and then stops and bends over in ripples of laughter and defeat.

The giant hotdish stands before us, the puddles of fat from the melted cheese twinkling with the reflection from the fluorescent lights. It has turned out perfectly, and we and all of our relatives will demolish it with relish. It turns out that the full poundage of our canned-soup chicken-and-cheese Midwestern heritage, the rich, dense weight of it, is too much for either of us to bear alone. I look for the other pot holder.

It'll take the two of us to pull this sucker out of the oven.

4

MEAT VERSUS VEGETABLES

You can generally tell how a woman was raised by the way she wipes down a countertop.

Some mothers of my generation shooed their daughters out of the kitchen in the hopes that they'd never have to toil in it and gave them little direct instruction. Others, like my mom, insisted that their daughters could "do *anything*" they wanted to do, but then continued to school them in the housewifely arts anyway.

When I was nine years old, my mom taught me how to wipe the countertop in the following very specific way: You soak the washcloth in steaming-hot water, wring it out hard with both hands so that it no longer drips, then stretch the cloth flat on the countertop and lay your hand on it, middle finger pointing toward a corner, that corner flipped back up over your fingers like a toboggan. This way, when you wipe (and if you haven't seen this demonstrated, let me tell you, it's a god-damned miracle), the corner of the cloth stays up over your hand. "With a flat expanse of cloth, you can pick up crumbs," my mom stressed, her body leaning into the surface, running her cloth-covered nail tip into the crevice between the stove and the countertop. Her face, hanging above the shiny surface, was smooth and contented. Not joyous, not sad, but what you might call Placid Wiping Face.

Unconsciously I absorbed the look of spine-tingling satisfaction she gave the gleaming countertop and knew it contained something even greater: hope for tomorrow and its many projects. If you're despondent about the future, you don't wipe like that. You let the crumbs lie.

The other way to wipe a countertop is to distractedly grab the wet cloth in a bunch, the sloopy ends dripping water, and run it along the surface, pretending you don't see the crumbs that remain—which is how Aaron does it, and how many people do it, and which still generally gets the job done.

But inside my mom lived many generations of female ancestors who elevated mundane household maintenance into a craft. Women who wiped their countertops with rags so hot they steamed, who bleached their cutting boards monthly; women who thought that walking away from a crusty dish to let it soak would be like inviting the demon himself into her kitchen. From my barstool perch on the other side of the counter, I watched my mom wipe the mouths of glass condiment bottles, digging the crud out of the rim threads before putting the lids back on. I watched her transfer diminishing leftovers into smaller containers before putting them back into the fridge. For jobs too fine for a washcloth, she grabbed the old graying toothbrush from the bucket beneath the sink and frantically brushed the tight corners. The level of detail to which my mom and her mom, Grandma Dion, cleaned their kitchens was borderline obsessive-compulsive, and yet it pretty much sums up the entirety of professional cooking. Via the simple act of wiping, they passed on to me about 85 percent of what I'd need later on to survive my years of cooking in Manhattan kitchens—which is to say, the percentage of line cooking that depends on your ability to keep shit clean.

AFTER MY SUMMER TRIP TO FRANCE, I went back to Danube for a second helping—five or so nonillustrious months on the entremet station—before quitting once again. Out of fear that I was becoming addicted to the Bouley brand of dysfunction, I felt I needed to move on to another kitchen to see what else was out there. My next cooking job was at Daniel Boulud's db bistro moderne (all lowercase), where everyone, whether subjected to housewife training or not, knew how to properly wipe down a countertop. Unlike at Danube, where I was often the sole woman, this place was flush with female cooks—and from what I could tell, they were all angry.

Jean-François, db bistro's chef de cuisine, assigned me to train with Julie, who was working the cold station but moving up to entremet. She was to be my handler, and she did not look real happy about it.

Upon first meeting, all cooks posture to each other to let the other know exactly at which level of the game they're playing. Men in the kitchen generally do this subtly, dropping clues of their experience whenever they find it convenient. Women in the kitchen get right to the point. The serious ones generally play to win.

Julie let me know right off that she had cooked for so-and-so and so-and-so, and also at Café Boulud for years, and was only working the cold station as a favor to the chef. They were short-handed because some pisser—naturally, a girl—had quit.

"Ugh," she said. "The last girl sucked. Let's see if you can do better."

I wasn't sure. The prep list was serpentine.

At the time, db bistro moderne was Chef Boulud's third restaurant. He shared a French cooking pedigree and initials with Bouley, but they differed in temperament. Boulud's comments were delivered at a higher volume, and he was more briskly businesslike. And because he also ran two other restaurants—Café Boulud and his flagship, Daniel—he was also less likely to be hanging around during service.

db bistro was in the theater district, meaning it courted the hell horde of pretheater dining: tables in by 5:30, out by 7:15. Unlike at Danube, there was no gradual slide into the dinner slam. And being newly opened, the restaurant was also mobbed with the usual New York City scene-chasers; there was usually one at each table who ordered the $27 db burger, a high-end ground-beef blend stuffed with braised short ribs and a center chunk of foie gras, topped with two petals of tomato confit, and a tuft of pale green frisée. Dubbed "the most expensive burger ever" by the press shortly after it appeared on the menu, the db burger pretty much had its own public relations team and absolutely required its own cook. There was one guy who just made burgers all day long, pressing the tri-ply meat cake into the clean lid of a mayonnaise jar to mold it, filling sheet tray after sheet tray with burger pucks. The rest of us put hundreds of portions of tomato confit—peeled plum halves that shrank slowly overnight in a bath of olive oil—into low ovens every night before we left.

Apparently I had not learned my lesson at Danube and had not found a mellower follow-up restaurant, if such a thing even existed in Manhattan. The schedule in this newly opened place was after my dad's own workaholic heart: It was thirteen-hour days if you were quick enough to finish your work and six-day weeks. And sometimes, if for some reason Jean-François couldn't finagle your day off, you lost that day and had to work fourteen days in a row. This happened at inopportune times, like during the Christmas holidays. Everybody got off for Christmas Day, though, because the restaurant was closed, and the lucky ones were even sent home with a Christmas capon from Daniel Boulud himself. I quietly shared my grumbling with my friend, the Scottish meat cook. He had introduced me to a special little snack of cribbed French fries shoved into a soft bun, "the chip butty" (pro-nounced "buh-*hee*"), and tried to raise our collective Christmas spirits by making an elaborate Scottish haggis out of lamb lights (lungs) and heart and tongue, assembled after he'd finished his significant prep list. Returning to work on December 26 at six-thirty in the morning, the Scot and I trudged up the steps together and he said, turning his cuffs back, his kind eyes drooping at the corners, "So I guess that was the 'olidays, then?"

Unlike the Scot, Julie didn't seem to expect days off. She continued to ride me, following me around like we were twins, pointing out where I should have transferred my slightly-too-small amount of lobster mayonnaise into a container of a more befitting size, reminding me to cut my labeling tape with a scissors so that it had perpendicular corners instead of amateurish ripped ones, shrieking when I tested the artichokes barigoule for doneness with a meat fork, which left two small holes in the olive-green flesh. "Pinch them to test! Don't leave holes!" (*We sliced them and the holes wouldn't even show,* I thought, *but whatever.*) Whenever I appeared calm and in control—clearly not hustling enough—she ordered, "Come on, lady! Move your dick!"

I followed her around, too. For one thing, I was learning an invaluable amount of precious info from her, every bit of which was making me a better cook, but I also trailed her in the way that the abused cling to their abusers. She didn't like it when I got too close, though, and when we were lined up in the tight alley behind the hot line she hissed, "I can feel your *dick in my ass,*" and bounced me back a step with a well-placed bump.

Dear Jesus. I could have complained and resisted her, but there was no point. Engaging would have just egged her on. So I decided to take that moment to internalize her teachings and truly improve. I heard her voice even when she wasn't around, changing out containers, religiously rotating my mise en place to be FIFO compliant (first in, first out), stretching my plastic wrap neurotically over the corners of the metal containers until not a wrinkle in the plastic remained, until the taut top looked as see-through as glass and its containment was totally invisible. I ripped apart forty live lobsters every morning the same way she did: furiously. I screwed off the big claw and threw it into the big claw bin, the small into the small; I swiftly spun the tails apart from the bodies, then twisted and ripped out the middle fan of the tail, taking with it the ropy gray intestinal tract. Then, firmly holding the muscular clenching tail, I shoved a wooden skewer up that same poop chute to flatten it out and tossed it into the tail bin while its little arms were still waving good-bye. I didn't stop to watch the arms stop fluttering; I moved on to the next one. And the next. Nor did I take a minute to clean the lobster juice spittle from my glasses in the middle of ripping lobsters, but instead waited until it piled up so thickly that I could hardly see, when I was done with all of them. I tried not to feel sorry for these creatures, as I knew that would slow me down. My lobster meat was fast disintegrating into a goo. It needed cooking, pronto.

If Julie's predecessors, such as Ti, had taught me to cook well fast, she taught me to cook well even faster, and for bigger numbers.

I was in the vegetable walk-in at the end of my shift organizing my day's prep when she came in. She leaped up to the top shelves to grab a nearly empty box of watercress, then the last of the carrot carton and a half-gone box of limes, manically taking to heart her own advice to keep things neat, and pitched everything violently into the center like she was making a pile for a bonfire. Something was really stoking her.

"I'm just so sick of this crap!"

Either she was taking the nearly empty vegetable boxes way too personally or she was choosing this moment to reveal something to me—but I shouldn't have been surprised, because we were in the walk-in. Displays of emotion had no place in the kitchen, but the minute the walk-in cooler's massive vault door sucked shut, the coast was clear. It was the private inner sanctum of the kitchen, equal to a therapist's couch. Like wolves howling into the arctic night, cooks stood in the purifying freezing air and expressed themselves, snatching a moment to slowly grab herbs and share their grievances, to disgorge some burning kitchen gossip, or, like Julie, to angrily smash every nearly empty box to the floor and unleash her hot fury, which steamed off her in waves in the cold fan-powered wind.

When she found a metal six-pan of white beans soaking, the wrinkly top beans rising up above the waterline, she started railing—not at me, but at some nonpresent incorrigible someone.

"These beans are improperly soaked!" She could have just said that someone didn't use enough water to cover them, but for her the incompetence went deeper than that. The amount of water wasn't just insufficient, it was improper. It offended her kitchen ethic.

"Not mine!" I backed up.

"Shut up, I know they're not yours. Do you cook beans?" she taunted, shaking the six-pan. We both knew I did not.

Julie threw her head back in the air and spun for the exit. "Thirty-one years old and I'm still doing this fucking veg shit!" she said, punching the button to open the door. The air pressure gasped, releasing her to the outside.

I made a quick deduction that she hadn't been promoted to the meat station, recently vacated by the giant I-forget-his-name-now guy, the sweaty one who kept the tip of his rolled-up tongue pressed to his top lip during service in a state of pure concentration. For some reason, you rarely saw chefs assign women to cook the main protein, even if that woman was a sous chef. Sometimes the fish, but never the meat.

Honestly, it didn't make sense to me, though. It seemed that Chef Jean-François trusted Julie. We all liked him. He was a fair guy. I looked around the kitchen at all the cooks' moving, bumping, swirling shapes and thought, It wasn't that Jean-François, or most of the male chefs, meant to be sexist. What was going on here was actually worse. It was a failure of the imagination. Promoting a cook to a position of greater responsibility involved squinting at that cook to see if you could imagine him (or her), as they said, "stepping up" into the harder job. It was the lazy side of cowardice: when the chefs looked back in time to their own line-cooking youths, they fondly remembered their own chefs squinting at them and gauging them sufficiently ready to step up, so they promoted the guy. Pleased with themselves to close this circle, they failed to see that it was an unfair eternal cycle.

Or maybe I was being too generous. They also knew the girls would take the sideways promotions to fill the stations that needed filling, good strong girls that they were. So capable and uncomplaining, just like a mother.

When I walked out, Julie was heatedly discussing this issue with Faye, our thirty-something "junior" sous chef. They broke the huddle when they saw me. The last thing they wanted was an all-witch bitchfest. They were too smart to dilute their power by embracing their lessers.

By the end of my seven years in Manhattan kitchens, I'd come to feel their pain. Like them, I nearly always worked the vegetable station and never the roast. Always a bridesmaid, never a groom. Only later did I realize that the vegetable station—the entremet—which I thought of as my gender-specific bondage, would be my revelation.

SOON AFTER, Julie left to be the head chef of a restaurant in Brooklyn—I cheered both her success and her evacuation—and I took over her entremet position on the line.

This was classic French food reimagined by Daniel Boulud, inarguably one of the great chefs in New York City. But due to the amount of covers we were doing, the multitude of people we were serving, it was the classics on speed. Escargots with garlic and parsley puree took three minutes. Chicken Grand-mère took two. There were two guys to my left, the Scot cooking fish, a new towering guy cooking meat—so much meat that he sliced the duck breasts and steaks with an electric knife, a tool I hadn't seen used since my mom buzzed through the Thanksgiving turkey back home. To my right was the burger guy, responsible for about a quarter of the main courses that flew out the door. His fries were as crispy and light as balsa wood, and exquisite. I ate many, many, many of them. I was cooking all of the garnish for the meat and fish plates, and when we got slammed, Jean-François hopped onto the line to help dig me out.

The first rush was over and I was replenishing the garnish for the chicken, which had experienced an uncharacteristic run in the first quarter of service. I was cooking fat blocks of bacon lardons in a sauté pan, starting them in a shallow bath of water, as the morning entremet had instructed me to do. Jean-François asked incredulously, "What tha hell are you dew-ing? Is this how you cook lard-ohns? In water?"

He was right. Why *was* I cooking them in water? With a chill I thought: *Because the morning entremet guy had told me to.* How could I screw up bacon, the ingredient that defined my childhood, the thing I watched my mom cook with such devotion? She'd drilled me on the bacon. Don't crowd the pan, she'd said. Don't cook it so fast, or it sticks to the bottom and its juices boil away. Don't cook it too slow or too much fat renders and it'll taste dry. You want to tease out the fat. The bacon should swizzle steadily away in its own juices until its edges constrict like a shrunken wool sweater and turn coconut-brown. These visuals were hardwired into me.

If I was screwing up the bacon, something was seriously out of whack. And at that moment I reached the very peak of my information-gathering phase; the stage of absorbing the lessons of others like an indiscriminate sponge had ended. Going forward, I'd follow my instincts.

Meat got all the glory, but the roast position seemed to me the most straightforward one in the kitchen. The protein had to be cooked to the correct temperature, no question; that was easy to see. And not that hard to do once you got in the groove, cooking identically sized portions of the same things night after night. Once it was sliced, it was truth time. The color told you whether to cook it harder the next time or ease up.

The garnish, though—the starch and the vegetables and the sauces—were all more subtly make or break. Oversalted or undercooked yellow wax beans? Those are invisible mistakes. Lack of soulful cooking, also invisible. And, crucially, in order to sing on the plate, the starches and the vegetables need to contain some soul. Undercooked fish came right back to the kitchen for refiring and was grudgingly reaccepted a few minutes later, but if a diner bit on the tough core of a carrot they registered it the way a carpenter does a nail found in the center of a board: with supreme annoyance, but silently.

Everyone, even the big bulky guys, referred to cooking the garnish well as cooking "with love," a phrase rarely applied to the protein. The

first time I heard it, I was taken aback. A big lumbering guy, reminisc-
ing about his days cooking at Alain Ducasse in Monaco, said: "The guy
I trained with, he cooked the vegetables with so much love . . ." and
shook his head, as if trying to dislodge a big, fat imaginary tear in his
eye, a kaleidoscope that turned the sauté pan before us into twelve
swirling gems of vegetable-garnish loveliness.

At the time I saw the world in much the same way, in terms of
colors, sounds, and shifting textures: silken scarves of hot squash
puree, dunes of homemade bread crumbs as mottled and cool to the
touch as beach sand. Fresh parsley puree of a stinging green, pure
liquid chlorophyll. The cackle of thyme and garlic hitting brown butter,
its reassuring scent rising up. I also admired the seared golden-
crowned scallops and the sliced pink duck breasts and the dark lobes
of venison split open to reveal their savage red interiors—but I fell in
love with the garnishes. In fact, nearly every emotion I felt during that
time was connected to the food; my relationships with humans were
secondary. (And I say this with deepest apologies to Aaron because he
knows it's true.) My egg-shaped silver plating spoon was an extension
of my hand, the plates an extension of my thoughts. I was pie-eyed for
the garnishes and knew nothing of current events. Even now, when
someone mentions a major happening from my line-cooking tenure,
I often look at them blankly. (Hanging chads from that contested 2000
election? No flipping idea.)

At the end of the day I fell into bed and a color factory of sauces and
purees washed over me: the bright yolk yellow of the corn sauce; the
milk-green of creamed favas; the inner glow of beets in red wine.

This is what happens to a cook when she spends so many hours
gaping at the contents of the pan before her, waiting for doneness. It's
not unlike the way a gardener watches her tomatoes ripen. Both end
points mark the moment at which a vegetable contains as much liquid
sweetness as it ever will. When perfectly cooked, a wedge of white
turnip will drip juices as if its light purple veins run with fat, and its

tissue will soften and taste like butter. On the raw side of things, an utterly ripe tomato at the end of August swings low on its vine, opalescent and suntanned gold at the shoulders, its voluptuous flesh nearly falling out of its skin.

To me, becoming a cook meant being able to spot that point and know when the time came to stop—to pull it, slice it, and put it on a plate. Raw or cooked, that is the vegetable finale. And to me and all my entremet sisterhood—both the women and the men—it looks pretty much like happiness itself.

5

HERRING DARES AND CHICKEN TURTLES

In 2003, Fort Greene, our neighborhood in Brooklyn, seemed bipolar, rapid-cycling between decline and boom—a symptom better known as gentrifying. The dusty-shelved corner bodega, an obvious front for a numbers joint, soon gave way to a slick sushi place. When the first posh pet-accessories store opened, we worried that our rent would soon be increasing and we were right: Two years after we moved from the illegal sublet across the hall into a cavernous two-floored space big enough for both our living space and Aaron's studio, the landlord nearly doubled our rent.

I wasn't deflated, just pissed. We'd re-created a mini-Minnesota in the building. Not long after Matt's death, Aaron's sister, Sarah, came home from the Peace Corps and moved into our second bedroom, and Sara Woster, our painter friend from Minneapolis, had moved into our vacated studio across the hall. (We called them Sister-Sarah and Woster, respectively.) Together with Rob, who came over to smoke cigars with Aaron in his studio a few times a week, we expat Minnesotans dropped into one another's apartments with frequent, casual, sitcom ease. We all spent much of our free time going to art openings. Rob was doing well in the art world; he had a gallery in Chelsea, had made it into the Whitney Biennial, and was selling sculptures for big sums of money, but he and Aaron were still working carpentry day jobs together and working on artwork at night. On Thursday and Friday nights after openings, I'd meet up with all of them at the late-late after-party, pulling up with greasy hair, my heavy cook's bag tilting me crooked, and try to catch up to their loose-jointed states by ordering a shot and a beer chaser, which I was usually too tired to finish.

But when New York bore down its realities, the time came for us all to scatter and find new homes.

Aaron and I found a new apartment one subway stop farther away from Manhattan, in Prospect Heights. It was a one-bedroom above a deli on Atlantic Avenue, Brooklyn's main thoroughfare, but the immediate neighborhood surrounding the building felt desolate and uneasy. The streets were occupied by scrappers pushing shopping carts full of cans and metal to the recycling center one block over. Outside the front door stood a thick cottonwood tree with a curious wet spot in the crevice of its first branch. Eventually we figured out why this spot was perpetually moist and named it "the piss tree"—for it provided all the neighborhood men on walkabout a shady place to relieve themselves. But the apartment came with a double-car garage at street level, big enough for Aaron's studio, and a large private roof deck. The rent hovered just above our upper limit. I wasn't sure. As we walked away from the building in the pounding rain, weighing our options, I saw something skittering to the side of my vision: a huge rat squeezing under the garage door.

We'd been in New York for more than three years, so I wasn't shocked by the rat. It just compounded the dimness of the moment, the blows of the giant raindrops on my boots. Where Aaron saw hope and a nice studio space, I saw a future shackled to high-rent digs on a dreary corner. My perspective could just as easily have been positive. We weren't destitute. Aaron was working a steady carpentry job that paid well, even though making art was still his main gig; every night he whacked away at a new group of sculptures. He'd just begun to paint the surfaces of his carved bas-reliefs black and to rub the points with metallic graphite so that the wood looked like poured iron. They were growing into a serious collection, starting to look like deranged frescoes made by a mad hermit in a hideout. He'd been showing in gallery group shows, but still, art wasn't paying the rent. My cooking job at db bistro sure didn't pay much. In this neighborhood, I wouldn't be able to ride the subway home after work and walk the three dark empty blocks from the subway alone; I'd have to blow money on nightly cabs.

"The apartment is pretty nice," I said. "But that garage is a shit-hole."

"I'll clean up the garage," Aaron said. "It would be a great studio."

"What if we can't afford it?"

"What does that mean? I'm making good money. You're working."

"I mean, what if you don't. What if you get a show and don't work," I said, not really questioning but dropping statements like bombs.

"You mean what if I become a working artist with a gallery and don't make any money? That doesn't make any sense." He looked at me with bewilderment. "That's what a working artist is: *working.*"

As we walked he let this sink in and then spun his head and groaned. I couldn't believe I'd said it out loud, either. It was exactly as he had suspected, the buried tension that hummed between us. I wasn't buying the dream. I would have argued that I was questioning the sustainability of the dream, but I knew that all he could hear was the sound of my heavy boots stomping on plan A.

"No, no." I backpedaled. "It's not that I don't believe in *you,* it's that I don't believe in the *art world.* I don't know if I believe in . . ." I keeled through the puddles and the water flew up in protest. I shook my head quickly, to dislodge the thoughts that were rising up in my head: *Maybe I just want a normal life. Boring and predictable. Salaries. Vacation time. Savings.*

"Listen, Amy," he said. "This is what I am. I'm an artist. I don't *do* anything else. I'm not really equipped to do anything else. This is what I went to school for, what I trained to be."

I stood there silently. I knew his work was really good, better than what was in a lot of the shows we saw. Aaron had spent all of these years deriding the notion of a backup plan—equating it to a dilution of one's purpose—and I had always agreed in the abstract, but now we were living it, without any kind of meaningful or realistic plan B. He was a sculptor; I was a cook. We had no financial cushion.

"I can't believe you actually said you don't believe in it," he said, meaning our dreams, the reasons we had moved to New York in the first place.

I was skeptical, but when he put it that way, I didn't want to be the one who, twenty years from now, could be blamed for derailing our lives onto the secondary track. I wanted our first choices to work. "I do believe in it. I do. We should take the place."

He nodded, didn't look at me, and briskly entered the subway stairs. He didn't believe me.

WE RENTED THE APARTMENT AND, soon after, Aaron's sister, Sarah, and her husband, Paul, moved into the apartment next door. Eventually Aaron would cut a swinging door into the fence between our adjoining roof decks, but first he cleaned up the garage. It was a serious project that involved screwing cement boards around its perimeter to block the rat superhighway leading into the deli next door. The rats, effectively priced out of their old neighborhood, quickly found new homes. Aaron whitewashed the floors and the walls, and one night we set up a table on which I laid a tablecloth and a landscape of fancy appetizers. He opened the garage door to the street. Just a month after that day in the rain, we were having a housewarming party and I was serving raw-milk cheeses in the rodents' former abode. What a taunt.

Upstairs on the vast garage-roof deck we erected a verdant ode to our rural life back home: We planted rows of peppers and tomatoes and cucumbers in empty Sheetrock buckets and constructed a raised bed for herbs, and in the center we dragged over an adolescent maple tree in a whiskey barrel in the hope that its canopy would someday shade our picnic table. Aaron installed a tightly wound screen door on the entrance from the kitchen and its quick slam behind us was like the punctuation to the rural language I knew.

A horde of friends came to our housewarming party. Even with people divided among the apartment, the deck, and the studio, the place felt hopping. A West Indian timpani band started going through its jubilant set in the lot directly behind ours, having rented the space in preparation for the Flatbush West Indian parade. They practiced nightly at 10 P.M., but this night it seemed as if they were playing just for us.

After midnight we heard this series of soft explosions, maybe fireworks, and through the open garage door we saw a group of teenagers running swiftly past. Ten soft pops, then more, almost too many to be a shooting—but it was. Aaron immediately slammed down the garage door, and instantaneously everyone began asking me for the number of our local car service. We were so new to the neighborhood, I didn't even know it yet.

When we opened the door a few minutes later to let people out to meet their cars, we saw that Matt, our friend from Minnesota, had been stuck outside when the garage door closed. He was still crouching behind the piss tree, all 6 feet and 4 inches of him not exactly hidden.

"I'm okay!" he shouted with an upraised palm, and bounced into the garage. "Could use another beer, though."

BY THIS TIME my résumé was as confusing as a Long Island Railroad timetable. It was riddled with exits and returns, mostly a lot of back-and-forth from the Bouley enterprise: Danube; back to Park Rapids for a couple of months; Danube again; db bistro moderne for four long months; home for a month for our wedding; back to Bouley again.

Like most New York City line cooks who were cycling through top kitchens soaking up experience, I always intended my kitchen stints to last the required year. Twelve months was long enough to appease the chef and absorb the techniques and flavors of the job, but short enough to maintain both your sanity and your relationship, if you had one. Basically, the rule was a baker's dozen: Twelve months were required, a good cook gave thirteen or more. My last stint with Chef Bouley—otherwise known as the time I returned to the dysfunctional family for one final helping—fell a little short of that.

After our wedding, it appeared that Aaron and I had miscalculated and couldn't quite afford the European honeymoon we'd planned to take. We had to forfeit the tickets to Paris his parents bought for us because we didn't have the money for food or hotels once we got there, even if we scrimped. We spent our would-be honeymoon at JFK airport fighting to get vouchers, to no avail. Our hopes and wishes, as outsized as ever, had once again surpassed our practicality. It was classic us.

As before, my feet beat a trail to the Bouley doors on Duane Street. I timed my arrival with the afternoon family meal and cornered Shea Gallante, the chef de cuisine, whom I'd known when I cooked at Danube, and begged for my job back.

He rolled his eyes. "Again?" And then with a sigh he admitted that he could use another cook. He took me to the office where Chef Bouley agreed to my hire—on the condition that I'd take on the added responsibilities of recording all of his recipes and turning the kitchen into a more well-oiled machine. Bouley was juiced up; he wanted a total rehaul, and for some reason he persisted in thinking that I was some kind of a great systemizer. "Reorganize all of the mise en place on the stations," he told me. "I don't want cooks stacking plastic cups of mise en place into tubs of ice anymore, it looks so sloppy. All of that prep should be in refrigerated underpulls. I want everything off the counters. And let's be neater. I want all of these cooks cleaning out their own blenders."

As we left Bouley's office, Shea gave me a sidelong glance, a lowly line cook who had just been given a curious amount of responsibility. Embarrassed, I blurted out, "Wouldn't this be your job? Why in the hell is he asking *me*?" He laughed, knowing exactly how difficult it would be to rewire the whole kitchen system. "I have no idea," he said, taking the stairs to the kitchen two at a time. "But now it's your job. You should get going on that."

I walked back into the kitchen and took a look at the mountains of dishes, a full day's worth, in the basement; the lack of under-counter refrigeration in the kitchen to accommodate this new "no cups" situation; a line cook, frantic before service, throwing his dirty food-processor container onto the top of the dirty dish mountain; two pale externs frantically assembling canapés for an offsite party; Bouley due to rush in the door at 6:00 with fresh produce for new menu dishes; the family of prep cooks calmly running through their lists; my own heavy meat entremet workload. The two-floor kitchen was too serpentine, Bouley too prone to throwing unpredictable grenades, and the family, who actually held the keys to the system, too stuck in their routines.

Overwhelmed, I failed to instate a new organizational system and after three months I gave notice—yet again.

As if for punishment, my final day coincided with the aftermath of an extermination bombing—the most unsavory day in the life of any Manhattan kitchen. Roy the head butcher impassively brushed piles of insect bodies off the counters with a broom. As I pulled out a cutting board from the bleach water, the fast teenage roaches that had somehow survived ran wild like hoodlums.

The day got worse. During that evening's service, instead of closing out my tenure there with my usual proficiency, I collapsed into an epic fail. Nothing went right. My disks of wild mushroom duxelles, gelled with agar-agar and served hot under the rack of lamb—which I had been *nailing* for the past few weeks—were all inexplicably dissolving. My simple butter-emulsified green vegetables—entremet 101—overreduced and broke into beads of excess fat. My timing was cocked a good ten seconds off every table.

Finally the meat guy to my right threw his basting spoon clattering into the pan with the chunk of wagyu beef, raised his head to Bouley at the pass, and hissed to me, "I can't fucking cook with you!"

Bouley walked over and clenched a hand around my shoulder, not exactly kindly and without his trademark smirk, and whispered, "I thought you just got married? You getting too much, is that why you can't cook anymore?" Then he looked at me quizzically, as if receiving a new idea. "Or maybe you're not getting enough . . ."

By this time I'd become accustomed to his carnal cooking metaphors—juice was juice!—and wanted to return the joke by saying that the temperature of my porridge was neither too hot nor too cold but just right, thank you very much, but felt muted by my poor performance. A captain called him back to the pass to greet some VIPs whose last private offsite party I'd worked with Bouley. The woman waved enthusiastically at me, calling me over, saying something inaudible to the chef. He looked at me with a false smile and answered, loud enough for me to hear across the room: "Yes, she's here. For now." I stood still halfway between him and the line, my plating spoon frozen to my pot. "Amy's like a little bird," he said, his fingers flickering in the air, "flitting from place to place." The most manic, improvisational, restless chef in New York was calling me out as an itinerant flake, and he wasn't wrong. I had to admit: I was a bird. A snowbird. A returning swan. I was always on migration.

DESPITE MY FLAMING DEPARTURE FROM BOULEY, I decided to stick with the fine-dining scene and cycle through the next top New York City chef of that generation: Jean-Georges Vongerichten. At the outset his style seemed to lie somewhere between the two DBs: a bit modernized-

French-classic like Daniel Boulud, a bit vegetable-juice-fueled like David Bouley. After my first night trailing at his flagship restaurant in Trump Tower, Jean-Georges, I found that his cooking also contained a thrilling streak of Asian brightness, pops of finely minced Thai chili, lime juice, and lemongrass. Greg Brainin, Jean-Georges's chief creative officer, hired me to work the line, and then just before I started, he decided to transfer me to be a sous chef at 66, an authentic Chinese place they were opening in Tribeca. When I met with Catherine (not her real name) in management she dropped my title to junior sous, reducing my modest salary even more and marking yet another time that the women were meaner than the men.

At this point, I had to laugh. Sexism was so predictable. Nevertheless, 66 proved to be the craziest, most transformative experience of my cooking career.

The kitchen was huge, clean, white, and modern, and visible to the Richard Meier–designed dining room through a bank of very large fish tanks. The staff was composed of both Chinese- and American-trained cooks. The Western-trained cooks handled the cold appetizers, the hot appetizers, and the more fusion-style main courses, all cooked on gas ranges. The Chinese cooks (most of whom had lived in New York for years) were divided into teams: the wok station, led by Chef Wei-Chin; and the dim sum station, led by Mei (pronounced Moy), whom we called Mei One. Wei-Chin and a few others stir-fried entrees in the woks, and Mei One and his team made all the dim sum, ran the giant steamer, and made the noodle and rice dishes. And each was definitely a team. Collectivity was their thing. If the management threatened to can one of them—as they did when Mei One was caught bullying a tiny, effeminate male back waiter in the locker room—they'd all threaten to go. The barbecued meats in the restaurant, however—the crispy suckling pig, the Peking ducks, the red-glazed pork char siu, all the stuff you see hanging in the window of a Chinese restaurant—were made by another Mei who worked solo. We called him Barbecue Mei. In all, there were four Meis.

Everyone answered to Josh Eden, the chef de cuisine, a New York–
born Jean-Georges veteran who went by the nickname of Shorty. And
in the beginning Jean-Georges himself was always in attendance, as
were Brainin and Master Chef Lam and Sun Tek, consulting chefs
from Hong Kong.

Right off the bat, this was the place the fashion and food worlds
wanted to be. The music was thumping; the tiny string of airplane-size
bathrooms quickly turned into long-term "powder" rooms. During the
opening week, it seemed every scallion pancake I served was destined
for Naomi Campbell or Martha Stewart or former New York City
mayor Ed Koch or someone similarly famous. One morning I arrived
to find a photo-shoot crew from *Vogue* swarming around a familiar-
looking top model standing in front of the fish tanks holding a live
lobster, her legs buffed to a classic-car high gloss. A prop stylist met
me at my station, hysterical with the question of the morning: Would
the lobster die after being out of the water for so long? It had taken
them thirty minutes to get the shot. I assured him not, covered the
lobster with soaked paper towels, and slid the lethargic crustacean into
my cooler. I didn't quite get his concern. The thing would meet its
steaming end within a few hours anyway.

Mostly, I cooked the hot apps, much-improved versions of Chinese-
American favorites: egg rolls, shrimp toast, gingered barbecued ribs,
corn-and-crabmeat soup. I also made a few more authentically Chinese
dishes: a whole stuffed blue crab covered with a lid of delicate, fried-
lotus-seed paste; frog's legs marinated in egg and potato starch, deep
fried, and showered with a light snowy pile of crispy egg and garlic
topping; wild mushrooms steamed with sake and ginger and spooned
over a disk of sticky rice. It was the best Chinese food I'd ever had.

Chef Lam, who was staying in an apartment over the restaurant,
was the first one to show up for work in the morning, and he sported
three strands of long curling hair from his chin. They said that he had
invented Shrimp with Candied Walnuts and Chili, the dish knocked

off in hundreds of Chinese restaurants around the world and at 66 as well. He spent his evening service cooking dozens of whole crispy-skinned garlic chickens in the wok, passing them between two wire spiders in the hot fat until the skin turned uniformly caramel brown. Then with his cleaver he reduced each blistering hot bird into bite-size pieces and adroitly reassembled them on the plate into the shape of a turtle. This chicken was a marvel of Chinese engineering, a balloon of juice contained inside a shell of brittle brown skin. My proximity to his chopping station drove me crazy, the crispy shards flying tantalizingly close to me but hitting the floor. Once in a while he passed me an odd-shaped divot of meat and skin, one that didn't fit into his turtle puzzle. I tucked it into my mouth, swallowed it as unobtrusively as a snake sharked down a tidbit, and nodded my thanks.

When it got slow, which it was wont to do in a restaurant with a menu of such breadth, its items spread out among so many cooks, I squatted behind my station next to the enormous Chinese dim sum steamer, downed extra dumplings on the sly, and contemplated drinking sake out of a teacup, as some of the other cooks were doing. I had never drunk anything but water on the job before and wasn't really interested in starting. I had never squatted on my heels before, either, but I tried to mimic the deep, comfortable-looking pose of the line of dim sum guys to my left. They laughed at me and passed a plastic prep container down the line until it got to Jacky, the impassive kid who ran the steamer next to me. He had introduced himself proudly as an ABC, American-born Chinese, different from the rest of them.

"They want you to try the chicken feet," Jacky said, handing over the container. The Chinese cooks snacked on chicken feet all day long as if they were potato chips, spitting out the tiny bones into plastic containers.

Mei One got up and came down the line brandishing a cup of dark liquid.

"Saucy," he said, beaming.

"He says you need to try it with the sauce," Jacky duly repeated. I picked up a foot and nibbled on the gelatinous joint. Through the thick coating of sweet soy sauce, it tasted like a chicken back without the crisp, but fattier. The pop of the cartilage in my mouth felt oddly foreign, and I thought I could feel the toenail in my mouth. I could tolerate the chicken foot but wouldn't be craving them. But I smiled down the line, raising my empty plastic cup.

They howled and slapped their knees, knowing I didn't really love it.

Jacky was my informant. He told me all kinds of things about the dim sum team. They liked to gamble in Atlantic City, for example. They headed out en masse on Saturday nights for the AC bus, returned early in the morning to take catnaps on the puffy laundry bags in a dark basement break room, and woke up just before service to make a restoring vat of congee, which they decorously shared with the crew. They cursed Shorty for making them use sea salt instead of "chicken powder," their prized salt-and-MSG mixture, and had hidden the forbidden canisters deep beneath their stations. They preferred Korean brothels.

And these guys could really cook. I watched Wei-Chin flipping the iron wok over its jet of blue fuel, controlling the heat with the lever at his knees. He rocked the wok line like a stadium drummer on the trap set: with raised knees, mad precision, and regular bursts of flames. I saw that stir-frying was not a process of addition, as I had previously thought, but a careful orchestration. I watched as he briefly fried the beef in oil, then scooped it out with a wire spider and set it to drain on a railing above the line. He poached his Chinese broccoli (*gai lan*) in water, then set that to drain as well. He whisked his hot wok clean with water and a stiff bamboo brush, then sizzled his aromatics—ginger, garlic, and whole red chilies—in a little oil, returned the beef and broccoli to the pan, and tossed the mixture in one-two-three high-rising waves in the air. With one hand he seasoned it with salt (a little) and sugar (a little more) and with the other added a pinch of cornstarch slurry from the pot at his side. The mixture turned immediately glossy, each separate piece wrapped in a thin vellum of sauce. This operation took about two minutes, start to finish. When it hit the plate, gleaming, I thought it was one of the most glorious things I'd ever seen.

I stood at the hot app station in the sweaty heat at the end of the night, when my defenses were down, and I let the movie stream of new techniques and textures wash over me. Chinese food seemed to contain so many more of them than Western food. The Chinese don't just have crisp: they have wet crisp (stir-fried lotus root, for instance) and they have dry crisp (the crispy pile of fried egg yolk crumbs I gently squeezed into a peak on top of the frog's legs). There was moist soft (tofu and steamed fish) and dry soft (the cloudy-white steamed bao buns). I wondered why we Western-trained cooks had so few ways to describe textures.

And the Chinese guys cooked brilliantly in a way that felt counterintuitive to me. To make lemon chicken, they dredged a flattened chicken breast in egg and fluffy white potato starch and then deep-fried it for at least ten minutes, about eight minutes longer than flattened chicken breasts usually need to cook through. Greg, the other sous chef, yanked it up from the fryer after a regulation three minutes, and Wei-Chin came over in alarm, motioning him to drop it back down. Implausibly, after the full ten minutes, when we sliced into it, the interior still ran with juice. They dumped tubs of liquid maltose, as clear and sweet as corn syrup but thicker, right into a vat of boiling peanut oil—sugar in oil, which seemed like a surging grease fire in the making—added piles of skinned walnuts, and then calmly ran their spider through the foaming head of oil. A few minutes later, each browned walnut emerged from the sugared fat painted with a thin layer of sweet lacquer. They were so delicate and crisp that they clicked lightly on the sheet tray as the cooks swiftly ran their chopsticks through the mass to separate them. When we ran out of suitable vegetables for family meal, they stir-fried a case of green leaf lettuce and somehow made it taste like cabbage. They ran water for hours through colanders full of shrimp, which we feared would bloat them and sap their flavor, but instead restored their original clean ocean snap. They resuscitated what smelled to us like soured fresh water chestnuts the very same way, chasing Shorty with the containers in their hands to show how the running water had brought them back from the dead.

The ways in which the Chinese cooks deviated from the script of my French-based training was confounding to me, but also revelatory. Years afterward, holding a pack of frizzle-ended supermarket green beans in my hands, I remembered how to fry them hard in oil until they shriveled and to top them with a porky black bean sauce. From these guys I knew that these dead beans held some possibility. The produce we used at 66 was always top-notch, but the Chinese dishes held clues to a past rooted in deprivation and resourcefulness. Like a Midwestern farmhouse cook and her April sack of storage carrots, they could wring sauce from stones.

SOME OF THE WESTERN CHEFS were getting sick of Chinese food; not me, but some. We put up two different family breakfasts each day, one Western style and one Chinese. Given this choice, I always ate the Chinese one. Greg, the other sous chef, asked me, "How can you eat that gloppy stir-fry for breakfast every day?"

What, this? Chicken with bamboo and vegetables? I loved it.

But one day Shorty, our Jewish, Manhattan-born chef, said, "God, I can't eat any more Chinese food. I need some chicken liver pâté." So he called for takeout from Russ & Daughters on the Lower East Side: smoked whitefish, lox, smoked sturgeon, sour pickles, chicken liver pâté, and pickled herring, its silver skin as shiny as stainless steel. He arranged this spread carefully on the pass. The Chinese cooks looked on in amusement.

"Pickled herring," Shorty said. "It's fish! Try it!" Dao, one of the dim sum cooks, took a piece and bit off one end, then spat it into his cup of tea in horror. The others tried it and all had the same reaction.

"NO GOOD!" Dao pronounced. Mei One tried it and had the same reaction. He was appalled; his body shuddered at the combination of sugar and fish.

"Wei-Chin, try the herring. Very good," I said. He chewed it carefully, spat it immediately into the garbage, and grinned slyly at me.

The tables had been turned. In pickled herring we Westerners had found our chicken feet. Similarly, its joys were largely textural. Good herring has a sensuous resistance to the bite. When cured perfectly—not too sweet—it holds the mark of your teeth, as fudge does. The sting of the pickle transported me straight to summer at our lake cabin, where my mom ceremoniously uncapped the plastic tub of silver diamond-cut fish bobbing in brine, setting my mouth to swim with juice.

We ate and ate, slurping it up lasciviously. The dim sum team laughed at us and animatedly tapped their short dim sum rolling pins on the metal counter, talking joyously about our bizarre food.

You had to give it to them: New York was not diluting their heritage. They walked around the city in a Chinese dome, eating Chinese food, frequenting Chinese stores, speaking very little English. They were there, in New York, but as prideful, conflicted defectors, like me. I talked up Minnesota as if it were the promised land, stubbornly wore an unhip hippie belt that reminded me of my former rural life, and insisted on calling soda "pop." I wanted to keep training in New York, had no idea how I'd cook professionally back home in Two Inlets, but felt a powerful need to keep up my allegiances. Like my Chinese coworkers, I sailed around the kitchen with my home in my back pocket.

My nostalgia was like a slipcover for a precious-but-ugly family heirloom. No amount of gingered crab could erase the truth: The meat and potatoes that had once defined me no longer sufficed. My palate had been whetted for more complicated flavors, more diverse populations, more chili fire. As I kneaded lotus-paste dough, I weighed my two homelands, the old and the new, and began to wonder which one would eventually win out. Unlike my Chinese comrades, I didn't see a clear path back.

I WORKED LIKE I WAS ON REPEAT, walking out of the apartment each day around 10 A.M. with my glass pint jar of maple-sweetened iced coffee, returning home each day by taxi at 1 A.M., fried and sweaty. When I cracked Aaron's studio door I was often met with a cloud of cigar smoke and the sight of him and Rob sitting on rocking chairs in the gray mist, yakking about art and listening to a steady soundtrack of outlaw country. Waylon Jennings, Merle Haggard, Gretchen Wilson. The rural narrative was part of our collective consciousness, our group persona. They were the country boys who had reluctantly come to the city to find work in the art world; I was Aaron's exhausted third-shift waitress wife. My feet throbbing, I figured I was about as tired as a girl in a country song. I considered seventy-plus hours a week an inevitable schedule but continued to whine about my constant suffering and threw a tantrum over any Sunday plans Aaron suggested that didn't include a nap. My day off consisted of cooking him a huge dinner so that he'd have leftovers while I was gone. My case was classic. I was a martyr.

I knew this, could hear myself saying the words "wish I could, have to work," and rued them, but at the same time I kept a list of excuses running in my head. Here's the funny thing about a cook's martyrdom: It really does begin with a generous impulse. Even though I spent my nights hunched over tiny tasting-menu-size plates, at night I dreamed of making giant pots of soup and serving it to the masses. Because of this, the martyr feels justified in her crabbiness. She's pulling these double shifts out of a deep desire to feed the people. But housed inside the shell of a cranky, overworked cook with a sore back and a perma-rash between her perpetually moist fingers, that originally decent nugget of generosity comes out as the most unrelenting and aggressive kind of altruism, in spools and spools of never-ending spaghetti. And no amount of logic can stem her ever-growing rock collection of hard knocks.

Aaron was getting plenty sick of the way my work flooded our life, but to his credit, he never suggested I quit. My insomnia was killing us both, though. When I couldn't get to sleep on Sunday night, my only day off each week, he wanted to either take me out to a bar and feed me shots of Jameson until I passed out or clock me on the head. I was willing to do either if something would just knock me out. Something in our relationship, and in our life, had to break—and finally did. The day came that Aaron's commitment to plan A proved him right.

I knew he had had an important studio visit that day, but I didn't expect him to call me on the kitchen phone at the restaurant. Shorty answered and handed it over with disapproval: "For you."

Aaron breathlessly told me what had happened. Zach Feuer, the art dealer, showed up at his studio with a friend, who happened to be Maurizio Cattelan, the famous artist. They were enthusiastic about the work and each bought a carving on the spot—and then called up two of Cattelan's main collectors, who came over and bought up the rest of Aaron's studio. Aaron would have a solo show at Zach's gallery in Chelsea in the spring, and the collectors were going to show his biggest carving at their own museum during the Art Basel Miami Beach fair in December.

He finished his spiel and I tried to take it all in.

"Oh my god, oh my god! Do we go to that?" I said, meaning Art Basel.

"Yes, are you kidding?" he shouted. "Ask for time off!" And we hung up.

I keened all over the line, making Shorty think that something horrendous had happened.

"Aaron just sold out his studio. I need to go with him to Miami next month."

"For how long?"

"I don't know, four days?"

He scoffed. No one requested that kind of time off. Ever.

"I'm sorry, but I have to go," I said. No way was I going to miss being with Aaron when things were happening for him. It had been too hard a struggle.

The next day Aaron came into our bedroom as I was waking up and dropped two hundred dollars on the bed. Zach had paid him in cash.

"Why don't you go buy yourself some jeans," he said in his best Merle Haggard drawl.

"Little lady?" I finished his thought, sat bolt upright, and clutched the money. I realized then the insanity of my sense of economic security, which has never had any correlation to hard facts or numbers but rests solely, as it has since junior high, on whether or not I can afford to buy a cool new pair of jeans.

Aaron's full-time art-making and regular sales transferred some of the family focus from my career to his, to my relief. What he did all day—carving wood, painting, strategizing—was stressful, a pendulum swing between the poles of doubt and the thrilling highs. It was a weird job, unrecognizable to those back home, but it seemed to fit Aaron's personality.

Within a month we were floating in the ocean in Miami, the day after walking down the marble staircase with Zach at the Versace mansion, a gaudy Versailles-like backdrop that tilted the entire moment into campiness. It was the height of the art boom. The art market at this time defied economics as surely as it defied the down-to-earth Midwestern practicality into which we'd been born—and we were feeling its crazy buoyancy. As I kneeled in the waves, it occurred to me that no one in Park Rapids, not even my young self, could have envisioned this scene for us. As the salt water soaked my burn-slashed forearms, I could think of nothing to say but the most pedestrian of straightforward utterances. The weight of Aaron's belief system that had brought us to this place, where we were both floating in an ocean, taking a well-deserved break from doing exactly the kind of work we both wanted to do, was so much larger than that, but words sometimes fail.

"Good job, Aaron."

I no longer cared if we had a—quote/unquote—normal life. Security was overrated. I'd take this one.

IT CAME AS NO SURPRISE TO ME that in the spring of 2003 Aaron didn't see his steady art-making as more reason to stay in New York, but more reason to leave. He called the Two Inlets Mill and started getting quotes for building a new studio in Minnesota. I knew I'd have a hard time stopping him. The seeds we'd planted in that place years before had grown their inevitable roots, and he wanted someday to be able to work from there.

When Aaron talked to others about our place back home out in the middle of nowhere, he framed it with sweeping arm gestures, as if it were a utopian kingdom, the absolute center of the universe. I'd heard his spiel a million times before. Imagine this, he'd say, spooling out his long arms. It's a crossroads of four great American landscapes. We're basically sitting on the source of the Mississippi, the watershed of the nation. Drive north and you hit the boreal forest; drive east, the hardwood forests; drive south and there's the edge of the glacial deposit. Drive an hour west and you hit the beginning of the prairie that stretches all the way to the Rocky Mountains *and that's where the West begins*. And where else do you have four such strong, distinct seasons? Every six weeks the wind changes and you have to get ready for something new. It keeps you going. It never lets you rest. We don't have just four seasons; we have more like eight.

In truth, the cold arrived in October and stayed until May, so I think he was forgetting to mention that winter reigned during at least five of those mini-seasons; Old Man Winter was the king of them all.

The next morning as we bungee-strapped straw bags onto our bikes in preparation for our weekly brunch-and-farmer's-market Sunday routine, Aaron paused in the premature, weightless Brooklyn spring. The air felt as temperate as blood, as the 110-degree water you need to bloom yeast—in a word, heavenly. Aaron shook out his bare arms in a motion that implied zero resistance, a total lack of gravity. Compared to Minnesota's plunging shifts between dry-ice winters and humid, suffocating summers, this lovely New York spring was too long and pleasant for him by far. Every seasonal change, he got restless like this. I could see it in the way his jaw twitched in the warm morning air, the way his eyes followed the garbage swirling in the curb hollows. His outlook defied common sense, but it was perhaps common to exiles who pine for difficult pasts. Back home, weather was temperamental, addictive, and central to conversation. Nature vindictively doled out blasts of winter and then apologized with the sun; we northerners walked collectively on a pile of eggshells, attuned to its moods. Surviving the petulant weather gave us a shared resilience.

Most people thought that living in Brooklyn presented similar collective challenges to overcome—the hordes of people, the steamy subway air, the inconveniences of doing one's laundry in laundromats and of walking a mile toting heavy grocery bags that dug channels into your palms—but Aaron overlooked all that.

Sensing that he was getting ready to complain about this present glorious sunshine, I preempted him. "It's a *perfect* day."

He quipped, flopping his arms, "It's an almost nonexistent day. It's like there's no temperature at all." Squinting into the bright, untroubled street, he leaned hard into his pedal and restated his devotion to our place in the woods with brief, auspicious finality.

"I need weather," he said, sounding a lot like one of the Norwegian-American farmers from whom he was descended.

6

TWENTY-FIVE PIES

I MADE AARON STAY PUT and tough it out. But I agreed to tentatively consider the idea of the studio back home, which he read as my consent to keeping the dream of our homestead alive. After finishing out my time at 66, I started looking for another job. I wanted to get back to a fine-dining kitchen, something with the intensity and intimacy of Danube.

Cru, a posh downtown restaurant with a book-length, instantly legendary wine list, fit those requirements—not coincidentally because the kitchen was staffed almost entirely with former Bouley and Danube cooks. The chef, Shea Gallante, former chef de cuisine at Bouley, assembled a tight seven-person crew of highly skilled haute-cuisine geeks, many of us bespectacled, most of us in our early thirties. The Austrian sous chefs back at Danube would have dubbed us "old," but I preferred to think of us as "veteran." As we prepared to open the restaurant, doing everything from painting the downstairs prep kitchen to curing the new copper pots, we felt like a small reunion band—a feeling that grew stale as our prep lists lengthened, our hours swelled into the high-eighty-hour-a-week range, and Shea stubbornly decided not to hire anyone he didn't already know and trust until we got reviewed by the *New York Times*.

Tall and driven, with a pomaded, gill-like hairline, Shea was like a star quarterback, pushing his team toward the avant-garde. And once again, as at Danube, all of the smaller size 36 and 38 jackets were quickly snapped up. By this point I was beyond cooking in gaping sleeves. When I asked Shea to order more small jackets, he said under his breath, "What are we, a kitchen of midgets?" *No, Chef,* I thought, *just a bunch of nerds and one short woman.*

Shea installed me at the fish station where, in addition to ripping and cooking thirty lobsters a day as I'd done at db bistro, I also made a fleet of tricky contemporary garnishes for the middle courses, most of which were on the longer tasting menu: sweet onion ice cream to go with the foie gras; liquid spheres of black olive juice to accompany the tuna tartare; a fragrant hazelnut praline to swipe beneath the lobster, its natural sweetness suppressed via a three-step caramelization process that relied on low-sugar sugars such as Isomalt. It was at Cru, finally, that I saw artistry and rusticity collide in the way I'd always dreamed of. Shea threaded cutting-edge techniques with traditional Italian-ingredient-centric garnishes, enrobing sweet farmer's-market peas in reduced pea juice and blending pureed polenta with a heady amount of perfumed Italian olive oil. Our ingredients were tops. Fish came in on the morning flight from Japan, some still in rigor mortis. We paid top dollar for the world's best chocolate, the best vanilla beans, the largest Umbrian truffles. We cooks shopped the Union Square Greenmarket before work on Saturdays. Shea ordered heirloom Carola potatoes from a farm upstate, kept them in a cool dark back room, and cooked them one by one for VIP tasting menus; he pushed the plain cooked potato through the wire mesh of a tamis until it stood up straight like straw-colored hair, then swooped it onto the plate, covered it with greenish olive oil, and sprinkled it with rough gray salt. The remnants I fingered out of the tamis on the way to the sink tasted as silky as butter. I had grown potatoes like these once, the very same variety, when we lived in Two Inlets, and I had squandered them.

When the *New York Times* review landed—a glowing three-star by Frank Bruni that immediately filled our reservation sheet—Shea still didn't relent, and the overtime (for which no cook in New York City ever gets paid) marched on. To put the hours/numbers into perspective, there's this: At the end of any regular night, empty bottles of Château Lafite Rothschild or Pétrus or Romanée-Conti regularly crowded the sideboard—bottles of wine that listed at tens of thousands of dollars each. After taxes, I took home less than $500 a week.

Not that I cared about the money. I'd long ago accepted that the economy of cooking did not compute to hours worked for dollars paid. My mind skips the details and instead recalls that time as a close-focus montage: the round blat of thick homemade almond milk on the toe of my shoe that I am too busy to stop and wipe away; the zippery shush of my muggy black work pants; the soft plundering of all the cooks' rubber-bottomed orthopedic shoes on the tile floor; the polyester sheen of chickpeas pureed with wobbly chunks of cooked bacon fat; the cool fleshiness of the two fat Medjool dates I'd hidden in the breast pocket of my chef's coat. Whenever I feel my energy lagging I reach for one, convinced that even one sticky date can give me a supersonic boost.

As we cooks stand at our stations slicing shallots or filleting fish or searing short ribs, our chitchat bobs vigorously in the air. We're pros; our verbal stream doesn't pause as our hands continue to strip thyme from its stem, push lamb sauce through a fine chinois strainer, or cut carrots into brunoise. I have for my fellow line cooks the same fierce, teasing fondness I have for my own brothers—which makes sense, as we are members of an extended restaurant family, and as the sole woman there my role feels vaguely maternal. Clearly in their sleep deprivation they have forgotten my female origins, because these guys unleash all their freaky boyness on me. For instance, they quote movies all day long. (The women I know do not do this; we don't quote dialogue or finish one another's favorite remembered scenes complete with the action noises—not at age eight, not at twenty-eight, and not even if it's *Caddyshack*.) They talk about their favorite songs as if they're making a daily mixed tape. They guess one another's first concerts. Mötley Crüe. Whitesnake. Red Hot Chili Peppers for the youngsters. "Amy," Kyle the meat entremet speculates, "I bet yours was Heart." Nope, AC/DC, but close. How could he know that my small-town-girl soul has always held a lighter in the air for Heart?

They talk about their girlfriends. A good one waits up and is a game companion for the unwinding process, including the requisite midnight snack; a tough one is already in bed and offers no sympathy.

"When I got home last night," Rich the pasta cook says, each word heavy, "*she made me a sandwich*."

"Aw, really? What kind of sandwich?" asks Kyle.

"Dude, it was great. It was piled with roast turkey and Swiss and spicy pepperoni and pickled peppers, with mustard and mayo, and she fried it in butter. It was three inches tall. The best sandwich I've ever had." Says the guy who's curing an inside barrel muscle of pork butt to hang in the downstairs walk-in cooler—homemade coppa, the most high-brow of lunch meats.

"Wow, that sounds so good," Kyle says, honestly impressed, as he stands at his station plucking the tissue-paper skins from shrunken roasted cherry tomatoes and dropping the squishy peeled fruit into a pint cup labeled TAISINS—his nickname for tomato raisins. "I can't believe she fried you a sandwich."

"I know," Rich says, blinking back emotion.

Making a sandwich for a line cook after work at one in the morning, even one composed of the kind of crappy deli turkey breast their professional palates would otherwise never touch, elevated these unseen girlfriends to beatific levels. It had never once occurred to me to ask Aaron to make me a sandwich. He would have, happily, had I requested it. I just had no idea that a sandwich made by other hands meant so much.

My FEEDING IMPULSE overflowed into my off hours. I never grew sick of cooking. I desperately wanted to cook Thanksgiving for Aaron and our friends, and begged Shea for the day off.

"Please," he said. "We all want Thanksgiving off. We'd all like to cook. We're open that day." And then he reconsidered: "Tell you what. You make pie, right, in *Minn-a-sow-ta*? You can have Thanksgiving off if you make me twenty-four pies. Not for service, just for us." That worked out to at least half a pie per cook. But I came in early and stayed late that week and made twenty-*five* pies: ten buttercup-bourbon, ten of my grandma's macerated apple, and five maple-pecan. I copped a buttercup-bourbon for my own Thanksgiving at home the next day. When I took the pie home and sliced into it, I was crushed to discover that the crust was overly sturdy, not nearly as delicate as the piecrusts I'd made when I was a teenager. My recipe remained the same, Grandma Dion's, but she would have been appalled. Clearly, hopping the fence from home cook to professional had turned my luck with the piecrust of my Midwestern youth. I might have mastered olive oil sablé and duck-fat pasta dough, but I was now on the dark side of pie.

Yet a few weeks later, when Shea asked me to take over the recently vacated pastry chef position, I wasn't surprised. The pastry chef's last day was coming fast and we had yet to hear who would take his place. I sat with Shea in the front bar room watching the rushing daytime crowd on Fifth Avenue and considered it. I had no experience in pastry, no bank of essential recipes—the formulas that are like gold to pastry chefs. It would mean more money, but with just a hundred-dollar increase, it was not bona fide pastry-chef money. I burned inside at the "girl salary." Still, as head of the sweet side, I would finally be a chef, in charge of my own menu. This was my chance to create original dishes. I thought of my recipe notebooks, heavy with ideas.

I looked out at the enormous waterfall of apple blossoms sitting on the bar and ran my thumb over the crop of bumpy pink eczema between my fingers, my permanent worry stone, and tried to think. After many months of eighty-hour weeks, I couldn't imagine how I would explain to Aaron that I was going to start over in a new, higher-pressure job, that I would need to work extra hours to assemble a menu, and that the small percentage of time we spent together would actually decrease. Every slurp from my takeout coffee cup echoed weirdly in the room and sounded about ten times louder than it should have, as if the cup were having trouble clearing its throat.

"I know you've never worked pastry, but that savory edge is where pastry is headed. I think you could do it. Nothing too flashy. A chocolate cake. A panna cotta. Five desserts total."

I was silent, which was unlike me.

"You can try it and if you don't like it, you can go back to savory, I'll make you a sous chef." I could hear him thinking, *If you'd just do me this one solid.*

Indecision numbed my tongue. I knew what this job would take and I honestly didn't know if I was prepared to pull it off. And ironically, the very minute that Shea had trusted me, I wasn't sure I wanted it. I reluctantly agreed to take the job—but only temporarily, until he could find a permanent replacement.

Somehow, without a single day of pastry experience, without a stash of tried-and-true recipes, working from morning until night with a skeleton staff—most of the pastry crew had abdicated with the former chef—I managed to serve five desserts to the Cru customers in search of a sweet conclusion to their multicourse meal. My approach to pastry was indeed savory and redolent of memories of home: I ordered some wood-parched wild rice from my local Minnesota parcher on White Earth Reservation, fried it until it popped like popcorn, and steeped it in cream and maple syrup for panna cotta. I pressed slices of kabocha squash and sugared Meyer lemon into con-

fited blocks of terrine to serve with the cheese course. I poached apri-
cots overnight in a bath of spice-scented duck fat. Remembering the
flavor of the anise hyssop that grew wild at our house in the woods, I
made a syrup from its purple flower tufts and drizzled it over translucent slices of plum carpaccio.

My first night on the pastry line, my ice cream quenelles looked
ragged, unsure of themselves. After they got better and I got rolling, I
was happy with the individual flavors, but the composed desserts
themselves were still in sketch mode—not working as harmonically
as I had envisioned them—and it pained me to send them out the
door. Devastated, my ego took the blows and kept on going, wobbling
forward like a smashed car in a demolition derby.

When the first hothouse rhubarb arrived, I went back to what I
knew, the thing that had gotten me the job in the first place: pie. As
was the current fashion, I deconstructed it: rhubarb confit, marinated
diced rhubarb in raspberry syrup, a crisp lid of pastry, a milky-green
sweet-celery ice cream. I added more butter to the pie dough than I
had to the twenty-five Thanksgiving pies and reversed the method; I
creamed the butter and flour first like it was a French sable. It wasn't
the fragile crust of my Midwestern childhood, but it was more tender.
I balanced the pastry disk on top of the rhubarb confit. I was hopeful.

When Shea came back to the pastry department to taste it, he shot
it down immediately.

"I think you should bake this crust until it's almost burned, dunk
it in milk, infuse it, and turn it into a cream or an ice cream," Shea
snapped, crumbs falling out of his mouth. "It's way too fucking dry."

"Without crust, it wouldn't be a pie then, would it?" I volleyed.

"Exactly. The texture is distracting. People want, you know, mum-
mum." He gummed his lips together dramatically. "Think toothless.
They need to end on something soft." He widened his eyes at me and
walked away, shooting me the very same disappointed expression that
Mario had given the pastry sous chef who gave him the *dumpf* plum

dumpling to taste years before at Danube. I wanted to defend the primacy of American-style piecrust, but maybe he was right. Divorced from its pie and its function as the sling vessel for a sluicy middle, pie pastry was a touch dry.

I crumbled up the pastry, threw it into a quart cup of milk, and tossed it on the walk-in shelf. I went back to the mixer and whipped up a Madeira-infused olive oil cake as plush as moss for a rhubarb upside-down cake, which eventually made it onto the menu.

After three months of running the pastry kitchen, of sampling cakes and custards and syrups over and over again, a sickly taste of defeat came to settle semipermanently in the back of my mouth, and I realized something: working pastry made me very hungry. And a little nauseous. I scavenged what I could to fill my hollow—stray meat from the walk-in, cheese trim from the cheese plate, bread from the basket—but eating didn't ferry it away. It was a strange, seeking, serrated kind of hunger, one that no amount of stolen duck meatballs shoved into stolen crusty rolls could fill.

ALTHOUGH MY DEFTNESS IN PASTRY was still up for debate, by this time I considered myself a full card-carrying member of the haute cuisine workforce, my self-transformation from civilian to professional complete. I knew how to break down any fish; how to make meat submit to full tenderness; how to confit anything—fruit, or vegetable, or protein—by gently coaxing out its natural juice, concentrating it, and encouraging it to flow back inside its bulging skin. The way I minced garlic illustrated how full circle I'd come. Back before I cooked on the line I took the word *mince* very literally and meticulously diced the garlic into tiny cubes with my dull, doltish knife. Later, in the subterranean Danube prep kitchen, when faced with an entire pint of garlic, I smashed the cloves against my board and ravaged them to bits with my sharp knife, as my fellow line cooks had taught me to do. By the time I reached Cru, my knife skills had caught up to my original nearsighted devotion, and I went back to slicing each ivory clove into thin pleats before dicing them into minuscule cubes, as you would an onion—but three times as quickly as before—so as not to get any of that sticky, bruised garlic juice on my board or in my sauté pan, where I knew that its old-tasting funk would flower in the hot fat. That was how picky, how fastidious, I had become.

So I don't know if it was the relentless parade of swirls, dots, and quenelles that ran like ticker tape behind my eyes, or the steady pressure from Aaron to go back home to Minnesota, or just basic fatigue, but one night, while I was staring into the blurry mirrored surface of the stainless-steel prep sink, digging out crud from its drain, the moment arrived when I knew that my tour of duty was over. My professional cooking tenure measured nine years, if I counted the Schwarzwald Inn. I was thirty years old. Possibly too old to remain just a line cook. Possibly too old to fight against Aaron's insistence on our original plan, our seasonal flight pattern between New York and home.

That night after service I blew into the office and gave Shea my two weeks' notice.

"This just isn't working for me," I wailed in distress. "I've spent years mastering savory. I'm just not skilled enough in pastry to keep putting out desserts that are 'good enough.' It's making me crazy."

To this news Shea simply said, "Fine," and looked away. "I've found your replacement." His reaction to my giving notice, typical of most chefs, nonetheless pinched me with instant regret and a deep sense of betrayal, as intended.

As a serial quitter, I was used to it, but leaving this job felt different. For years, I'd just put one foot in front of the other, marching from one top kitchen into the next, amassing more fine-dining experience than any cook needs, until I reached a fog-filled fork in the road. My urge to go home was just as strong as Aaron's. The only thing I knew for sure was that while he pined for the landscape and the head-spinning weather, I itched to cook the hours-old vegetables from my garden.

At the news that I was quitting my job so that we could spend the summer in Two Inlets, Aaron wasted no time in flying back home to check on the studio and to plant the garden. He called me with his giddy report: "You won't believe how much the apple trees have grown! The plums are starting to bud out, and those black currants my dad planted took, too."

Meanwhile, I resolutely finished out my two weeks in pastry, quenelling perfect ovoids of salted caramel ice cream, filling sesame tuile cylinders with light poufs of olive-oil-passion-fruit curd, day-dreaming of the fantasy European-inspired country restaurant I wanted to have someday, scribbling in my notebook sketches and reci-pes that I would make when I got back to Minnesota, all of them exercises in raising our rural ingredients to my new standards. Braun-schweiger wasn't that different from mortadella; it could be made into a buttery mousse. The apple-saffron puree I'd been making would taste even better—stronger, brighter—if I used our crab apples. The luscious smoked lake trout of my childhood could go anywhere salt cod could go: brandade, fritters, Spanish croquettes.

Even though my pastry stint was clearly not a runaway success, I knew that cooking—meaning the job, the driving pace, the commu-nity of food freaks—had saved me. I'd been on the opening teams for two Manhattan restaurants, and on the first-year teams of two others, an experience that had pretty much served me my ass and my motiva-tion on a platter all at once. The long hours and devotion had been worth it. Every mistake I'd made—and I'd made most of them by this point—had taught me how to dodge it in the future. I'd become more receptive to an ingredient's needs. I knew that when I went home, I'd finally be able to give my heirloom Italian garden zucchini the respect it deserved. I thought back to a postservice meeting Shea had held during the opening weeks of Cru, when he thanked us for our over-overtime and our commitment to the team with a backhanded compli-ment: "But of course none of you are doing this for me. No one would be crazy enough to work hours like these unless they have bigger plans to be a chef of their own place." We all nodded. I remember pausing with the cold ring of a postservice beer glued to my lips, wondering: Is that true of me? Will we stay in Brooklyn long enough to make my dream of cheffing a place come true? How would I ever find the resources, or the strength, to open a small, artful, ingredient-driven restaurant—the only kind I could envision having—in the wilds of rural northern Minnesota?

Now that feeling returned, more insistent: *Had I really sacrificed seven sleep-deprived years to the Kitchen God so that I could become a better civilian home cook?* Like Shea said, that would be crazy.

Despite the fact that my tour of duty was nearing its end, my food fixation kept on growing. It felt insatiable. The better I got at the job, the needier I became. I was always craving more: better raw materials, brighter spinach, tauter fish, shinier eggplant, more feral fruit. The original cooking habit that became an affliction was now morphing into something of an addiction. And when an addict reaches her bottom, she wants only one thing: to start over at the beginning with that flush of first attraction. This cooking enterprise had begun, and needed to culminate, with my roots. Not just the geographical roots of my home, but literally in the dirt. With the horseradish. Parsnips. Potatoes. Onions.

Leaving Cru for Park Rapids was what my line-cooking buddies would call "not a strategic move." Any restaurants near the level at which I'd been working were in Minneapolis—two hundred miles away. Unless I wanted to return to the Schwarzwald Inn—and I did not—I wouldn't be able to cook professionally there. Thankfully, Aaron's art sales, together with the cheapness of our country place and the subletting of our New York apartment to cover its rent, bought me some time.

Thinking that I might have to fall back on my English degree and try to somehow write recipes and food stories for publication, I permitted myself to jot down sensory details about the kitchen in my notebooks—notations I'd previously refrained from making, considering them contraband, a mark of traitorship. One, my gray notebook, was filled with pages of cooks' dialogue, the real illicit stuff. On the last day I realized that all of my notebooks were missing. I searched the kitchen frantically and eventually found two of them hiding behind the electric slicer—but not the gray one. I interrogated everyone about its whereabouts, ending with Shea.

"You got some hot recipes in there, huh? You didn't type them up?" He couldn't stop the light from rolling over his face. I thought he looked as guilty as hell. This guy, who indulged in a practical-joke exchange with a chef friend that culminated in a padded envelope of express mail containing a "special kind of chocolate" that turned out to be the other chef's line cook's fresh turd . . . Even if he had killed the game for breach of decency, and sanitation, still: *that guy* would never steal a cook's notebook.

I never did find it, or discover who took it, but I'm pretty sure it was blatant sabotage. I loved these guys like my brothers. They could all be such little shits.

As I walked back to the pastry kitchen and packed up my tools—bundling into my knife roll my sharp Japanese knives, offset spatulas, needle-thin cake-testers, the precious espresso plating spoons I'd stolen so long ago from Danube—the move home began to feel distressingly real. I was struck with the uneasy feeling that, as always, my idea of Minnesota-home was double-sided. It was not just one place but two: our home in the woods in Two Inlets, and its nearest town, the Park Rapids of my youth. Through the door cracked open by my memories of those natural flavors—the domineering wild raspberries, the sweet, grassy chives, the searing horseradish—other flavors rushed in, and as they came at me they grew progressively older and more troubling. The oily-bellied smoked lake trout I loved was there, along with the deep sweetness of my mom's beef braised with onion soup mix, but they were followed by a march of powdered apple cider, canned black olives, mucky cream-of-mushroom-soup casseroles—the cheap, industrial, stereotypically Midwestern flavors that, as much as I wanted to deny it, were folded up into my taste memory and my history as well. Specifically, the American cheese—sitting in a lurid pool like a melted sun, the cheese sauce that at one time so efficiently glued my mom's pork roast, broccoli, and spaetzle together on the plate—and my family together at the table, had come due for a proper reckoning. I'd spent years trying to erase those homely flavors from my past, but when I gave my nostalgia an inch, it ran down the road a mile. Like an archaeologist picking in the hard-packed clay, I felt a need to return home to excavate the old flavors and all the feelings I'd ever tied to them.

It occurred to me briefly that anyone with more sense would have just let the past stay flapping back behind her and moved on—like every other reasonable small-town girl who had moved to New York to find her people.

7

THE SWEET SMELL OF HOME FRIES

PARK RAPIDS, MY HOMETOWN, is marooned way up in northern Minnesota, hours away from any big cities, but its location is fairly epic if you're into American geography. Our town sits just a few miles from the headwaters of the Mississippi River, right on top of the Laurentian Divide, the invisible landmark named "The Height of Land" by the local Ojibwe people. On a map, the dotted line of the divide is what stakes the direction of water to flow in two directions, either north to Canada or south to the gulf, so the river veers sharply upward before heading back down all the way to the gulf in the shape of a shepherd's hook—basically turning the country's great waterway into one long, drawn-out, ever-thickening question mark. Park Rapids is positioned right in the crook, in the spot where the river hesitates before figuring out which way to go, at what might be called the river's most dubious juncture.

Even though the prevailing spirit in this community of three thousand inhabitants is overwhelmingly rural, I didn't grow up in the country. I grew up in our town's most aspirationally suburban neighborhood, within biking distance of Main Street, wearing side blinders to the wilderness. Believe it or not, given my childhood isolation, four hours from Minneapolis–St. Paul, I thought of myself as almost urban, because I was not a country kid; I was a townie.

My relationship to the place has always fluctuated dramatically between love and loathing, often with the seasons. During the six months of winter, snow covers everything like a silvery wash of old paint. Gray ruffs of plowed snirt (what they call snow-dirt) decorate the roads, and the sky is opaque white—light in color but heavy. The bears hibernate and so do most of the humans, although even the most homebound of us must surface to go to the grocery store. Tiny houses, some just two rooms wide, crowd the neighborhoods, making for a whole street-string of contented, fat-bellied houses exhaling round puffs from their chimneys. The smoke of local scrub pine—common jack pine and tamarack—smells cheap and perfumey, like pipe tobacco.

The town doesn't have that haunted, ghostly feeling of so many eastern small towns, no glint of former grandeur or long-lost wealth. It was never rich. Its industry is freshly aluminum-sided. Prosperity here feels self-sufficient—proud, but not extravagant. And come winter, when the lakes freeze over and the tourists leave, the town's world seems to contract.

The blanket of winter snow highlights all the landmarks. Paul Bunyan and Babe the Blue Ox statues loom tall in neighboring towns, graphic monuments to a real, still-happening logging era. Present-day loggers and sawyers clomp around town in beige coveralls and loose boots. I remember standing behind one of them in line at the Farm & Fleet store when I was around ten years old, close enough to catch some of his foreign scent, a strangely intoxicating mix of pine juice, musky chain saw fumes, and sweet sawdust.

Then suddenly the snow mountains thaw, marking the end of winter. And during the three-month flash of summer, when the ditches light up with spring-green voltage, when the blue surfaces of the lakes shiver in the wind and the sun beats down onto your arm hanging out the car window, and when the tourists flip-flop around Main Street in swim tops under summer dresses, Park Rapids transforms. The people brighten like flowers in the sun, and the whole town feels quite nice, real Americana. Not ritzy, but resort-town fancy in an old-fashioned way—almost posh.

In addition to the pine trees and the clear lakes, we're known for potatoes. Notorious nitrogen hogs, potatoes take a lot and give little, and they enjoy the sandy glacial soil that surrounds my hometown immensely. One of the largest French-fry producers in America, our town's largest employer, welcomes all visitors driving up from the big city, its series of white buildings at the south end of town stacked tight like a bread pan of rolls. Each fall, they fry hundreds of thousands of pounds of fries a day over there, and I remember that seasonal stench, smelling like the belch of the great agricultural machine, stretching out like a tarp overhead as my brothers and I played kickball in the yard. All the neighbor kids insisted that the fries we ordered at the local Hardee's, given their initial fry just down the road, tasted better than Hardee's fries everywhere else. French fries were revered and considered a local food.

Even then, long before I made food my world, and though my fondness for Main Street was strong, I turned up my nose at the deep-fry emissions. There's something about realizing as a teenager that you're launching your life from the middle of nowhere that lends itself to grandiosity and tightens the collar of your nostalgia, a tautness that turns every pop song coming through the radio into a possibility for rising up. I grew up knowing that not only was nothing extraordinary expected of me, but that it was, in fact, gently discouraged. There was a proud monasticism in those clomping boots and resolute faces, and it had something to do with the harshness of the landscape. The people were tough. The "norm" was good enough. The weather, along with some leftover prairie practicality from the homesteading era, colluded to place bets against the dreamers. I harbored this feeling alone until I met friends who felt the same thing. My parents, having grown up in an even smaller town themselves, were oblivious to this notion; they did nothing to either support or dispel it.

With private rebellion, I fantasized about my adult self who left my hometown long ago and was now triumphantly coming back with new eyes. I imagined surprising everyone with my swooping return—just a brief stopover, a holiday homecoming like in the movies—revealing the depths of my fondness for my little town. These histrionics were supported by the 1980s playlist booming from the car radio, from John Cougar Mellencamp's "I was born in a small town," to Journey's "Just a small town girl/Livin' in a lonely world . . ." Coming and going could contain so much precious drama. I made myself cycle through departures and returns until the daydream became a sort of simulated homecoming bulimia, a future I put myself through over and over. That was just how inevitable my leaving felt.

Not unlike the swinging temperatures here, the disposition of the place sways theatrically. It's moody. Malleable. Dependent on perspective. Like many American small rural towns in the middle of nowhere, Park Rapids's character is formed daily, in the imaginations of those who walk its streets. I discovered later that it can be anything you want it to be.

THE IDEA THAT HOME COULD BE SPLIT, or double-sided, came to me early. In a sense, I was born with it, because from a young age, when I thought about my hometown there were always two: Park Rapids and Pierz, an even smaller town a two-hour drive south, where both of my parents came from. Because they had moved to Park Rapids as adults, my parents thought of themselves as "imports" and their children, like anchor babies, true Park Rapidians. Pierz, still home to most of the family, was their hometown; Park Rapids was ours. In my mind, the two towns were as subtly indivisible as the pith from the peel, the flesh from the juice.

There are three kids in my family—me, Bob, and Marc—and I am the oldest. My dad, Ted Thielen, was an only child, and subsequently the influence of his family took a backseat to my mother's more assertive, matriarchal side. My mom's family was thick with women, and none of them were shy. My grandma Dion, the eldest of seven sisters, had three daughters: Joan, Renee, and my mom, Karen. My aunt Joan, who never married or had children, lived in an urban part of St. Paul. Aunt Renee stayed in Pierz, married Keith Thielen (my dad's first cousin, once removed), and had three kids, all boys, in such tight alternation with my mother's output that it almost seemed competitive. Regardless of our double dose of Thielen genetics—think of it like *Seven Brides for Seven Brothers*—the women alone would have laced the family tight. For much of my childhood, I identified as a cousin, as one of six as opposed to just three, and the only girl among them.

In my memory these women are all crowded into the kitchen arguing over the contents of the pot on the stove, their voices joining to scale an imaginary mountain peak of volume. They're evangelical about everything but religion. We're believers, of course, good Catholics, people who observe the minor church holidays like All Saints' Day and keep fans of palms on the wall year-round. But there was no proselytizing, no reference to the great mystery. That sort of talk was reserved for household details, and manners, but mostly for food.

Their belief system could be summed up in three ingredients: butter, fermented pickles, and bacon. We really believed in bacon. Meat in general, actually. My uncle made the bacon and smoked all manner of pork at the family meat market in Pierz; he was the third-generation Thielen to run it (and later, his three sons, my cousins, the fourth). The place is so infused with years of pent-up woodsmoke that everyone who works there exits smelling like a smoky treat; dogs go bonkers around my uncle, yipping and chawing at his fingers. Every member of my family has consumed at least twice the normal lifetime supply of double-smoked ham, country sausage, Polish sausage, smoked wieners, and bacon, so much so that my forty-something living body might just be proof that the fear of nitrates is a contemporary myth. Homemade hot dogs, even if ingested in ridiculous quantity, will not hurt you. Pink smoked pork is holy.

All the women in my family cook bacon slowly, reverently, as if performing a devotion. They cut each piece in half and lay it in a latticed pattern in a warm cast-iron pan, then stand watch over it, jockeying the pieces until the edges all turn crisp and the middles turn tawny but remain pliable. "You don't really fry it," my mother instructed. "You want it to sweat a little first, then you flip it. Keep it moving. Take it out when it's still soft." Bacon cooked crisp enough to crumble is considered a sacrilege.

Bacon had nonedible uses, too. Say, for example, that you got a sliver in your finger while gathering kindling for a summer campfire, my grandma would have a solution: She'd cut a two-inch length of bacon from the fatty swelled end, salt it heavily, lay the meat over the foreign body, and wrap the finger tightly with gauze.

"Now go to sleep with this," she whispered. "And when you wake up . . ." She paused and twisted her lips into a wry pout, foretelling something supernatural. "The *sliver* will be *lying* on the *bacon*."

I was doubtful but slept in a log position, my mummified finger propped on a pillow, smelling like breakfast all night long. Sure enough, the next day, before I even got out of bed, I unwrapped the layers of gauze, flopped the bacon over, and there it was: a tiny wooden shard lying on a sweaty slab of smoked pork.

I was a believer.

Both my dad's and my mom's families had deep roots, many generations, in Pierz, reaching who knows how far back into the old country—which included a large part of the butter-loving, German-speaking portions of present-day France, Austria, the Czech Republic, and Germany itself. The origins of one branch of the family, my grandma Dion's mother's side, were a bit more mysterious. They'd emigrated from Silesia and Bohemia, the Czech side of the Hapsburg empire, and arrived in America with decidedly Eastern European tastes, a wicked dry sense of humor, and possibly a dose of mystical powers. My mom always said, "Wherever Great-grandma was from, they treated poppy seeds like gold . . . ," her voice trailing off dramatically. Sometimes I'd hear her and her sisters saying something about "gypsies," which when I asked them to expand upon, warranted a swift change of subject.

My grandmother very effectively cultivated this mystery by never saying a single word about it but dressing up in a gypsy costume on regular occasions and lending out her ability to read the palms of the walking public. She wore a fur stole, the fox's face attached to its tail midbite, a flouncy red skirt, and armfuls of stacked bangles. As she read people's palms, she spun long convincing stories, made meaningful eye contact, and tightly grabbed both of their hands. She sat in corners doing this at the grand opening of my dad's car dealership, fiftieth-wedding anniversaries, town festivals, and prom after-parties, never once telling any of us in the family whether or not her powers of intuition were real or fabricated. Sometimes, weeks or even months following one of these readings, a stranger would tap at her door, asking for another consultation. She never read the palms of her family, further deepening her powers.

"Where was Great-grandma from?" I asked Grandma Dion once, leaning forward on the counter.

"She was German!" she spat. "We all spoke German in the house. Plattdeutsch!"

"What did she make, Grandma?" I asked.

"Acchh," she said, "she made roast beef, you know, and boiled potatoes, and at lunch we made hash from the leftovers of both, nice and crusty in a cast-iron pan. Everything fried until it was *very crisp*!

"She made poppy-seed coffee cake, of course," she continued, pointing to the coffee cake sitting on the table, a black gush of rich poppy-seed filling oozing out of its cut sides.

We mixed-European-breed Midwestern mongrels are always outed by our coffee cake. Sour cream—probably Polish. Cardamom with icing—had to be from some part of Scandinavia. Our poppy-seed streusel pointed us to origins somewhere east of Germany. Between the poppy seeds and the stiff lace-edged potato pancakes and the fortune-telling, my best guess was that we hailed from a place somewhere between old Transylvania and the hometown of the Brothers Grimm.

Wherever this homeland was, it gave birth to fermented sour dill pickles, our family dish célèbre. My aunt Renee was the first to give our collective obsession a name. "I don't have a sweet tooth; I could take or leave desserts. What I have is more like a sour tooth." More precisely, we're fermentation fiends. My inner harpsichord trills to the thought of those fizzing sour pickles—their acidity softer and yet more probing than the vinegar kind. Just thinking about them makes everyone in my family, myself included, drop their heads, close their eyes, and softly stamp their feet. We all grew up not only eating them at every family occasion but also drinking the briny juice whenever we needed a little pick-me-up.

"DO NOT cut them!" Grandma Dion would shout. She was not into spears or slices; intact pickles were the only shape allowed. I held my knife stiffly in the air. "Cutting lets all the juices out!" As if they were water balloons.

Grandma always kept rows of her fermented pickles in her basement cellar, but everyone in the family quietly acknowledged that her younger sister Helen really made the best ones. Aunt Helen, the second-born of the seven sisters, spoke with a loud, hoarse swagger and was a fantastic storyteller. She'd spin crazy tales for as long as you had the patience to sit, flipping between true stories, fictional tales, and absurdist fantasy without transition, forcing us to distinguish fact from fiction for ourselves. The hardest hugger I've ever known, she squeezed us kids as if to juice us, her sharp rings burrowing into our soft skin.

The pickles she brought to Easter and Thanksgiving were always perfectly fermented—mouthwateringly sour, never too salty. Like her sister, she put them up in glass jars fitted with rubber seals and old zinc lids, and Helen's were screwed on so tight that we suspected rubber cement. To open a jar, she'd cover the lid with one of those soft rubber can-opening disks (a giveaway imprinted with the church's seal), crank it hard, and spring the pickles free. Tons of bubbles hopped from the surface of the brine, like baby frogs in wet grass. The carbonation was as strong on the tongue as a sip of pop on a hot day. But the pickled cabbage at the bottom of the jar was the best part, the connoisseur's reward. Whenever I dug down to it with a fork, Aunt Helen would interrupt whatever story she was telling—her *spiel,* she'd say—to shake a bejeweled hand at me and nod her endorsement of my cabbage-diving before turning back and continuing on.

Our reverence for butter—used in great quantity—completes the family holy trinity. My mom's butter dish was always there in the center of the kitchen, a prima donna presiding over all. I remember charting the two sticks' diminishment through the day: going, going, gone . . . then miraculously replenished. Even throughout the fat-phobic eighties, never once was an ounce of guilt attached to its use. Just as my grandma did, my mom made a proud "acchh" noise in her throat—automatic dismissal of any imaginary detractors—as she scooped it up in huge, glossy lumps.

Here's how my mom made toast (a little procedure that endeared her to Aaron the first time he saw her do it): She waited at the toaster until the bread caramelized, then spread butter on its surface in dramatic whorls, like icing. Then she stabbed it with the tip of her knife, making potholes for greater absorption, and stood over it until the butter melted and filled every yeasty pore before reapplying a fresh topcoat of butter and sending it to us across the counter. As we ate it, the warm fat often dripped down onto our wrists, which made her beam and say, "Butter's good for your brain."

Where others used milk or stock to moisten, she used butter: on dry mashed potatoes, on top of lasagna, on leftover braised beef. Nothing went into the microwave for reheating without a dollop of the yellow pomade schmeared on top. My mom's dish of room-temperature butter was more than a mere cooking fat, it was an ointment, filling, spackle, emotional salvo, as essential to combatting the deep Minnesota winter as lotion. Her dishes got butterier whenever she felt the need to soothe us; and when things were bad, they fairly sobbed with butter.

8

GIVE A GIRL A KNIFE

THE OVERSTUFFED, RUST-COLORED WING CHAIR sitting in our living room was as high as a throne in a pulpit. Naturally it was where Father Reid—our priest at St. Peter's Catholic Church and backyard neighbor—sat when he graced us with his presence for happy hour, which he did a few times a year. He never called ahead.

My mom jumped when she saw his tight grin and triangular nose in the high square window cut into the back door. It was rare to see any face at all in that window when the bell rang, as this entrance was used almost exclusively by neighborhood kids who were all too short to show. "Eeekk!" she squealed. "Fa-ther! You should have called!" She wiped her hands dry on a towel before opening the door.

We all knew that he had come for one of our parents' famous brandy Manhattans. Probably two.

Following a sip, ice cubes fracturing, he closed his eyes and let the black low fringe of his hair settle against the fuzzy high back of the chair.

"You like school?" he asked me, a shallow question deserving of only a nod. I was not going to try to pull a single story out of my wild fifth-grade life.

My mom returned to the kitchen to put a lid on her rice. "You're welcome to come in here, Father. I have to clean the pea pods," she said, her voice blowing out into the living room. He glanced her way but stayed put.

"You go on doing what you're doing," he rasped, gave me a weak smile, and stopped pretending to care. His beaklike nose floated up into the air and his face clouded over, as it did in church when the woman from the office got up to read the parishioner news.

Now at 6:45 in the evening on a Friday, in the dark of winter, Father Reid was gone, having minutes earlier toddled down the rounded, snowy back steps and across the yard to the rectory. A house full of nuns lived right next door to him, but apparently they weren't much for liquid company.

In the kitchen, my mom peeled apples. "I thought he'd never leave," she said. Her simultaneous respect and disdain for the church always puzzled me—why would you ever do something you didn't really want to do? I never got that. I looked at everything, including religion, with what my mom called "a jaundiced eye."

My mom held a paring knife, wooden-butt-first, in my direction, motioning me to help. I knew bare-nothing of chores at this point and had shown zero natural aptitude for anything householdy. I was a sniffly, snotty, allergy-ridden kid, known in school for honking into a Kleenex and then stuffing it up my sleeve, grandma-style, right in the classroom—and also a bit of a klutz. When my mom called to me from the shower for some shampoo from the bathroom cabinet, I reached in and the whole clutch of toiletries went down like a spray of tilted dominoes. The woman who prided herself on her economy of movement, a homemaker choreography so smooth it was nearly mechanized, popped her head out of the shower door and sighed. But miraculously, cooking was something I could sort of do.

I took the knife—an old one whose short blade had been sharpened over the years into the shape of a bird's beak—and tried to copy the way she sliced apples for the pandowdy for the church bake sale. Never once did she tell me to be careful. "Cut it like this" is what she said. She held the trimmed quarter loosely in her left hand and deftly sliced, her knife passing through the apple to rest on the pad of her thumb. Through red skin to pink skin, and back again, without incident. Thick apple triangles fell in a blur into the bowl below.

"Or if you want, you can make chunks," she said, steering the apple quarter this way and that, cutting quickly. *Shiff shiff shiff,* pyramid-shaped pieces fell into the bowl.

"The knife won't cut my thumb?" I asked. The skin on my thumb looked thin and pink as it bulged softly around the blade.

"Never!" my mom said. "Trust me, I've been doing this for years." She reached for another apple piece and lobbed the last two into my workspace. "My knives aren't all that sharp."

She ran her hands in the stream of the faucet, shook them off against the sink, her rings clicking reassuringly against the steel, and then wiped them half-dry on the kitchen towel. My mom's hands were usually damp and water-chilled.

She dumped a hill of sugar on top of the mound of apples. It shushed on the landing, trickled down into the crevices, and let out a faint stink—white sugar's peculiar processed funk. I knew to shake the cinnamon hard so that it whiffed out of the holes like a sneeze. My mom dribbled in vanilla extract from the cap and then gave it all a brisk stir. She worked from memory, with a knowledge that was housed in her hands. It was kind of like watching a veteran carpenter build a house. The crust flopped into the rectangular glass dish and her fingers deftly shoved the dough into the corners. She listened to my endless stream of middle-school drama, humming assent in all the right places, as she popped the apple pandowdy—more like a slab pie with a puffy, light pastry encasement—into the oven and started trimming mushrooms.

I never imagined that someday I'd have that same facility with a knife—although she assumed it. You give a girl a knife; that's just what you do. Eventually, hopefully, she might learn how to use it.

Someday she might even consider that knife an extension of her hand, as wedded to her finger as a nail.

"Amy, go get me the wooden salad bowl from the basement."

Her voice was sharp, like a prod. I was annoyingly slow with errands. Prone to daydreams. And it was while doing just that, protractedly loitering on our split-level steps, salad bowl in hand, that I remember being paralyzed by the most unremarkable and vivid of childhood memories, one that illuminated nothing in particular, but yet somehow everything. There were dust motes floating in the sun coming in from the window, jigging in the air. I was ten—ten!—and I would never be ten again. But then I thought maybe I could come back to this moment someday if I tried to remember it. So I blinked my eyes, hard, including in the frame the steps and the junction where the three flooring treatments met: the brown patterned basement carpet, the tan foyer linoleum, and the green living room shag carpeting, its sea anemone arms waving, the air above it sparkling with bits of ordinary-like diamond dust. I've always wondered why I chose that moment to single out for memory, but now I know that the image didn't matter as much as the place itself. Sitting on the stairway, the purgatory between floors, was a real time-and-space eraser. I was a split-level child of the '80s; maybe I was fated by architecture to a future of feeling torn between two geographical places.

"Amy! Salad bowl!" (Also by design, the split-level required parents to project their voices, turning them all into hollerers.)

A while after I'd left the kitchen to reinstall myself on my favorite chair, my dad walked in the door and commenced his evening routine. After unpeeling the tight black overshoes from his wingtips—he called them his "rubbers"—and hanging up his coat in the coat closet, he stood on the landing and waved at me, his hand up high in the air. Shy with emotion, Dad felt more comfortable declaring his love for us in grand pronouncements, usually on a schedule: once in the morning before work and then again when he came home. "He-ya, Amy!" he shouted. "She's the best girl there is! It's love!" I leaned harder into the chair in preteen mortification.

My dad was a car dealer, as his parents had been, but he embodied a quieter version of the cliché: He had the sport coats and dress pants, a pocket protector of pens at his chest, and the cigar—but none of the stereotypical car dealer's bluster. He spoke quietly and evenly, unless he found something to be excited about, at which point his volume rose, as if someone had bumped the stereo knob and unwittingly turned it up. We knew that he could carry dozens of eight-digit car VIN numbers around in his head, and that the bottoms of his wide feet were smooth and pale, almost custardy, having been worn to a rubbery softness in his wingtips as he pounded the asphalt car lot all day long. His fingertips were smooth and dry from pushing paper. As for the cigar, in lieu of smoking he merely chewed it, discarding the earthen black plugs in an ashtray.

When he came home at 7:00 after a long day, he was officially off duty. He didn't mow grass or change lightbulbs, and he didn't ever think to pull our heavy living room shades shut while he was watching TV, so that by the time darkness fell outside, the enormous picture window was like a television itself, broadcasting our wide-screen suburbanlike existence out onto the street. Every night my mom swept by and huffily tugged them closed.

At this hour, we fell into our roles. My brothers, hopped up on the snacks they'd stolen from the back candy table, played loudly downstairs. I twirled around the living room, practiced my splits, and watched TV as my parents canoodled over their drinks.

Reclaiming my usual post in the rust-colored chair, I jumped on the warm upholstered seat to work out the priest juju and then leaned backward over one of its beefy, bodybuilder wing arms, my support for going into a full backbend. Just as my dad eased his feet every morning into his stiff wingtips with a shoehorn, I used this chair to ease out. To unwind. As the tips of my hair brushed the floor,

my gut rose into my chest and the throbbing in my belly lessened
a bit.

I hung like that until it was clear that upside-down was no longer
working. I was really starving.

FROM A KID'S PERSPECTIVE my parents were just a high-strung, dramatic couple and perfectly matched. When they got along, their tastes
dovetailed. They squabbled over major details of their life, but the
minor things—the dailies—they largely agreed upon: cocktail hour,
vacations without children, and a pound of meat per person. They
never, ever, fought about the steaks.

Steak was a weekly administered rite in our house, and on special
occasions we ate surf and turf: rib eyes and lobster tails, lit by candle-
light, with those little spitting butter warmers, the whole deal. Consuming this much steak was no common thing in our town; many
people lived here because our proximity to state forests and open land
gave them the opportunity to hunt and fish to their absolute saturation. Ground venison was a mainstay for many, and judging from the
enormous display of ground beef at the grocery store, the town consumed a fair amount of that, too. But my dad had grown up the only
child of car-dealer parents in a white stone house on the Mississippi
River, eating prime rib roast and popovers, so steak was what he knew.
My mom had been raised in a tiny rambler eating cheap chuck roast
cooked in slabs to mimic steak, wearing clothes her mother had sewn
("I didn't even know my dress size until I got to college"), and was happy
that they had the means to buy all five of us our own slabs of beef.

As was popular back then, we had an indoor grill, a wrought-iron-
rimmed beauty tucked into the back corner of the kitchen. Standing in
front of it was my dad's honey spot. When he got to grilling, he had to
turn on the fan, whose suction was so powerful that you could feel it
gently pulling at you as you walked by. My mom, who tended to super-
vise any cooking taking place in her domain, trusted him with the beef.

To gauge doneness he didn't poke the steaks, as a pro would, and he didn't slice into them like an amateur; he watched them. As the steaks seethed over the flames, the heat drove its force from the edge to the center of the steak until the middle began, ever so slightly, almost imperceptibly, to bulge with juice. That's how you know they're done—when they begin to puff. My dad stared rudely at the steaks, never leaving his post. Sometimes I stood a few feet behind him and watched him watch them. Ever since, I've never understood how someone could put a piece of meat on the grill and walk away. Beyond the risk of overcooking, why would you ever want to miss the sight of the transformation?

As my dad grilled, my mom finished the steaks' pea-pod-and-mushroom garnish, which had been perfuming the house and driving me mad for what seemed like hours. She cooked the white button mushrooms slowly with a ton of roughly chopped garlic and a grenade-size lump of butter, and when they'd shrunk to the size of brown flower bulbs and began to stick to the pan and caramelize, at least forty minutes later, she threw in the pea pods. The second the pods turned bright green, the mixed buttery juices of both were ready to be spooned out next to the meat.

At the age of ten I was considered a full person, due a whole steak, so I sat down to an entire rib eye splayed out across my plate. (That was my mom's style: finding the space to put the potatoes and vegetables was your own problem.) Through some dogged knife work, you were expected to reduce the meat to scraps and to chew on the burned edges of the fat, too, which my parents rightly insisted was the best part. My steak was perfect, cooked just slightly—a mere shade—south of medium rare, at the point when the livid juices ran and pooled in the slash of your first cut.

When we sat down to the table, my parents were uncharacteristically quiet. My family mumbled the prayer. *Bless us so lord and these eye gifts for what we are about to receive from our bounty through Christ by lord*

Amen. Mom looked at us expectantly, desiring our cogs to start turning and pass the food around while it was still hot. My dad wordlessly assisted by spinning his hand in a fast spiral from the wrist. Despite the cooperation, I could tell that their tempers were up. My parents were silently antagonizing each other, my mom's every mundane comment an elbow to Dad's ribs, his reticence gathering in pressure. This night would not end as some others had, with them rocking together in the living room to Neil Diamond booming from the hi-fi.

My brother Bob, whose overboiling enthusiasm was usually irrepressible, stared at his plate, disappointed. He was easily disappointed—unless he was happy, and then his optimism was so great it bordered on fictive. When we watched TV, he was startled to see the same actors in different shows and sometimes asked me if I thought the actor was really going through the same struggles in real life. *How can you not know this?* I thought, my grip on narrative reality never wavering. He was largely viewed as the honest one, the one all the women in our family considered our shining hope for the priesthood; I knew him as the one who pinched me slyly and never got caught. I was thought of as the craftier of the two, mostly because I never learned to hide behind my emotions; I was the perpetually naughty three-year-old who had bitten her baby brother on the back when he arrived to steal her spotlight, and I could never live it down. But—touché—I wasn't as much of a believer as he was, either.

I looked at my brother Marc, his precocious youngest-kid wit now failing to crack up the table as it usually did. His smile waned, as if he just realized that not everything was funny. I ate my rib eye and chewed the last bit slowly, surprised to find that the growth of negative space in my gut hadn't been resolved by twelve ounces of beef. I looked over at Bob's uneaten steak, asked him if I could have it, forked it from his plate to mine, and ate most of that as well.

Up to this point, I'd never overeaten. Like a wild animal's, my body met its need/use ratio and there wasn't an ounce of anything extra hanging on my muscles. My legs were like smooth tan saplings with joints. I was starting to dabble with obsessive snacks like butter-logged bagels, scrambled eggs overcooked until they formed a brown crust, spicy giardiniera pickles, and canned black olives, but they were still aberrations in a mostly birdlike daily diet. But in this new uncomfortable fullness I could feel the shape of a second kind of hunger, one that reached past borders of appetite. In addition to need, there was this heavy sensuous thing called want, and it was both thrilling and terrifying.

That night after Bob and I went to sleep in our basement bedroom, I was woken by the sounds of my parents' subsumed fight from earlier unfurling its flag. I opened my eyes in the buzzing blackness and crawled into my comfort cove of distant observation. I luxuriated in their voices, in the predictable accelerations, the well-worn volleys, the familiar notes of their outrage. Rubbing the husks of my dry heels together beneath my blankets, I listened hard and kept score, making notes on character motivations like a dramaturgist watching from the wings.

When I turned over, I saw my brother Bob sitting cross-legged in the triangle of light coming in the doorway, his back straight and at attention. Having had to listen to this for two years and two months longer than he had, the dream of the perfect family had begun to fizzle in me; but it was still actively churning in Bob. I got up and joined him in the doorway, but I knew that we were sitting too close, paying too much attention, and that it was more tolerable if you closed your eyes.

A cloud of acrid grill smoke drifted in on their voices, smelling like a clump of rib eye had fallen between the grates to smolder into a petrified knot. The smoke in the house was a benevolent cover, the lingering symbol of their extravagant passion, the beauty that made their surges tolerable—and honestly, probably the only reason I remember this moment with such clarity.

Like the charred fat on the steak, like the mushroom juices that seeped into my potatoes, their dark nighttime emotions felt familiar,

comfortable, and essential. Like a gold standard, their fighting provided a heavy counterweight to our mostly lighthearted childhood.

I wouldn't fully understand the importance of sadness until later,
when I learned to achieve a precarious balance in the kitchen, in the
bowl in front of me. The joy of lemon cannot stand alone; it needs
sugar or olive oil, something to bring it back to earth. Vinegar literally
cries out for fat. Fat falls flat without salt or sugar. Chile heat sings with
brown sugar. And bitterness, well, that needs it all: acidity, bacon, butter . . . and a little caramelized, crusty scudge from the bottom of the
pan—a bit of sweet, dark sorrow—doesn't hurt.

9

THE PERPETUAL POPCORN POT

THIELENS WORK TWELVE-HOUR DAYS. Six days in a row. Fifty-two weeks a year. With a hangover or without. Thielens, by nature, are not lazy.

Against this busy backdrop my childhood lassitude stood in dark contrast, particularly during my fifteenth summer, my last gasp of pure, uncomplicated leisure. I'd somehow been able to put off getting a summer job until it was too late. My mom, perhaps aware that my life as I knew it would soon be changing, let it slide.

As we did every spring on the first weekend of warm weather, we moved to our cabin on nearby Long Lake. It was just a fifteen-minute drive from our house in town, close enough to commute to during the last month of school. That summer I finally indulged my reading habit to its limit. What began in early childhood as a way to tune out my parents, to unplug my auditory sense from the familial white noise, had become a full-blown fetish. Atypical in my family, the open book in front of my face was not only obsessive but, admittedly, also somewhat anti-family. Worst of all, even though it wasn't technically lazy, it *looked* lazy.

And so I read like a sloth during the day, when I wasn't swimming. I read books in bed late into the night, sometimes all night long, desensitizing myself to my hysterical fear of bugs until the thrumming of June bugs against the window screen no longer spooked me. I lazily brushed off the tiny gnats that keeled over on my pages, exhausted from their inability to penetrate my hot, glorious lightbulb.

One day my dad, watching me read in a chair, not moving for hours, threw me a book, one of the few I'd ever seen him read. "*Iacocca.* A good American story. You should read this." I promptly sucked it up and its follow-up, *Talking Straight,* and forever after absorbed the commitment to Buy American. "We've really got to buy local, Dad!" I said, freshly convinced that his injunction that we buy everything in town—so that people in town would buy cars from him—was the only way to live. "The girl's got it!" he shouted, admiring his budding young capitalist. "And remember," he said, "every price is negotiable!" (Having watched him haggle unsuccessfully with a sales-person over the price of a sport coat, I knew it wasn't always true.)

I was obsessed with books, but indiscriminate. Having little guid-ance in that department, my literary inhalation was akin to setting up a shop vac in the woods: the lightest materials flew in first. At eight or nine, I started plowing through my mom's downstairs paperback library, which was chock-full of fat James Micheners and historical fiction series. By the time I was fourteen I'd moved on to a shelf of books that was similar but more sinful. Then I found some truly saucy books, like *Scruples* by Judith Krantz and everything by the chaste-covered LaVyrle Spencer (who changed my view of turn-of-the-century one-room-school teachers forever: Sluts, every one of them!) as well as the slim flight-attendant classic: *Coffee, Tea or Me?* I skipped the few real classics she had, like *Anna Karenina.*

Somehow I knew there had to be more. I went to the town library, where I checked out novels by Erica Jong and other feminists from the 1980s, whose fierce energy I liked, though I didn't understand yet what they were fighting.

I checked out *Gone with the Wind* and read it in a single sixteen-hour jag, turning pages steadily throughout the day, then the night, then the cool hours of the dawn. I fell asleep around 7 o'clock in the morning, missing *The Price Is Right* at 10:30, my main reason for waking up before noon that summer, and then slept for fourteen hours straight. I called my friend Chelsey to brag about my binge. As we talked I weighed myself in the bathroom, reporting that I had lost two pounds in two days. We were just beginning to weigh ourselves. Books were good for everything.

Like we did, Chelsey and her family moved to their lake cabin on nearby Big Sand for the summer, and our buddy Sarah (Aaron's sister) lived year-round on Fish Hook. Together with our friend Cara, who grew up on a Christmas tree farm east of town, we cycled among cabins, taking turns lying on air mattresses in different lakes. As we floated in mine, our feet brushing the soft tops of the weeds, Chelsey and I reminisced about summers past when we would pack up picnic lunches and take them into the Norway pine plantation. Wearing canteens on our hips, we'd walk until we found the perfect portal in which to enter the fairy-tale forest, the entrance that took us from the bright sunshine into deep faux-night. The Norways had been planted in tight, unnaturally even rows, and their high canopy blocked out the daylight. They had friendly, long needles, much softer than the mean quills of the spruce. After we found the patch of forest bottom we were looking for—so perfectly carpeted with fallen needles that it looked like clean barn bedding—we'd unfurl our cheese sandwiches and black plums wrapped in paper towels. The single butterscotch crispie bar we'd brought to split crumbled a bit under the weight of its thick chocolate-bark top as we passed it back and forth, bite for bite.

We talked about going on a picnic in the plantation again, but we never did. I remember realizing that my powers of pretend were fading. We were gearing up for our junior year in high school and would have to bring real details and real experiences to the fight. Other-worldly was momentarily out.

BUILT IN THE 1940S, and bought by my mom and dad in the 1980s, the cabin was resolutely my mom's place. No matter that the relationship between her and my dad had been crumbling all winter at the house in town, at the cabin she spun for us the myth of the perfect family. There we lived out an idyll: days on the boat, nights by the fire, sunsets and dinner bells ringing from the trees, and pink flamingos. Lots of pink flamingos. Flamingo toothbrush holders, clocks, letter openers. She stuck an entire flock of them in the yard, as if declaring it the entrance to Margaritaville. Out on Long Lake, Mom's fantasies were central.

The centerpiece inside our cabin was a fieldstone fireplace with a rangy deer head above it. Out back sat a dusty screened-in fish-cleaning house in which my cousins and I gutted and filleted and flicked fish eyeballs at one another from our fish-scaling forks. On the lake side, mature white pines pocked the gentle slope down to the water, where an old-fashioned boathouse with an attached deck loomed out over the shore. From that deck, my brothers and cousins and I fished for suckers in the spring, our hooks baited with chunks of fatty leftover steak. If it was dark and still enough, if the air wasn't raking the water, we could see the blimplike suckers clearly in the shallows, swift black demons swooping in for the meat.

In the early years, Mom left the cabin untouched, and she and her sisters and mother spent many a weekend there installed around the kitchen table, drinking gin and tonics and playing cards. As if to enforce the casual vibe of the lake, the women all put their pajamas on right after dinner—groaning as they shucked off their clothes that they just couldn't *wait* to get out of their bras. (Their equivalent of letting down their hair.) The men must have been around, but I just don't remember them.

Like all prerenovated cabins, the grubby original turned out to be more fun than the redone. Small and dark and postered with relics from someone else's dreams, old cabins come equipped with a freeing fortlike glee. Without the cultural tradition of these shacks, the upper-Midwestern character would be wildly different. It's all the thrill of camping, but with ice cubes.

In the name of improvement, my mom chucked the dusty deer head, added on a couple of bedrooms, and put down practical gray berber carpeting throughout. She kept the fieldstone fireplace, though, because it was stacked by hand by someone else years ago. On cold evenings, not unheard of even at the height of a Minnesota summer, we made what we called pudgie pies right in the open hearth, layering white bread and ham and cheese into the pie iron, then carefully cracking an egg in the middle before locking the two sides together and holding the iron in the fire to cook it all into a buttery, turtle-shaped pie; it was kind of like a French charlotte with American breakfast filling. For this totally blind cooking process, the pudgie-pie cook had to rely on her instincts. I liked my bread almost burned and my yolk soft, so I bravely held my iron down in the orange-and-silver coals and pulled it out only when tiny droplets of butter and melted-cheese liquid dripped from the iron.

On sweltering nights, which the dramatic northern summer could just as easily produce, we sat in front of the fan with our feet in buckets of cold water and watched movies. My mom made us big bowls of heavily buttered popcorn and then stood in the kitchen frying up half-slices of bacon, which she passed around on paper-towel-lined plates. She bought it from the family meat market in Pierz, never in less than five-pound bundles, and it flowed throughout my childhood like water. "Another pound, kids?" she'd ask, until it was gone. As she fried and flipped, the dog sat at militaristic attention at her feet.

When my dad came home, his face was often shadowy with his work, the numbers, spreadsheets, and complicated personal interactions still churning in his head. His was a difficult job, a shuffling pattern play each month, and we were unreservedly proud of him. Unlike us, he was not "off" for the summer. He changed into his only pair of shorts and tan walking shoes, still wearing black dress socks up to his knees, tilted the fan toward his recliner, and sat down with his paper. Because his mind functioned best with all points firing, he found it relaxing to stretch himself out in his recliner in a numbing blitz of simultaneous media—watching TV, reading the newspaper, and listening to the baseball game on the lo-fi AM radio all at once.

My mom's opinion of my father was in free-fall that summer, so she asked me to serve him his libations—now ice water instead of his previous Chivas Regal, following the premature heart attack he'd had the previous fall at the young age of forty-one. He was the kind of guy who quit things cold turkey. She peeled and sliced thick wedges of raw kohlrabi and handed me the bowl with a shaker of salt. "Give this to your father." His predilection for the raw, wet salted chunks was an indicator of his family's German roots, and the only food craving I remember him having. Once, I caught him munching on a salted wedge of what looked like a potato and asked him, "Why are you eating raw potato?" He replied flatly, as if the answer were obvious: "Because your mother ran out of kohlrabi." Dad accepted even the shiftiest of substitutions: When a restaurant failed to stock ginger ale, he routinely told the waitress to give him a glass filled one-third with Coke and two-thirds with Seven-Up. It tasted nothing like ginger ale, and when I told him this he said, "At least the color is right." My taste buds were more demanding, like my mom's; his were clearly more zen.

At the cabin, as the raucous outside leaked dangerously into his precious interior downtime, my parents' after-hours fights gathered steam. As the heat wave continued, one day we were surprised, but not really, when he didn't drive out to the lake after work but instead stayed alone at the house in town. It was quiet, air-chilled to his liking, and the dog, who loved nothing better than to sit on his La-Z-Boy-propped legs, went with him.

In October, we moved back in with Dad at the house in town, which I hoped would set everything straight. Football had started for the boys and I was in the school play.

My mom and I fell into the habit of sitting up after dinner to snack on her sinful buttered popcorn and page through mail-order catalogs, me drinking water, her drinking red wine. With her own future swirling uncertainly, she took to talking a lot about the family's past and then vaguely about my future, insisting that I could do *anything* I wanted to do. The narrative my mom spun for me involved college and then moving away to get some kind of job in the desk-and-cubicle world before eventually settling down with a nice—*preferably rich*—man and having children. I pictured the first part, living in a city, working in an office, wearing a low-cut pinstriped business suit straight out of the pages of Victoria's Secret, this catalog being my only window into the cosmopolitan world. I didn't know what I'd be doing exactly, but I thought it might involve signing contracts and having heated, triumphant meetings.

In my mom's programming of me to become the independent woman she herself wanted to be, her strategy was repetition. She told me the family stories, of strong women and stubborn men, over and over—with much variation in the details, revising them nightly as she saw fit. I was insatiable for the stories. And weirdly, I forgot all of them in between the tellings—like, total amnesia—which dovetailed nicely with her desire to repeat them. She sewed lead weights into the hem of every telling, giving each one the gravitas of new truth, and I believed the latest version as much as I believed in fiction—which is to say, completely.

She squirted herself a glass of wine from the box of Merlot sitting in the pantry and began talking. Her first story often recalled her dad, who had died of cancer when she was just three years old, and her most vivid memory of him, when he'd propped her up on the ledge of the kitchen sink and showed her the stars and told her he'd always love her. She told me about his mom, her beloved grandma Bertha Dion, a short, stout French-Canadian woman who could cook an enormous feast seemingly without effort. "She'd just be tinkering softly around the kitchen and then, suddenly Bam! Dinner for eight would be on the table." All of Great-grandma's gravies were elegant and thin, never thick and cloudy. She never turned the flame so high that fire shot up the sides of the pot, she never fried anything so hard that it spit grease (as her own mother did). "Everything was cooked on low heat." When she made chicken fricassee, the whole mushrooms shrunk to tiny slick knobs and the slow heat nagged at the joints of her meat until it just "shrugged off the bone." She was kind and soft and gracious, my great-grandmother, just like her food.

In contrast, my mom's mother's side—German-Bohemian farmers and dramatic, high-volume storytellers—seared their meat until it browned, and correspondingly, had tougher skins. "They're funny— you know that," my mom said, "but *horsey*."

"Grandma told me the last time I was there," I added. " 'Be fun, be lively! The last thing you want to be is a dud. Those people are THE WORST.' "

Addie Dion knew just when to throw a joke to take the edge off; her hard life had gifted her with perfect comic pitch. The eldest of seven girls, she quit high school to help her mom cook and raise her sisters, and was a widow with three young girls by the age of thirty. She was immensely capable and didn't have time to waste on delicacy. While she could take notice of the sweetness in a shy person, over time she grew intolerant of introverts, of those who had to be drawn out slowly and coaxed to say what they wanted or needed. Unlike the Scandinavian reticence that made up the stereotypical Minnesota character, she was direct, often to fearless, comic effect. Like a good, fatty piece of bacon is said to have a streak of lean, my grandma had a bawdy streak of lewd, in that old-time way. Take, for instance, her greatest gag, the "Drinking Nuns." A dozen found photographs reveal the premise: Mother Superior and her three daughters "Sister Joan, Sister Karen, and Sister Renee" in four perfectly rendered nun habits Addie had sewn, parked at a blackjack table in Vegas, heartily enjoying their first-ever brandy Manhattans. It was a serial bit, and they were loyal to their parts: just a few innocent nuns from Minnesota out on a ripper, "lifting a few." Nothing was safe from her teasing, not even the almighty Catholic Church.

Sensitivity was not her strongest suit, however, and my mom, with her big expressive eyes, was easily the most sensitive of the bunch.

"What she means by that is 'Have a good *bar* personality,'" my mom said, rolling her eyes. "Like she does."

"Sometimes, even her food was coarse," my mom said, "like those hard knoedel she always made." Just like her personality, Addie Hesch Dion's cooking was generous and full-throated—and sometimes even catch-in-the-throat.

The moral here was that the Germans, you see, were hard and coarse, just like their dumplings. The French, my mom's father's people, with whom she had a special kinship, were soft and benign, just like their sauces. My mom's cooking, although heavily influenced by her mother's German roots, also bore some resemblance to the little French-Canadian lady's: her gravies were strong but pourable and shimmered faintly with a surface glitter of fat; her potato soup was not like the local version—thick as sandcrete—but instead more bisquelike, each floating potato distinct. When my mom ordered a creamy soup at the local diner, she also ordered a glass of milk to stir into the soup by the spoonful until it was thinned to her liking. When she moved in the kitchen, she slid as smoothly as Grandma Bertha, like a slow pinball.

"I always wanted to be a chef, you know," she said.

"You did?" I was surprised. "Why didn't you?"

"My mom said it would be too hard, that I wouldn't be able to handle it," she said quietly, sipping her wine. "But there was this program that sent you all the way to France! I brought the pamphlet home and my mom said, 'Oh! You'd be way too scared to go to Europe.' And so I didn't go."

It didn't sound right to me. Even though I was as loyal to my mom as a serf, it was hard to imagine my adult self so blindly heeding her advice.

"So I became a teacher," she said with a sigh, heaving over the lump of practicality. "And then a few years later I had you!" she finished brightly. "I couldn't wait to quit my job and stay home and cook a big dinner every night." I knew she was speaking the truth.

As the level in her glass dipped, the dumplings became harder, the sauces thinner, the men increasingly egregious, and the women saintlier.

ONE NIGHT MY MOM POURED TWO GLASSES OF WINE: one for her and one for me. I raised my eyebrows but said nothing. It was unspoken: Once my mother started talking, we were French, like her father, and the French drink wine, apparently even the fifteen-year-old daughters. As we sat there eating popcorn, my mom flicking through her bowl in search of slightly burned old maids only partly exploded, me looking for the big, yellow-sopped buttery ones, we paged through catalogs. Then she said, "We should go to the mall in Fargo soon and stock up on any clothes you think you might need because I don't know how much money we'll have after this." She was so flippant about it, so self-assured, that it couldn't possibly be real. *My mom was leaving my dad.* I gathered up the clues in her tales of women wronged, her growing inventory of my father's failings, and stored the bud of their impending divorce in its green, tough, unflowered state, hedonistically allowing myself to ignore it in order to grab on to what seemed essential at the time, the words *mall* and *money.* I was a teenager, my desperation for new jeans that tragic.

I remember the resulting trip to West Acres Mall feeling buoyant because we bought freely, but also heavier. Our usual order at the

Country Kitchen—cups of thirteen-bean soup and a bran muffin, split—tasted denser, lined with doom.

One night soon after, my mom made boiled pork and sauerkraut for dinner, an assemblage that really deserved a better name. Even though she talked the talk about French food, her best dishes pulled from her mother's German side. Scented with garlic, thyme, bay, and allspice, her pork roast—a muscular picnic cut—simmered in tangy sauerkraut juices for four to five hours until it was as tender as tuna. It had the power to stir you deep down, in the way that only long-cooked pork can. I halved the baseball-size potato dumpling that had been poached in the pork broth, smeared butter on its firm ragged interior, and nibbled on the fluffy cloud edges. It was my favorite meal. I had three helpings.

My brothers and I did the dishes as always, and then our parents called a family meeting.

Matter-of-factly, my mom told us that she and our dad were separating. Dad was moving to the lake cabin, we were going to stay at the house in town—"for now," she said ominously—and their divorce was likely. Large tears rolled out of my brother Bob's round brown eyes. My youngest brother Marc's face, a transparent superconductor of his every passing thought, projected shock and confusion. My dad didn't look up. I was grateful that he didn't make eye contact because I knew that my eyes would reveal that I already knew.

Suddenly the phone rang in my room, my own private line. I was a teenager—it rang all the time. In a move that I have regretted ever since, I walked away from the table and down the hall to answer it.

Even worse, I still went to play rehearsal that night. During the break, Cara asked me if I wanted to split a package of Gardetto's pretzel mix from the vending machine, as was our nightly habit. I held my taut belly and told her I'd had three helpings at dinner that night and was way too full.

She said, "Again? Why'd you eat too much for dinner again?"

I didn't really know the answer to that. I was eating to fill a new and foreign space.

OUR DAD MOVED OUT TO THE CABIN THAT WINTER, and eight months later, we'd move away, too. My mom had chosen our escape route, one that felt sufficiently dramatic enough to match the high tenor of her big life-changing decision, and planned a move to a suburb of the Twin Cities, a place we'd visited a mere double handful of times.

That August before my junior year of high school, we moved into a sprawling apartment complex that probably housed the same population as the town we'd just left. It contained all the coziness of an office complex. I'd had my driver's license for precisely two weeks, had only driven dirt country roads and around the ten-block radius of Park Rapids, and had yet to master what for me was the hardest part—steering—when I launched myself as a hidden hazard onto the interchanges and merge lanes of the Minneapolis–St. Paul freeway system.

My Park Rapids friends and I burned up the USPS with dramatic, overly descriptive letters. Cara wrote that she often saw my dad driving around town with our dog, Buffy, in his lap. It's so cute, she said, but also kind of sad. The dog's paws were up on the wheel, as if she were steering.

I figured Buffy was better at it than I was.

I have just a vague recollection of going back to visit my dad at the house in town. The rooms were clean but painfully bereft of my mother's housekeeping. Plastic bags of dry-cleaning from Modern Cleaners hung on his doorframes, indicating that my dad now ferried all his clothes to the dry cleaners, including all of the dress shirts my mom had previously spent hours ironing. He sat in front of the TV in the evenings with the curtains wide open, so that anyone driving past on Eighth Street could see him. And he ate out a lot, alternating nights among the four restaurants in town. The one thing he made at home was popcorn, which I knew because I saw the smaller of my mom's two dedicated popcorn pots on his stove, both of which my mother credited with making her popcorn so irresistible. Golden and heavy, the exterior of the pot was covered with a flaky layer of oily black crud and so caked with it on the bottom that when you shook the pot against the metal burner, sparks flew. The inside of its lid was stained with brown oil residue, as sticky as pine pitch, and impossible to scrub off.

It was amazing how that smaller one, hardly more than six inches in diameter, could produce the enormous bowl of popcorn that it did; it was the clown car of pots—just when you thought everything was tipped out of that thing, the popcorn kept on coming.

Back when we used to sit at that counter, popcorn had always been the savory dessert after our lavish meal, but here in Dad's empty house, it might have comprised dinner itself. Were the two precious popcorn pots laid out in the divorce degree, as in: I take the kids, you keep the dog; I get the speedboat, you get the house; I'll take the big Club Aluminum pot, you keep the small? The minute I saw the small popcorn pot on Dad's stove, the permanence of my family's division descended on me all at once.

A few years later, while rooting around the cupboards at my mom's place for stray stuff to fill my college apartment kitchen, I would snag the other one.

10

OLD FIVE-AND-DIMERS

I'M SIXTEEN YEARS OLD and I love my mom with an almost scary fierceness. It blooms in me like a mushroom cloud of seething milk right before the boil.

Her opinions seep through me until I am soaked with them. They make me feel full. I take everything she says as the last word on the subject, from the way she cleans raw pork chops by scraping off the bone grit from the saw with a butter knife, to the way she singles out the best romaine at the grocery store, her finger tracing the head with the curliest edge. I try to eat the way she eats: ever so slowly, sucking on a single square of chocolate for a long time as if it were a lozenge. I love how she pushes a grocery cart through the store and then out over the icy parking lot—with urgency and feeling.

I watch her assemble an outfit for a night out, lounging on the silky discard pile on her bed as she tries on each ensemble with this belt, then that one, this necklace, that heel. Her body is exactly like mine, but grown; her kneecaps are smooth and rounded, her ankles small and bony, her wrists too small for most bangles. I stand by as she drapes eye shadow onto her deep-pocketed eyes, the silver dust clinging to the wide awnings of her lids. I love the way my mother smells, how soft her skin feels just above the knuckles.

I am happily, completely, my mom's spawn. She is my world or, more specifically, my country, and now, in the time of my parents' divorce, the country is at war. My parents, who fought regularly but never seemed to hate each other, have turned into vicious adversaries. In a panic to assemble some foot soldiers, my mom shares details to get us to join her side—which we do, given that my dad's influence in our lives measures just a drop compared to the ocean of our mother's, and that my dad refuses to talk about the divorce with us, never presenting us with his defense. I feel guilt over this years afterward, but we were just kids; it wasn't a fair contest.

My quiet dad grows even quieter. The invisible force field that has always surrounded him now turns so hard that I can almost see it, and because we're not sharing a house any longer, I lose even the small bits of affection that I used to glean from just being in his presence. He makes regular, awkward trips to the city to take us to professional sports events or to formal dinners. By this point my mother has taken on a character role, the wronged woman, and she is "spitting mad"— even though we are pretty sure the divorce was her idea. Midway through their three-year court battle, my brothers and I lose interest in her character, and in his character, and for once in our lives feel a unanimous desire to flip the channel and watch a new show.

That the divorce's eventual outcome takes my mother by surprise is an understatement. The judge does not seem to agree with her request for lifetime maintenance, and it turns out that in addition to raising us and ferrying my brothers to early-morning hockey practices and weekend tournaments, she will also soon have to get a job. When I come home from school, I sometimes find her in bed. It's so unlike her that I worry. I crawl in next to her and listen to her rail against the evil cards our dad's lawyer played that week in court.

Finally, one day she gets up early and decides to enroll in a college class to renew her teaching license. This does not mean that her fury has dissipated. It means it has solidified into a mantra.

"Kids! It's time for a new family motto," she says, as I riffle through my memory to recall any previous mottos.

"Fuck it!" She was referring to the divorce, to the move, to all our struggles to adjust, to our collective fear of an unfamiliar future. "Fuck! It!" she says, laughing, her new blunt haircut shaking. We look at her in shock, and then at one another with cracked conciliatory smiles, because even though the subversion was hers, she means for us to share it.

SOMEHOW IN ALL THE FIGHTING over monetary details, the big question—*Why can't you just get along?*—was neither posed nor answered. We never did find out why they split up. Being kids, all we really knew was that we were now living in a new town.

After six months in the office-apartment complex, my mom moved us into a big beige house in a freshly constructed suburban neighborhood so twisting and dizzying that the developers must have been high when they plotted it. Our house was identical to two others in the neighborhood, and more than once I pulled into the wrong driveway. Driving in circles along the endless meandering snake paths of my new streets, I felt out of the bottom reaches of teenage lostness, not yet understanding that the visual sense I was missing in my environment was *soul*. My mom sought out only the freshest of Sheetrocked starts for all of us, but I couldn't help but feel the lack of history there: Park Rapids could feel gritty, at times about as glamorous as carpet worn down to the plastic mesh, but it was nonetheless storied. And when we lived there, so were we.

My brother Bob shot up about a foot, grew out his hair in the back, and won a rare freshman spot on the varsity hockey team. A true northerner, he found his footing on the ice. The familiar, funky, dry-aged-beef odor of his and Marc's hockey equipment thawing out by our fireplace, the fresh layer of animal-boy sweat drying into a shellac on top of the last one, remained the only reassuring indicator of our former home.

Marc, at only ten, was a powder keg, tossing off insults at every provocation, as if he were walking around with tiny sharp rocks in his shoes. Wielding my own wicked tongue and using my language abilities to full press, I appointed myself family judge and chief arbitrator. I spent lots of time telling everyone what they should be feeling so as to cover up the fact that I had no idea what to feel myself. Sometimes my brothers listened to me, and other times they sneered that I was just like Mom, walking around the house with a tissue lodged between coffee cup and saucer as she did, and about as bossy. Mostly, when I wasn't eating bowls of oily leftovers, I drove around and got lost in suburbia, blaring the alternative radio station at top volume. My adolescent rebellion—"Smells Like Teen Spirit"—had been curtailed out of necessity, but it was still active, like a buried hot spring.

Walking around loose and unknown in my enormous new school, I had my first taste of anonymity. Despite this, I made deep instant friendships with an already established crew of theater goofs, and we spent a lot of time studying for our AP English exams, smoking loosies and drinking strong black coffee in Minneapolis's late-night coffee shops. My mom insisted that I must be out partying, that there was no way in hell we could be hanging out that long in cafés.

But I was a good girl. And, suddenly, a very hungry one. At home we ate, with more sickly comfort than ever. Feeding hungry, emotional suburban kids—the three of us and, eventually, many of our friends—became my mom's specialty.

To outsiders, every dinner looked like a holiday. The spinning wheel of my mother's arsenal, which up to this point had always pulled in a fair number of ethnic outliers like stir-fry, spun tighter and tighter until it began to land each night on one of our richest Midwestern favorites: chicken marsala with mushrooms and spaetzle in brown butter; grilled pork chops served still a little pink in the middle and cloaked with horseradish sour cream; butterscotch bars caving beneath the weight of their thick chocolate tops. She began to make even larger batches in advance prep for the preteen raids on the fridge that so thrilled her. "Marc's friends came over and ate that entire gallon of chili and *all* of those apple dumplings!" was a common boast in those days. I can't remember her ever saying that she herself was hungry, but rather that it was "time to feed these kids." The woman who made more food than a single family could eat had one wish for it: She wanted it gone.

Her cooking, and our belief in its eminence, was fast becoming the family glue. My abdomen-thorax regions grew permanently round and remained so, in a state of full-on satiation, for the next three or four years. To my mother's credit, never once did she acknowledge my weight gain, even as my short frame skip-counted from size 4 to 10 and then 12, and not even when I begged her to admit the truth: "Agree with me, I'm getting fat."

She dismissed this with a wave of her hand—"You're absolutely not!"—and countered with the only words of eating wisdom I've ever needed: "If you feel that way, then cut out desserts, and don't take seconds."

She refused to ruin food for me, for which I'm forever grateful.

WHEN IT CAME TIME FOR ME TO APPLY TO COLLEGE, my main goal was to distance myself as much as possible from the fallout from my detonated family. I found a small liberal arts school in a village in Ohio—as insulated as Park Rapids but even smaller—called Kenyon, whose old stone buildings and ancient literary pedigree seemed like the perfect place to launch a small-town girl's literary calling. Feeling hopelessly foreign, a Midwestern duck swimming in a pond of East Coast kids, I threw myself into my classes. To offset my social anxiety, I counterintuitively returned to my comfort zone: I got a perm. (I still believed the Midwestern adage that curls make round faces look thinner.) By the time summer break rolled around, I'd come to see my college foray as an indulgent, expensive escape from the family drama, a luxury that I probably didn't deserve.

Moving back into the house in the cul-de-sac, I saw that they were doing about as well as I was—surviving but not exactly thriving. Marc wore his new angry-teenager costume 24/7; my mom began buying better wine but still in jumbo sizes—cheap magnums instead of boxes; and my brother Bob seemed to be taking the divorce the hardest. He'd been sending me long handwritten letters all year, some of them updates, some of them wildly inventive poems. One night we sat up and talked about them.

I thought his writing could have been really good if it weren't for his syntax, a curious mixture of biblical and Middle English. While I had lost my Catholicism and my ability to pretend years ago (at around the same time), Bob remained in possession of both his Bible and the full scope of his imagination. In narrative terms, I was reasonable, boring nonfiction; he was fantasy fiction. The secular, liberal English major in me changed his every "morn" to "morning" and "ye" to gender-neutral "they," and sent them back for revision. And now I was feeling guilty for having so mercilessly edited my brother's work— little more than diary entries.

"I actually don't think you need to change anything here," I said.

"Whatever. The individual words aren't as important as the meaning of the whole." He sighed. I was the one in the family known for her achievements, her aptitude, and yet in his eyes I was often so dense. "Look at the last line."

It said, "So be it."

So be it? "Is that some kind of answer?" I asked.

"Yeah. When it comes to our family, none of them will ever change. Your problem is you expect too much."

As a devout child of psychotherapy, I found that hard to accept, but the undeniable truth was that after that he dealt with our parents' divorce, the move, and his own coming-of-age with the kind of finality and wisdom it would take me many more years to find. Unlike me and, to a certain degree, our brother Marc, Bob had no desire to return to our hometown to dig in our family's wreckage for fossilized clues. He shut the door to the past and remained close to both of our parents, but never returned to Park Rapids for any length of time; I kept my door open, just a crack, and every time I went back I walked all over my past self, nose to the ground, sniffing for clues.

For my sophomore year, I transferred to Macalester in St. Paul, another liberal arts school—but this one was only twenty minutes away from my brothers, my mother, and her kitchen.

MACALESTER COLLEGE PULLED IN lots of East Coasters from moneyed backgrounds, but I gravitated toward the more informal Midwestern-ers. I roomed with an enthusiastic social-activist lesbian-theologian from Milwaukee and a wisecracking poet from Minnesota who was deep into Sylvia Plath's language of melancholy. The poet and I wrote endless pages of confessional poetry and smoked cigarettes until the silver ash mountain in the ashtray overflowed onto the floor. All three of us spent hours playing drinking games with the boys in the base-ment apartment, who then sculpted a living-room couch from our empty cases of cheap Wisconsin beer. (Huber Bock, to be specific, which in retrospect might have contributed to my thickening torso.)

Everyone in my family, save my mom, thought that my pursuit of an English degree in an expensive liberal arts college was pure extrava-gance, and told me so. "For that, why don't you just go to a state school?" asked the ever-practical Grandma Dion. In a way, they weren't wrong, for I basically spent my college years fine-tuning my god-given aptitude for procrastination.

I'd wait until the eleventh hour to start writing a twenty-five-page term paper, then drive down to my mom's house and stay up all night long and write the thing in a single sitting, fueled by hefty servings of the food I revered. I came back toting bags of leftovers, which my hungry roommates leapt on.

Installed in my first apartment, I also started to cook on my own. Whenever the pressure of a writing deadline loomed uncomfortably in front of me, I'd dodge it by jumping into my car and driving to one of the nearby Asian markets. I'd happily plunk down forty of my pre-cious work-study dollars at the Thai market to buy everything to make chicken coconut-milk curry and green beans with pork and fish sauce for eight of my closest friends—and another day's reprieve from writ-ing my paper on Flannery O'Connor, William Faulkner, and the South-ern literary consciousness.

I cooked outside of my mother's arsenal. I did a good rendition of spaghetti carbonara, with an obscene amount of bacon fat and freshly grated Parmesan cheese. I cut carrots and parsnips length-wise into spears and fried them hard in a sea of butter until the edges browned to copper and the insides gushed when pressed, and then poured the fat, burnished sticks over white rice. If I had a deadline the next day, I could be found at three in the morning crouched in the living room pureeing squash soup in a blender because the socket in the kitchen didn't work.

But I also regularly overcooked pasta and spent long minutes peel-ing garlic and mincing it into minuscule cubes, returning to the stove to find my onions frizzled down to a crust. I stopped trying to replicate my mom's chicken marsala, because the meat never turned out as velvety as hers. When stir-frying in my thrift-store wok, I particularly hated the metallic fumes that rose up when the soy sauce bubbled on the hot metal, burning upon contact. That wasn't right. How and when are you supposed to add the soy? I fretted more about my steep learn-ing curve with cooking than I did about my classes.

The disasters in the kitchen piled up. As did the dishes, because I so rarely did them.

THE SUMMER BETWEEN MY JUNIOR AND SENIOR YEARS of college was a tremendous bust. Just three weeks after scoring my first job in food service, as a back waiter—beverage pourer, basically—at a high-end Italian spot in Minneapolis, I was fired. Not after breaking my sixth glass, or even after clownishly dropping an entire magnum of champagne on a guy at a very special table of four, but only after I nervously proceeded to pat him down hastily with my side towel—all the way down, into the crevice of his lap, not even thinking about where my towel was headed until I saw his wife's burning expression. Shaking with mortification, I would never attempt to work front-of-the-house ever again. I left my white button-down shirts in my locker and ran.

Adding to that, my boyfriend of four or five months was breaking up with me. Or, rather, he wasn't even bothering with that, but just openly starting to date another girl. ("You're going to Minnehaha Falls with Kristina? Can I come, too?" I'd asked.)

Having never been so thoroughly dumped before, I was clearly confused, and dramatically heartbroken, for about a week. My pain was more theatrical than real.

The heat didn't lessen from day to night that summer. Compared to northern lake country, city nights feel strangely indistinguishable from the days. Up north, after the sun dives behind the trees, the wind and the temperature both drop and the waves on the lake flatten to reflective glass. I missed the lake. I missed nights spent sitting on the dock, talking with my friends in low voices because we knew that the water before us would amplify our every sound wave. I missed the Park Rapids sign that announced our population: 2,961. I missed our double-wide Main Street; I missed the sight of the dumb potato plant belching fryer steam, my friends, and even my dad's dorky announcements of love. I just wanted to drive north and go jump in a lake. It was all I could think of to do.

Mom's lake cabin had been the first pawn to go in the game that was the divorce—first point, Dad—so I couldn't go there. Our house in town, where my dad still lived, looked exactly as it had after my mom's final garage sale. At the end of that day her face had taken on a weird clownlike glee as she watched the effects of their years together march out the door in the hands of new owners. As the house emptied and she began to feel the reality of her fresh start, she grew bolder, ordering my brothers to run back into the house and grab paintings, doodads, all of her seasonal fake-flower arrangements, whatever, and slap a dollar tab of tape on each one of them. My brothers, bouncing to the beat of the adrenaline in this, sprinted in and cheerfully obliged. By the time it was over, she'd sold most of the house's decorative aspects. She'd basically sucked the woman out of it, leaving him with—not kidding—light squares on the walls where the photos had been and bare mattresses in the rooms, which he'd truly had no idea how to cover. When we came to visit him, you could almost hear him thinking: Where does she keep the part that goes under the sheets, the pad thingy? I was welcome to stay in his forlorn, air-conditioned house in town, but it would be no jump in the lake.

Two weeks in advance of a high school friend's wedding, I called up my friend Sarah Spangler to ask for an extended visit. Sarah was in the wedding, too, and if I could think of a house that better fit my nostalgic ideal of life in Park Rapids, hers was it. Built at the turn of the twentieth century, the Spangler place was so close to Fish Hook Lake it nearly squatted on its shores. More bookish and environmental and Scandinavian-outdoorsy than my parents, hers filled their house with plants, piles of *New Yorker* magazines, and a constant soundtrack of classical music. Also unlike my house, theirs lacked a glorious supply of leftovers, and her dad's environmentalism extended to the furnace, causing Sarah and me to walk around on Saturdays after sleepovers in afghan capes. But still, their house felt like a lakeside refuge. I'd stayed there for a week while we were moving, and maybe they'd let me bunk there again.

I called their house three, four times but couldn't reach Sarah, who was working two jobs. Each time my call was answered by her older brother, Aaron, and each time our conversation lasted an abnormally long time, especially as I couldn't recall a single verbal exchange between the two of us. He was four years older; if he knew me at all, it was as one of the cheerleaders he'd cautioned his sister not to hang out with in high school.

Now he was back in town himself. He caught me up on all its changes in the past four years while we'd both been away, both of us digging our hometown with a strange expatriate enthusiasm. Over the phone line I fell hard for Aaron's conversational prowess. In his orbit the most mundane details, such as the renovation of the town's Dairy Queen, felt worthy of discussion.

"We got a second traffic light," he said.

"Over by the Holiday stationstore?"

"No, for some reason they put it by the Pamida."

This is so weird, I thought. *But oddly comfortable.*

The fourth time I called, he asked, "Can I ask—why do you keep calling?" I explained my plight, that I wanted to come home but didn't have any place to stay. "Oh, just come up," he said.

"Really? You don't think Sarah would mind? Or your mom?"

"Nah, it's fine." In those days teenage friends of the Spangler kids—Matt, Aaron, and Sarah—would often show up at the sliding glass door, knock, and walk right into their '70s-era gold-and-orange kitchen. That summer I was one of them.

If there was someone I had assumed would never, ever come back to live in Park Rapids, it would have been Aaron. Easily voted "most likely to get out of town" in his senior year, he was one of a handful of local kids who had been turned on to punk music. He lent Sarah mixed tapes of pounding music we'd never heard before: Black Flag, Sonic Youth, Motörhead. He fronted his own band. He studied both the hardcore ethic and its aesthetic—the casual, open-flung shirts, the ratty, gnarled flop of long hair, the loose Converse Chucks—and practiced them devoutly. He didn't jibe at all with the sonic and cultural testosterone of the *Top Gun* 1980s, or the conservative town for that matter, and so he sought out his own symbols, a lot earlier than most of us did.

I hold on to a vivid memory from childhood that contains the both of us, an illicit *meet* between the rebel and the cheerleader if you will, although he still refuses to confirm it.

I was in the ninth grade, co-captain of the boys' basketball cheerleading squad, sitting for my biannual perm at the Family Hair Affair—a tradition that began for me in kindergarten and mercifully ended my senior year of high school (save that single backslide during college). The stench of the solution was a perfect blend of rot and ammonia and it needled at my eyes. Aaron sat in a chair behind me, in my mirror's purview. The salon's owner, Mavis Davis (her glorious married name), and her constant cohort, a six-foot ice blonde with a Brigitte Nielsen crop, stood over Aaron. These ladies loved—they absolutely *lived*, as my mother would say—to cut it short. Mavis roughly lifted up hunks of Aaron's heavy dark hair and loudly discussed how they might remove the enormous rat's nest that was knotted at the back of his neck. Or maybe I'm remembering it wrong and they were holding up his hair and talking about how they could remove the image of a spider that had been shaved into his head beneath his long flop of top hair. It's all a little hazy now, and Aaron swears that he never set foot in the Hair Affair after middle school, but I know without a doubt that I sat in that white vinyl beauty-salon chair suffocating in a stinging cloud of perm-fumes and spied on my future punk husband while he was in consultation with Mavis Davis.

AFTER COLLEGE AARON WENT TO ART SCHOOL and exited with the intention of being a full-time artist. ("That's different," the hometown murmurs.) A few of his sculptures sat in the Spangler yard: One was a small wooden chair surrounded on three sides by wooden-framed windows. I tried out the chair when I first got there. The old wavy glass threw the woods into a squirmy, surreal abstraction, instantly defamiliarizing the landscape. On their porch hung another of his pieces, a large relief carved out of wood, with a glossy blue river flowing through a rough, tar-covered townscape. It was not-pretty in a foreign, intriguing way.

He'd been living in Minneapolis for years, and yet here he was back in town, by day working at a local sawmill, by evening building a house out on his parents' land by Two Inlets and reposing nightly on the Spangler back porch playing country songs on his guitar. Sarah and I joined him after dinner, curled up in sweatshirts against the cool summer night, drinking spiced tea. Eventually Sarah, a morning person, went to bed, giving us two night owls the tree perch to ourselves.

"So what's your house like?" I asked.

"It's just one room, and tall. Kind of like a warehouse live-work space, but in the woods. Full of scavenged wood and windows I've been collecting. I'm still putting up the logs on the inside, straight-cut slabs I bring home from the sawmill." He smiled. "I don't really know how to build a house, you know. I'm just making it up as I go."

It seemed a little doubtful to me that he'd actually moved back to Park Rapids to make art like a hermit, and I told him so.

"It's Two Inlets! Not the Park Rapids we grew up in." He crossed his legs into a triangle and lit the ivory bowl of his pipe. "George, the sawyer at the mill, has so much vernacular knowledge. He's cutting logs on this old saw from 1910 and he judges how to cut a log by how it *sounds* on the first cut. I'm learning so much basic stuff there, things I feel like I should already know."

He pulled up his guitar from his feet and all of a sudden tipped his head back and started singing. No tentative porch sing was this. It was more like a solo in a musical, a song woven right into the conversational fabric. I was a little taken aback, not yet accustomed to the way Aaron naturally just breaks into song.

"Last winter I bought a tractor-powered saw-mill . . . I wanted to make my living cutting boards to sell . . . but she don't want to live in the town I grewed up in . . . so I'll just take my tractor back . . . to the auction barn . . ."

" 'Grewed up'! Who sings this song?"

"It's mine. Old country songs have bad grammar." He kept the rhythm on his guitar and popped right back in.

"We fellll in love, I bought her a ring, but she found out . . . that all I had to offer her . . . was this piece of ground. She says we woooon't be married now . . ."

"Shallow lady!" I interrupted.

"I have nothing to call my oooooown . . . and I . . . just lost . . . my trac-tor to . . . the auc-tion barn . . ."

"Oh no, not the girl *and* the tractor!"

"Listen to the song, you're like a heckler in a bar," he said.

"All alone, allllll alone . . . living on . . . my daddy's land . . ."

And then he tipped his head back so far his eyes shut, and he fell into a soft yodel that grew louder, longer, and ever more woeful.

"Yodeleyheeee-hooo . . . yodeleyheeeee-hoooooo . . . yodeleyheeeeeeeee . . . yodeleyheeeee—EHEEEE-hoooo . . ."

His voice filled the entire porch, all the way to the corners. It was a vulnerable howl, and I wanted to cry. How could she turn her back on the romance of the guy and his tractor-powered sawmill?

When I slipped into bed beside Sarah that night in her old bed-room, she rolled over and sleepily groaned, "Oh boy, were you up all this time talking to my *brother?*"

AROUND THE TIME I ARRIVED at the Spangler house, a stray dog started showing up. This surprised no one because odd dogs often came for the summer to join the pack of them that ran the beach, tore around in the woods, and rolled in the dead fish on the shore; they'd gotten three of their dogs that way. I nicknamed this one Schnoz for his out-size lab nose and quipped that directions to their place must be written on the hobo dogs' bathroom wall. During the day I read books by the shore, my hands buried in Schnoz's woolly head.

When it came time for me and Sarah to go to our friend's wedding, Aaron decided to crash it, and he arrived in style. When he stepped out of his low, old-man Buick in cowboy boots and a tight parchment-colored vintage three-piece suit, his shadowy blue eyes found mine and the round gears of his jaw shifted under his suntanned skin. I had never before been so curious about a person.

Within weeks, he was back down in Minneapolis. He and his friend Rob were planning to pilot Rob's houseboat all the way down the Mississippi, from Minneapolis to New Orleans. Rob's boat on the river looked more like a little log cabin with a woodstove in the center than a river rider. As at Aaron's house, its walls were nearly choked with paintings and found objects, and the two of them spent their free time tweaking the interior for their trip. In the meantime, Aaron picked up day work with a stone mason and dated me. After going to art openings and museums and rock shows and his favorite diners, we'd sit on the steps outside my college apartment and talk for hours. One night, after he left, my roommate, the theologian, said, "Holy shit, when the two of you get together you take on this really strong accent."

The cadence of the talk I grew up with, which I didn't realize had faded, was coming back.

Aaron and Rob had spent all their time perfecting their houseboat abode and none working on the engine, so when it failed to start up, their Mississippi trip was called off. I was secretly glad. Aaron was staying most nights at my place, anyway. He had been sleeping on a pallet of blankets in his cement-floored warehouse studio space, so giving him a proper bed felt like the most practical thing to do.

The first night we spent together we stayed up in bed until the wee hours, watching the light of dawn creep up the window shades as I lay there in his arms, trading memories of Park Rapids school lunch. We recalled the windowless dungeon that was the middle school's basement cafeteria and the route there that took us through the dark boiler room, pitted with surprise puddles of water that soaked our white Keds. We joked about the way the gruff lunch ladies, in their housedresses and hairnets, clocked out perfect balls of mashed potatoes onto our plates, the synthetic potato-bud mash as smooth as nylons. These shared fruit-cocktail and hamburger-gravy memories were amusing to him, but the fact that we had grown up eating the same crappy lunches absolutely slayed me. I howled and curled into a fetal position, doubled up with recognition.

In the mornings, we listened to the radio in my bedroom—K1400 AM, an oldies station for seniors that played "The Music of Your Life."

I started wearing a robe. In the mornings, we'd get up, eat basted eggs, and then I'd send him off to work with a tub of bean soup stuffed with three kinds of smoked meat from the family meat market: country sausage, bacon, and the pink bits whittled from a long-simmered hock. He'd look at it with a smile—"This should get me through!"—accustomed as he was to lean turkey sandwiches with sprouts. This gave me a charge, as I was already hanging part of my self-esteem on my cooking, well on my way to becoming a feeder.

I felt timeless with him and blurted this out one day, immediately wishing I could take it back. *Shit,* I thought. *I don't even know what that means.* Mercifully, Aaron understood. He said he felt the same.

THAT CHRISTMAS, when I was back in Park Rapids to see my dad, Aaron introduced me to his house. Located four hours from Minneapolis, twenty-five minutes from our hometown, five minutes from the nearest gas station, and a mile down a snaking dirt path, Aaron's house was so lodged in the woods that it felt like we were traveling back in time.

It was so rough and so wild, even the road was homemade. To make it, Aaron had followed the faint stamped-down line of a deer trail all the way through the eighty-acre piece. After cutting the trees with a chain saw, the small brush with a gas-powered brush cutter, and the high grass with a machete, he was able to heave and bounce down the road in his four-wheel-drive Ford.

But now, when we came to the driveway, he stopped. "What's wrong?" I asked.

"Snow's too deep. We have to walk in."

"Too deep for the four-wheel-drive?"

I couldn't believe I wasn't wearing decent winter boots. City living had made me soft, my footwear unfit for anything but a shoveled sidewalk. I felt hopelessly un-local. The snow swooped across the driveway in an even wave, broken only by the fine string of oval hoof holes left by deer delicately plucking their way across the road. We were doing the same, but indelicately, me tromping in rapidly soaking leather boots, Aaron in proper winter mucks.

"It's just another half mile," he said. Halfway there, the cold wind invaded my lungs and I realized I was having an asthma attack.

After stopping three times along the way, we arrived at the end of the road. There, on a hill above a wide, frozen waterway, stood his house. It looked old, like it had been there a long time. He explained how he'd built it, over the course of two years, without any electric power. He'd dug the foundation with a shovel and then started raising the sides: four large log poles on each side, spaced eight feet apart. It was basically a pole shed. He planned the ceiling to be fourteen feet high, so that it would feel lofty inside, even though the footprint was only twenty-four by fourteen feet.

The padlock on the front door was unhitched. Aaron turned the latch and pushed open the nine-foot-tall door, a giant's entrance into a tiny house. We walked in and were met with the spicy aroma of fresh wood. It was like walking into the inside of a barrel and smelled exactly like the woolen work shirts he wore to the sawmill.

To the left there was a shipman's alcove kitchen, its shelves holding a few colorful spice jars, boxes of tea, and metal canisters of sugar, flour, and cornmeal. Taking up most of the kitchen was a huge vintage white stove with four wide burners and a lake of shiny white enamel between them, with two identical oval rust holes burned out on each side. A large speckled black kettle sat squarely on one of the burners and on the other, a wire cone-shaped contraption.

"What is that?" I asked.

"That's my toaster."

I'd seen this artifact, along with the water kettle, in antiques stores before, but never in action. Here, they made sense. The ceiling in the kitchen was a network of rough beams he'd cut with a hand saw, with open joints and wedges shimmed in the corners to make them as level as he could. Freshly constructed in 1995, the place looked like it could have been built in 1895.

To the right of the entrance, a homemade wooden ladder descended into the room. It led up to a small bedroom, anchored with a rusty metal bed ("pulled from my grandpa's chicken barn," Aaron boasted) covered with a patchwork quilt. Beneath the loft sat a vanity, with a shadowy mirror and a chipped enameled washbasin on top. I guessed that that was the bathroom.

Aaron built a fire in the woodstove in the center of the house and dropped a pile of snowy logs at my feet, on which I propped my boots to let them melt off. Outside, the sun was dropping. He lit an oil lamp, tinting everything orange. I shivered, not with cold but with the engrossing weirdness of the place. If I hadn't known him and his family all my life I'd have thought I'd just entered a madman's lair.

I looked up. The flat ceiling, fourteen feet up, was covered with overlapping pieces of rusty sheet metal ("the backside of old trailer house siding," he said). The blotches of maroon, orange, black, and pink swirled into a surreal pattern like the one that forms on the back of your eyelids when you squint in the dark. The house was sided with rough board-and-batten, but the interior was made of shiny logs, which he explained were the extra slabs that he'd taken home from the mill, stripped of excess bark with an axe, varnished thickly, and nailed onto the walls to create a faux-log-cabin effect. Though he'd fully intended to put down a wood floor over the wide plank subfloor, he fell in love with the dirty patina the floor had taken on during the time he'd been working on it with his muddy work boots, and instead decided just to preserve its finish with four layers of heavy varnish. In the flickering firelight from the oil lamp, the dark pine boards shone like lacquered dry coffee in a forgotten cup.

Nearly every inch of space on the walls was filled with stuff: paintings, photos, iron tools, lake buoys, record covers, deer hides. Crude handmade wooden weapons hung ominously amid the sculptures and paintings. The tables held a granny's menagerie of tchotchkes—trinkets, figurines, little glass boxes with taconite pellets, quirky old coasters, brooches, geodes, music boxes with yellowed gloves draped over them—a nice collection of everything you might have felt like buying in an antiques store but put back at the last minute. Each treasured knickknack held its own orderly slot. Everything wore a lacy shawl of dust.

The nearest electricity box was more than three miles away. He poured me a glass of water from the jug he'd brought in and explained that there was no running water, either, because the pump he'd attempted to pound in the kitchen had come up dry. And no phone. He laid the eggs and the bacon, the loaf of bread and the coffee on the kitchen butcher block. We were marooned, with just these resources. And yet it was the coziest place I'd ever been, like the fantasy house that children dream about as they sit in their forts, wishing them to come to life. Most adults forget about those places as they grow older, but not him.

We slept there that night, crawling the ladder to the loft bedroom. I pulled out the lace-up petticoat top I'd bought in a vintage store, which suddenly felt a little too historically accurate. *My fantasy is out of the bag now,* I thought, as I fastened the long line of pearly buttons and crawled into bed. Aaron piled the heavy quilts on high. When we turned off the oil lamp for the night the mice began to play a game of pinball in the rafters, and immediately Aaron corrected his mistake.

"I always play night music to drown out the mice," he said as he went downstairs to put a Fritz Kreisler violin tape into the boom box. The high notes of the violin kicked in, swirling into the dark like a voice. We lay there, taking turns rolling over toward the window to look out at the soft drifts of moonlit snow.

Aaron said, "Ever since I was a kid, I've been afraid of the dark. I used to think it was a monster"—he held his arms up—"*chasing* me."

"You're not afraid now, are you?" I asked, a little scared myself.

"I'm starting to get over it," he said. "It's better with someone else out here."

The next day when we were ready to go, we let the fire die down, shut the door, turned the latch, and hung the open padlock on it. As we walked back to the road in yesterday's trampled footprints, I turned around. The loft window formed one eye and the window in the door another, making a crooked, lovable face. It was hard to believe we were going to leave the house out there all alone. It was already a character.

And although Aaron hates it when I say this—because it's so sugary—when I looked back at the house, I thought its board-and-batten siding made it look just like the one on *Little House on the Prairie,* ladder to the sleeping loft and all.

A FEW MONTHS LATER, the long, record-breaking cold winter of 1997 came to a close. To celebrate the temperature's rise to zero, we drove around with the car windows down. The sun was shining, and in an instant we were old-timers, happy, and constantly together.

I was graduating that spring but hadn't yet formulated a plan. Many of my friends were moving to New York, and others were headed on to more school. I figured I'd work a year in Minneapolis, then probably go to grad school myself to become a professor. The English department felt more like home to me than any other place. I knew Aaron intended to keep making art and that he'd want to move back into his empty house in the woods that summer, but he was keeping his specific plans for the future close to his chest.

Then one day, as I was sitting on my bed reading *The Making of Americans* by Gertrude Stein—a famously unreadable book, but one that effectively drills the dream of the pioneers into your head over the course of two thousand pages of repetitive nonsense—and Aaron was sitting in the wooden chair next to me, embroidering a tiny baby-quilt art piece with the logo for the fictional Two Inlets Knife and Gun Club, his absurdist ode to the rack-and-gun culture of our home, I started to cry, my tears projectile.

Aaron kneeled by my side, imploring me to tell him what was wrong. What was it that he had done?

"Nuh-thing!" I wailed. I didn't know. Or I couldn't say. I couldn't see. I finally coughed it out, the words that hadn't yet gone through the pipes of my brain but had been keeping me from breathing deeply.

"I wanna go up there!"

"You want to go up *where?*"

"I wanna move up to the house with you!"

"My house? In Two Inlets?" He was honestly shocked.

"Yes!" I shouted, wiping my face. I glared at him through puffy eyes. "Why didn't you ask me?"

"I—I don't know. I didn't think you'd want to live up there."

He looked at me, slumped on the bed, fully depleted and about as unvarnished as I'd ever been with him or anyone else. "All the guys up there told me that I'd never get a woman to live at my place," he joked.

"Some guy says women can't live in the woods and you believe them?"

"I'm sorry! I didn't think it was really your thing. Honestly, I thought I'd have to build a rambler at the front of the road to get you to move there with me. The road is so long and terrible."

"It's terrible," I agreed. "But I don't care. I want to go up there."

"You really want to live up there, sweetie?"

"Yes," I exhaled. "I do."

For some reason, going back felt like the very definition of moving forward.

I had said it: I wanted to go home. It was hard for me to admit, but moving away from my hometown two years short of my high school graduation had somehow messed with the flow of my natural exodus. The city, where I'd found the culture, the books, and the people I'd been looking for, wasn't enough. I didn't even like that damned town, and never thought I'd want to go back and live in it, but I couldn't shake the feeling that I'd left something behind there that I needed to retrieve. Aaron, a post-high-school flight risk like myself, felt a similarly inexplicable urge to go back to the town to which he'd never expected to return. He didn't put a name to it, and neither did I, but I could feel the energy of what pulled him.

Somehow in fusing our two minus-forces we had made a strong magnetic positive. The charge between the poles of our two homes—rural and urban—remained strong and tight with tension, setting our insane future migratory life together in motion.

11

ARE WE GOING TO BAKE THIS BREAD IN MY LIFETIME?

THAT SPRING, after we decided to move in together, I took Aaron to Pierz, my parents' hometown, to meet Grandma Dion.

Addie Dion, my mom's mom, lived in a green rambler the color of lime Jell-O on a side street a block off Pierz's Main Street. For years her sprawling backyard was taken up with an equally large garden, whose far edge reached the backside of Thielen Meats, the meat market and smokehouse owned by generations of Thielens on my paternal side. (As it often goes for two fated families in small towns, the path between doors was beaten well before the formal link took place.)

Like many a Midwestern house, Addie's had a formal front entrance decorated with Catholic statuaries that no one ever used; the tiny side entrance into the kitchen received the heavy traffic. You walked in and pried off your boots in a precipitous two-foot-square foyer, walked up two steps into the bright yellow glow of the kitchen, right into the kitchen table wedged into an alcove. The move that felt most natural was to sit down, which most people did. I cannot recall that table without people stuffed around its perimeter, all talking, eating, and drinking in a liberated fashion, and its top was never bare.

Every opportunity to turn a plain day into a more delicious one was taken; my grandma took levity where she could get it. Losing her husband to leukemia left her with three daughters under the age of four, very little cash to sustain them, and no choice but to run an incredibly tight household ship. In a house where the loss of the father whispered in the corners, the food at the center of the table set everything right with the world. Her cooking was thrifty but extravagantly rich, heavy with meaning and flavor.

Whenever I arrived, Addie sent me to the cellarlike basement cold storage room for provisions. I pulled a jar of fermented pickles from the shelf, its zinc lid frosted with salt. My reach was short inside the ten-foot-long chest freezer, so I heaved my belly onto its edge to retrieve the frozen sugar cookies and foil-wrapped chunks of poppy-seed coffee cake—a little lost balance and I would have been interred in a giant coffin. She laid out these items with dishes of sliced ham, salami, herring, crackers, and cheese. And always in the middle of the snack chaos sat a fat square of butter from the Little Rock Creamery a few miles down the road. Waxy and dense and pale, it was "very lightly salted," she liked to point out. It tasted just like the famous butter of Brittany.

Some nights she made beef soup with shaggy clumps of tender meat and tiny curled fists of tan natural wild rice, its broth as clear and brown as weak coffee. Or slabs of coppery-pink Thielen Meats ring bologna cut into pointed rounds and fried until the edges crisped sharply like a new penny. This peppery bologna wasn't bouncy, wasn't made from suspicious meat scraps like the stuff sold under the same name everywhere else. In fact, Uncle Keith insisted that it contained "nothing I wouldn't eat," and he's a rib-eye-eating sort of butcher. It melted in our mouths.

When we had eaten all of it, she ran the heels of her homemade white potato bread through the oily pan juices. "Try this," she ordered.

"It's what we girls on the farm used to call dip dee." The bread, slubbed with ropy sausage juices, was transcendent. It was best followed up with a cleansing forkful of her paper-thin-cucumber salad, properly bludgeoned with freshly cracked black pepper and shivery with vinegar.

She delighted in all seasonal delicacies. When spring's little silver fish ran in the freshwater streams out of Lake Superior, she was promptly in attendance at the smelt feed at Flicker's Bar, the same bar in which she'd worked as a cocktail waitress as a young widow. The bar owners brought in the tiny fish by the pickup load and then had a party to get them ready: while drinking beer, the bar crew gutted thousands of fish and cut off their heads by the half dozen with an office paper cutter. Line 'em up and *whish*! Headless fish ready for their batter. It was exactly the kind of food theater that Addie loved.

ADDIE CAME FROM A TIME when cleaning and cooking were indivisible, and her housekeeping bordered on an overabundance of caution. If there was a bunch of pens in a drawer she would gather them together tightly with a rubber band, putting the kibosh on their potentially uproarious scattering. She repainted the walls in the house every year, just to "freshen them up." In her garage, a tennis ball hung from a long string attached to a wooden rafter over a rectangular carpet sample, perfectly positioned so that when she inched her car into the garage she stopped when the tennis ball was hanging directly over the center of her car hood, at which point her gas tank would be directly above the carpet rectangle. Untold cement stains were prevented this way. Her rags—*her rags*—were bleached until the chemicals ate holes in the fabric.

It was the same story in the kitchen. She and my mom spoke reverently of the women who kept their houses so clean that "you could eat an egg cooked on their floors" and less so of others who were such pigs that anything they cooked "couldn't be sanitary." ("Soap is free," Addie liked to add, a holdover from her farm upbringing.) It's no wonder that the best bakery in the area was called the Sanitary Bakery. To me, the name brought to mind maxi pads rather than great doughnuts, but I got the point: Cleanliness was good. Sanitation was the goal. Add bleach and you had the triune god.

Beneath the veneer of her cleaning, Grandma Dion's hospitality was a lot like my mom's—aggressive, good-natured, and generous—but possibly a little more insistent. She was a bit of a food pusher, Grandma.

"Want some sauerkraut hotdish?" she'd ask, pointing to a layered casserole of noodles, ground beef, sauerkraut, and cheese. If you declined, she snorted with genuine shock. Despite the name, it was quite good. The rusty browned shoulders of ground beef bobbed in the sauce, and the lingering tartness of the kraut made the pads at your jaw shudder and tingle. Digging up a deep forkful made a rich sticky sound, as if the hotdish were taking a deep breath, and that sound was a comfort in itself. No one with any sliver of hunger inside them would rightly turn down her sauerkraut hotdish, which she often served to us kids to-go: in Dixie paper cups impaled with plastic forks. This she considered a snack, and we were strongly urged to take it.

She had a word for people who turned down food just because they weren't particularly hungry, who denied themselves the pleasure of eating in the interest of keeping themselves fashionably bony: *gemikli*. It sounds like its definition. "You know, not thriving," she'd say with a scornful smirk, "undernourished." The implication was that people, especially women, who kept themselves thin didn't know how to feed themselves, had no appetite for life, and, worse yet, were vain. The subtext here is that when you really know how to cook and to feed yourself, food is not your enemy.

Her behavioral code was forged during a time when "getting your fill" was an art, not a caution. This included drinking, too. Uptight she was not. If anything, she pretended to drink more than she actually did, just to foster a spirit of generosity and goodwill. Like a speck of dirt in her house, all excesses around her table were swiftly swept away. Temporary muck, nothing to worry about if you could function in the morning.

And that's exactly what she was doing the morning after I brought Aaron to meet her: flipping strips of bacon stacked three deep in a cast-iron pan, calmly making breakfast like we hadn't all been hanging out around her table until three in the morning. She was clanging things around to make noise, to let some of us know that she was already up and working. The sound of her whacking her spatula against the pan's edge, along with the familiar scent of that bacon's sharp smokiness, dragged me from sleep.

So did her voice. "Aaaay-meee . . . Are we going to make this bread in my lifetime?"

She was in her late seventies, so I got her point. I clomped down from the bed and stumbled across the hall to find Aaron. He was sleeping in what was known as "the green room," for it was unspoken that we shouldn't sleep together as we had for the previous year out of respect for the Catholic church I so rarely attended. I looked into his eyes. His face, against the backdrop of the foliage-printed drapery, was tinted limey. "Your skin looks green," I said, my speech slow. "But maybe it's just this room."

"I don't know, but you don't look so good, either."

"Holy shit, I have to go make bread now. I don't think I can do it." I fell backward next to him on the bed.

"Kidlets!" Addie barked sharply from the kitchen. "It is time to rise and meet the day! We have got to get this show *on the road*."

"How can she be up? What time is it?" Aaron asked. We had been up half the night drinking with Addie and her boyfriend, Izzy. Tall and lean like Aaron, with a vintage-looking ivory forelock, Izzy was a retired salesman who had a stockpile of personalized freebies at the ready: pens, money clips, pads of paper. His positive energy was best described as rollicking, a whitecapped wave that spilled over to consume my grandma's occasional dourness. Izzy's high cheeks shone pinker every time he said, "Well, that is just wonder-ful!," which was often.

At twenty-one, I had never been more in love with Addie and her larger-than-life outline, or with her ebullient Izzy, or with my own boy-friend, who had been willing to accompany me for what would be the final episode of my informal cooking training. Addie called these ses-sions "workshops" and in my early teens I had come to her house to learn how to make pie, and fermented pickles, and poppy-seed coffee cake—the most renowned things in her repertoire. Now I was here to make her white bread, for which she was not too shy to say that she'd earned the grand champion ribbon at the Minnesota State Fair when she was just a teenager, triumphantly beating out a bunch of outraged middle-aged women. I can't say I wasn't afraid of screwing up the bread. I knew that she wouldn't let me off easy. Of her six grandchil-dren, she often reminded me, I was the only girl of the bunch.

At one point the night before, I had gotten up to change the record in her enormous turntable console. The last thing I remember clearly was cranking on the turntable's arm to start the second side of *Anne Murray's Greatest Hits* and feeling pretty sure that I had broken her record player. Then, somewhere in between the beers we'd cracked at happy hour and the brandy Manhattan nightcaps we'd sipped at the kitchen table, we had driven to the bar—which now, the next morning, I was starting to isolate as the moment we got into real trouble. After dinner, as my grandma and I did the dishes—she carefully washing, me drying every crevice in each crusty glass with a flour-sack towel that was simultaneously stiff, bleached with holes, and overly fabric-softened—Aaron, the human jukebox, played his guitar. He pulled out the old country hits he knew she and Izzy would like, his clear tenor bouncing around the linoleum kitchen and surrounding us until we felt like we were back in a rural dance hall in 1952. One of his own songs really fired Addie up. *"I love the Ponsford life—I heard Marie—she was hollerin' loud, she was just calling her dog's name out—dumb dog got sprayed on the porch once again, when will that dog learn the skunk won't give in."*

"Whoooo!" she called, cranking her rag hard to wring all moisture from it and slapping it over the faucet neck. "What do you think? I'm pretty sure we can make last call at the Rooster!"

The next thing we knew we were piling onto the wide bench seats of Izzy's Buick and floating down the highway to Genola, one town over. Just as we liked the same music, we all liked a spacious Buick. We spilled out at the Red Rooster, where Aaron played his guitar and held the bar's frontline captive—or they held him captive, depending on how you look at it. His stack of wooden chips (good for future drinks) piled up dangerously in front of him as the crowd begged him to play "Small Town Saturday Night" over and over again. When we got home, we handed over the chips to Addie, who officiously dumped them into a small urn full of drink chips sitting on her dresser.

At the end of the night, after she had finished sipping on her perpetual brandy Manhattan—a wise routine that involved watering down her drink in pace with the dwindling hour—she covered it tightly with a small square of plastic wrap, smoothed down the edges so tightly that a dime could bounce on its taut top, and put it in the refrigerator.

What strikes me as funny now about this habit was not the obvious Depression-era thrift but instead the hope it held for future good times. The assumption contained in the watered-down refrigerated elixir was that it would get consumed during some upcoming happy hour. Maybe tomorrow's.

LIKE A PACK OF PROFESSIONAL FEMALE COOKS, the women in my family are tough on the ladies. They expect a lot of one another. Even though I was unshowered and unsteady, I plodded into a loose skirt, kneesocks, and a vintage button-up shirt and strode into the kitchen. I was hungover but ready.

The winter sunlight shot low through Addie's kitchen and bounced off the shiny white Formica, calling the day to order. At the counter she was apronless. There were so few ingredients before her—just a sack of flour and a can of Crisco—and she moved so quickly that I feared the whole operation would be over before I could shake my eyes open. I knew she never measured anything, so I had to watch closely. I took out my notebook.

Still in my senior year of college, I was accustomed to taking detailed notes. "How many cups of water is that, Grandma?" I asked her as she poured cloudy liquid into the bowl.

"Stick your finger in this. As warm as a baby's bath," she said, and I stuck my finger into the water. "And it's potato water," she said, and then looked up. "Jesus Christ, put the pencil down and just pay attention." She pawed out a lump of Crisco and threw it into the warm water. It started to melt into a reflective ivory pad on top of the water, as pretty as a cheap opal. "You don't write out a recipe for bread."

She crumbled a moist-looking plug of fleshy cake yeast into the water. Below the surface it dissolved quickly and smoothly. "I bought this cake yeast at the bakery in town. That dry yeast in the grocery store doesn't always work. I buy it and bring it home and half the time it's as dead as a fart."

I made that mental note. Two rounded cupfuls of flour went into the bowl and she started stirring forcefully, whipping the batter until a shaggy lump rolled woozily in the middle and stretched out arms of dough that clung to the inside of the bowl as if holding on for dear life.

"You've got to beat it," she said, exhaling, "until you see the gluten working." Her arms were a blur. "You try it."

I was surprised by the force required to stir from the bottom. My arms, not strong with experience, were feeble.

Addie baked by feel and eye rather than by formula. She added more flour, even more flour, and then suddenly came an amorphous flop. A puddle of dough was on the counter. She started kneading, yanking the outer edge and suturing it to the middle, sealing it with the force of her palms. It was like braiding, but from only one side. As she worked it, the dough started to perk up. I poked it and it felt alive, like it had muscle tone. Its surface was as smooth and cool as well-hydrated skin.

"You want to knead it until the gluten gets tight," she said, leaning into the dough, "until—do you hear that? You have to knead it until it starts to squeak." The middle of the dough emitted a high-pitched *eek*. Now I can recognize this sound as the reaction of two tense sheets of dough slapping together, like a valve squeezing out pent-up air, but back then it sounded like the lump was hiding a lost mouse that'd taken a fatally wrong turn.

As she flipped and pummeled the dough, I was well aware that this was the bread that so many immigrants had made from their bumper crops of wheat. Crusty brown on the outside, with a white interior sponge and tiny even pores, this white bread posed no chewing challenges to children or seniors; it was as easily digestible as their new American life, and its high, caramelized tops just as photogenic.

To my knowledge, few immigrants came bearing recipes for this lofty white bread in their trunks, and yet this was the one that so many Plains-state Americans, no matter where they came from, learned to make once they got here, from the flour that they grew and milled and the boiled potatoes that accompanied the noon roast. Unlike in the old country, Addie explained, in America they ate meat for lunch, usually with mashed potatoes, without exception. When the milky potato-cooking water was drained off, they saved it. What wasn't added to the gravy was set aside at room temperature where, after being fed a little flour and left to sit, the potato-water slurry turned into sourdough starter. Any surplus potato water that remained after that, they fed to the pigs. Nothing was squandered. While hers wasn't a yeasted starter, my grandma's porridgy potato water contained an underground history, a pretty clear record of what it felt like to "make do" out on the prairie in Pierz Township. I had always thought the phrase meant you settled for what was subpar, as in making do with a hill of cornmeal and a chunk of salt pork, but I had never before considered the obvious: When you grew your own corn and cured your own side pork from your own barnyard hog, you didn't settle for something dodgy on your table. Making do was more literal: It meant *making* and *doing*. Creating something uncommonly beautiful from the honest country materials you had on hand.

After this I felt like I had to ask about the origins of everything. "White flour then, Grandma?"

"Yes, of course white flour!" she said, as if whole wheat was not to be trusted.

But then she tipped her head. "Back on the farm in Buckman we used to get our white flour with the germ in it. Big twenty-five-pound sacks of it. It spoils in the summer, though. That's why we switched. The bleached never spoils."

"I bought some of that last week!" I bleated.

"Good! Yes, with the germ. The flavor's better. You'll see flecks in the bread. It's the germ, not bugs in the flour.

"But most of the time," Addie continued, rubbing the bowl with Crisco until it shined, "I don't even do all this. I make my bread with Rhodes dough. And it has to be Rhodes! Not that other garbage brand they sell at Coborn's that doesn't rise."

I had to admit, I felt a little bit cheated. I'd been led to believe that I was eating her famous blue-ribbon potato-water bread all along— when I was usually eating bread made from commercial frozen dough. Most of the magic must have been in the kneading and the rising, because even her Rhodes bread was memorable. I suddenly saw where my mom had picked up the habit of sometimes changing a quantity or two before passing on a prized recipe to a friend. She'd inherited the proprietary-recipe gene from Grandma. But Addie couldn't do that to me now because I was forbidden from writing anything down. In my notebook, following "add the potato water" was a great blinking expanse of white paper.

When I eventually wanted to reproduce her homemade potato bread, quite a few years later, I was forced to call on my sense memories, which came dribbling back to me: the long, stretchy gluten arms, the tight squeaks emitted during kneading, the *whoof* of living, breathing air that escaped when Addie punched down the first rise, the way she coiled up the dough before tucking it snugly into its twin bed of a loaf pan. I called up the taste of the nut-brown heel smeared with butter and its stubborn chew, my teeth on it like a growling puppy that wants to prolong the pleasure of someone tugging on her toy.

Along with the bread came other memories, older ones, of the leggy bird marionette that Grandma piloted into the kitchen to entertain us young kids, its big head drunkenly veering toward me, nodding enthusiastically. I remembered sitting on my mom's lap, the edge of the kitchen table pressed deep into my belly. As the adult voices swirled in the atmosphere above me—my dad laughing deeply, my grandma coy, my mom smiling sideways—I felt invisible. I nibbled on a rectangle of poppy-seed coffee cake, giving its rubbly streusel top my full attention, and even though I felt as inconspicuous as a fairy, I could feel that my consumption of it gave my grandma great happiness. I was eating what she wanted me to eat. Being good.

I don't remember ever seeing my mom eating the poppy-seed coffee cake. In fact, I think she had stopped eating it for a while—the same way that as a young adult I stopped eating my mother's wonderful homemade caramels. It didn't matter that they still tasted like buttery liquid happiness floating down the throat; they transported me on a direct flight back to my youth, from which I needed some distance. Maybe that's why you have children after all, to provide new recruits who can be counted upon to take down the signature sweets. There comes a time when you need to bring in the fresh troops.

YEARS LATER, I went to see my grandma in the nursing home in Pierz. We were sitting in the hallway in chairs lined up against the railing for

what she called "another one of these damned mock tornado drills."
To break the awkwardness of our hall exile I asked her, "How do you
make a piecrust with leaf lard again?" It was a question to which I
pretty much knew the answer, having made a couple according to her
phoned-in instructions, but I wanted to hear her tell its story. She sat
there a beat, then pursed her lips.

"You don't know how to make a piecrust?" she hooted. "And you
call yourself a cook?"

I was somewhat prepared for this. In her old age, her comic bossi-
ness had settled into a more cantankerous groove. At "the home" no
one wanted to sit with her at mealtimes because she complained so
much about the food. She hardly ate, and on the days that one of my
cousins could take her out to Patrick's Bar, she ordered just a single
egg roll—"fried very crisp!"—washed down with two White Russians.
Some days, she didn't even bother changing out of her housedress.

She had probable cause to jab me. After she moved out of her
house, my visits became, regrettably, less frequent. I cursed my inat-
tention, but it just wasn't the same without her kitchen, and we both
knew it. There were no basement runs to send me on, no jars of pickles or bags of frozen sugar cookies to retrieve. When Addie left her
house, she lost her household machine and, with it, a lot of her spirit.
I was in mourning for that.

She wasn't done with me. "I don't know why I spent all that time
cooking. Acch . . ." Her disapproval ratcheted up in her throat. "I wish
I had spent more time talking to people and not so much time feeding
them." She had concluded what she wanted to say and looked down
the tunnel of the hall.

My obsession with cooking, my passion for digging into the historical topsoil of every recipe I loved, many of them taught to me by
the woman now sitting before me . . . what she was saying made no
sense. Except maybe as a provocation.

"You don't mean that, Grandma," I said. I thought of her tiny
kitchen table encircled by well-fed revelers clinging to her freewheel-

ing hospitality like so many rescued souls around a life raft. "You love feeding people."

"At one time," she said, closing the book on the subject.

No, I thought. *Sitting around an overflowing table with too many people in a too-tight nook had been her life. I'd been raised to see that as living.*

I knew one thing, that she was like me, or I was like her. Our automation was everything. Her cooking hands, my mom's, and mine all functioned as the turning motors for our minds. The legacy she passed on to both of us, the compulsion to make wonderful food no matter how much extra work it required, was as heavy as a professional responsibility. Once she broke her flow and started sitting all day without a purpose, she lost her taste for the work, food, life, everything.

I kissed her on her white floury cheek, soft and deflated, and she smiled up at me, grabbing my small warm hands in her cold rock-jointed ones, and we said good-bye. For years before she died it felt as if I was always saying good-bye for the last time, again and again.

The conversation we had that day followed me around for a long time, like a challenge. She had obviously been trying to remind me to focus on the people I was feeding instead of the food; she knew the domineering nature of her own cooking complex well enough to try to save me from the same fate.

But one day something else frizzled into the light: What about the recipes? Her holy box of recipes, many of them hand-lettered in her bloomy cursive and imprinted with a scrawled "very good" in the corner . . . How could she say they didn't matter to her?

Her recipes—which old early American cookbooks sagely refer to as *receipts*—patiently stacked in long-forgotten metal recipe boxes, remained the only hard paper evidence of the dinners she made for us and the memories we shared around her table. As I shuffled through them, I saw that her gift, as a frugal, widowed mother of three, had been to cook as if there was no end in sight to the food. As if it were bottomless. That kind of irrepressible generosity couldn't be stoppered; it was still flowing like a slow leak through my mom and me.

Despite what Addie said about cooking being a waste of time, she slipped it to me that she believed the reverse to be true. Her surliness was the key: If something deep down inside her hadn't known that all her cooking had been worth it, she wouldn't have brought it up.

12

THE OLD TIME OF
MY YOUTH

THAT SUMMER, I packed up my life in Minneapolis and moved with Aaron up to Two Inlets for the gardening season.

We took Highway 10 north, chasing and racing trains the whole way. Driving the 1973 Buick Centurion, we were soap sliding in a bathtub and felt like we owned the road—two clichés that rightly describe how those old boats make you feel. Both wide and long, the Centurion had aerodynamics designed for road tripping in the pre-air-conditioned era. Even with all the windows down, the wind just gently sniffed at the very ends of my hair but otherwise left me alone. In a car like that, dignity rides on the open air. We could smell the muggy musk of the corn in the fields the whole way up.

By the time we arrived at the little house out in the forest, the sun had just sunk, taking with it all possible light. Without any electricity, the night sky covered us like a heavy black quilt, and wouldn't pull back its cover until dawn.

Twenty-five minutes from Park Rapids, our hometown, the place was, as they said locally, "out there." The bark of the nearest neighbor's dog was just a muffled *bok* in the dark; the moans of the wolves sounded closer. The clucking of the wood frogs out working on the creek, a concertina of mallets knocking on hollow logs, was deafening.

Parking in front of the house and leaving the car lights on so that we could see, Aaron and I made our way down the hill to check on the small fenced-in garden that we'd planted over a weekend a couple of months back. Maybe it was beginner's luck, or the pent-up minerals in the freshly turned dirt, or a gracious pattern of summer storms and heat, but the plants towered over the fence. The tomatoes were unrecognizable from the baby starts we'd planted. Aaron lit a kerosene lantern and leaned it into the mass of vegetation. The tomato foliage had grown into itself, working its limbs into knots. It smelled like a pungent mix of green grass clippings and wet locker-room floor, like nothing I'd ever encountered before. Miraculously, shiny green tomatoes hung heavy on the vines. The cucumber plants had fuzzy, pointed leaves, skinny limbs with prickly caterpillarlike fuzz on them, and, cooler yet, fully grown cucumbers. Pickle-size. I reached for one, surprised by the sharpness of the short quills covering the fruit. The pepper plants hung with pepper lanterns. The beets sported crowns of greens. The peas had pods on them. And on and on.

At a time when everyone wonders what a young college graduate will make of her life, I moved to the woods without any amenities. This was not the bucolic woods of the East Coast corridor, managed for generations and planted with cows, but the ten-acres-and-a-trailer *backwoods* that surrounds my gritty northern hometown . . . This was like hitting a big fat pause button. There was to be no big-city career in my near future, no immediate upwardly social movement.

My mom and most of my friends considered my move to the woods to be a phase, as they'd never known me to willingly take a walk on any kind of dirt path, beaten or not. It was pretty much the most unexpected move I could make—and I knew it. That was the part that thrilled me. Walking to the outhouse under the cover of a night sky so tarry that the white roll of toilet paper actually glowed only heightened the audacity of it. I felt as if I'd just made a tremendously exciting wrong turn, onto a tiny road, in the pitch-black dark.

We lugged Adirondack chairs inside the fence, each cracked a beer, and surveyed our little kingdom. For all of the vegetable eating I'd done growing up, we'd never grown any ourselves. My lack of knowledge in this area was thrilling. I was twenty-one years old. We might not have had any power—no lights or running water, not even a phone line—but I remember it as an electric time, when all connections were firing. The road ahead, cooking out of the garden, stretched out long in front of me.

THE MOSQUITOES WERE OUR ALARM CLOCK; humming at a high pitch, they dove into our ears and then teased us at close range, hovering close enough to reveal their hairy legs and garters. This was before we rigged up an army-issue mosquito netting over our bed, as both princess tent and impenetrable bug-free zone.

When Aaron and I now talk about this era we tend to list everything that we lacked, in context with everything we eventually acquired. Our life at the house was the real-life definition of the timeless feeling I felt we had together, and the changes we made to it over the seasons compressed the nineteenth and twentieth centuries like a paper fan. I can describe it in many mini-eras.

This was the oil-lamp era, before we got the used solar panel from Aaron's buddy Dave and the old car battery and inverter from Bruce and were able to rig them to power the laptop and two electric lights (though not both at the same time). This was before we pounded the sand point well, when we were still hauling water back to the house in five-gallon plastic containers, which we filled at our neighbor Marie's spigot or at the faucet on the outside of my dad's car dealership in town—inconspicuously, after hours. This was before the porch and its beneficent mosquito screens. This was before Aaron built the new outhouse, when we still used the old spider-filled one Aaron had pulled off an abandoned farm.

This was before we had a phone. That first summer we'd stop at Tiny's Meats, the small meat market that sat alone on a treeless patch of ground a few miles down the road, to pick up some ham steak and any phone messages, if applicable—until Barney, the owner, shook his head and told me he couldn't take any more of my messages. My mother's reminder call, to "tell Amy to bring Grandma Rose's pink glass platter when she comes to the city on Saturday," might have pushed him over the edge.

To ease off Barney, we made most of our outgoing calls at the pay phone attached to the Two Inlets Country Store, four miles down the road. The small store and bar (selling weak 3.2-percent beer, per Minnesota law) was, and remains, one of the three public points in this small community, an unincorporated burg populated largely by descendants of the original homesteaders and native families. The other two landmarks are the Spanish-style Catholic church, complete with a fieldstone altar built to mimic the grotto of Lourdes in France, and the Two Inlets Mill, a bustling, old-school sawmill. By the time we arrived, Aaron had already worked a winter at the mill, throwing slabs in the planing shed. The cozy store was where we bought our gas, eggs, cream, sugar, and other dry goods and occasionally did some drinking around the horseshoe bar.

Back at our house, cold beverages were hard to come by. I kept our perishables in an old propane fridge we dragged home from a friend's hippie homestead south of town but never actually turned on, because everyone said that the propane pilot would suck all of the oxygen from the house and kill us. So we stacked the vegetable bins with blocks of ice from the store, turning it into a semifunctioning new-fashioned, old-fashioned icebox—cool enough to keep smoked meat and dairy from spoiling. Fish or chicken, not for long.

Starting as we did with zero connection to modern life, we added back amenities as we could afford them, at an inching pace. At the end of the first summer, after Aaron took out a bank loan for the five thousand dollars the telephone company required to run a line down our long road, we got a phone. I sat up late one night talking to my mom, the spiral cord wound around my body, and I remember trying to correct her semantics, to get her to call our place a "house." Her habit of calling it a cabin drove Aaron crazy. "It's a house!" he insisted. The distinction seems ridiculous now, but I got his point. A house is a primary residence, a cabin is a secondary seasonal one, and his feelings for this place demanded primacy. We were unapologetically dramatic about it—being, after all, still in our twenties.

"I don't mind cooking without running water," I told my mom. "My kitchen's kind of like the kitchen Grandma grew up with on the farm in Buckman." She was not impressed.

"Sure, it's great if Aaron's doing all the water hauling!" she said. "What happens if you're out there alone?"

My mom thought I could conquer any urban mountain and rule any office kingdom, but she doubted my ability to haul water; that pretty much summed up the fretful stance she took to my growing self-reliance. She must have forgotten that I had minored in women's studies; I *wanted* to haul water.

I didn't know how to tell her that I felt like I'd been given the chance to pass through a wormhole into an older, wonderfully unspecified time. I tried to persuade her that we weren't thinking small; we were dreaming big.

My dramatics brought about the opposite intended effect. Being a mother—and being *my* mother, for whom the details of modern domesticity reign supreme—she tearfully confessed: "I'd happily call it a house and not a cabin if it weren't what it is . . . which is more like *a hovel!*"

I glanced into the kitchen, cataloging the things that would look awful to her: my gross open bucket full of compost; my black-bottomed pans fired sooty from the hot yellow flames of the propane burners, which unlike her, I ran on high; the rough wooden windowsills whose burrs caught on the dishcloth and couldn't be properly wiped; my favorite rusty peeler. I imagined her standing beside me as I cooked, watching from the wings as I rinsed out a bowl with a dribble of cold water, wiped it, and used it again—because I didn't have hot running water—and the woman who believed that everything had to be sanitized in a 145-degree dishwasher looked crestfallen. She didn't even have to be present for me to feel her thoughts bubbling up in me. I knew what she'd say: *Rust!* That's not even sanitary.

Okay, I thought, this was perhaps not where she imagined her daughter living upon graduating from college—a rough-hewn log cabin with gaping floorboards out in the Two Inlets State Forest. Not only did it lack power and refinement, but it also lacked distance from the town from which she had so dramatically fled with us in tow, a town to which I—to her puzzlement—had so enthusiastically returned.

I forgave her the digs about our house. The place wasn't her style. But I couldn't help but scowl into the darkness at her for moving me away when she did, for deepening my nostalgia, for complicating my life with this need to go *home* to this place that held little hope for my future employment.

"It just feels like home," I said meekly.

"But it's not even the same Park Rapids you grew up in. You were a *town kid*." And then she sighed and said with more tenderness, "Honey, home will always be wherever I am." I knew exactly what she meant, that *home* was me, Bob, and Marc, sitting around her table, eating her pork roast, her spaetzle, her gravy.

I worshipped her pork roast, but after we hung up, I thought, *No, I'm sorry, Mom. Home will not always be where you are.* My home was a place. The proximity of where we sat, just twenty-five minutes from my hometown Main Street, mattered to me. I didn't yet know exactly why, but it mattered a great deal.

"HEY, AARON, will you take out the buckets under the sink?" I pleaded. "They're full again."

"Sure—but don't you want to get outside?"

This was one of Aaron's constant refrains. He didn't understand how I could stay inside the dark house all day while the sun was shining outside, when the tasks of the garden were calling. Habit, I guess. Odd for a girl who had moved to the woods, but I had always considered myself firmly an inside person. I'd never been very nature curious. My directionals were always better in malls than they were in the outside world. I was really good with up, down, right, and left; north, south, and the rest never really took.

Initially I rebelled against this call of the wild. Like a turtle coaxed to stick out its head, I pulled it in more tightly and curled up defiantly in a big chair with my book. Eventually, our way of life forced me to leave my chair to go to the edge of the woods to dump pots of frying oil, to the herb bed to get thyme, to the garden for a hot chili pepper, to the shed to get oil for the lamps or wood for the stove when it grew cold. To the outhouse to pee.

Sometimes on these forays I'd pause and look at the creek that encircled us. The widest part had to be a mile across, but it was no swimming hole (unless you liked gambling your limbs with snapping turtles). It was more like a nature preserve, the geese and swans and redwing blackbirds holding court by day, the wood frogs and splashing beavers and crooning wolves taking over at night. I sat down in the grass under one of our birch clumps with my cup of coffee, the trees' papery bark flapping like loose skin, the flickering sunlight warm on my arms, and it felt good to be small. Just an inconsequential animated speck in the great big woods. The animals were doing their own thing. The birds swooped down around me in gangs to peck competitively at the ground, oblivious to me. The dandelions opened up with the sun but pulled in their yellow arms at around dinnertime, hiding their blooms just when I was getting ready to go looking for their greens. Every plant in the garden had its own companion look-alike, a weed that had sprouted next to it in an attempt to pass detection: feathery fronds among the carrot tops, purslane under the round potato leaves. They were survivors.

I finally understood why so many locals called their houses a "place" and why they would give it a name, as if it were a living being. The interior and exterior walls of our rough board-and-batten siding were rightly, fluidly, connected.

At times, the boundaries needed enforcing.

Standing in the kitchen one morning, I felt a tickle on my ankle and looked down at the gaping floorboards at my feet and into the sand beneath the cracks. There, a sharp spire of green leaf jauntily rose. *Was that a blade of grass?* No, the leaves were too thick and too stiff.

It was corn.

A cut kernel must have popped off my cutting board and landed directly below the sink, where my vigorous sloshings sprinkled it with water and the sun beaming through the window gave it a rooting chance.

I laughed and let it live for a day. The next morning I skewered its roots with a butter knife, dragged it out, and dropped it in the compost.

MY DAD WAS GLAD I WAS BACK IN TOWN, if mildly suspicious. The man who had known me previously as a sore teenager gifted in passing on late Macy's bills found my new rustic life a little incongruous, but, to his credit, never said so. He simply shook his head and pronounced that we were "living on love out there." What we were living on, literally, was a blooming vegetable garden and a fantasy that was part hippie and part nineteenth-century homesteader.

The feeling that we inhabited a different era, or maybe the twilight zone, persisted when I went to town that summer. Walking Park Rapids's Main Street, crossing the double row of parking in the middle of the street, the scale felt off to me, as if I'd dropped into a miniature diorama. The streets looked too wide, the stores too small, the people as faux-familiar as television characters. There was my fifth-grade sex-ed teacher, ringing up my order at the coffee shop. There was my brother's hockey coach—never could remember his name—waving me down. Faces came back as if in a dream, characters I should have remembered. It had only been six or seven years since my mom had moved us to the city; to the residents of Park Rapids my absence was just a sliver. I retreated back to our house, and to 1895, and fired up the oil lamps.

The truth was, if the place hadn't been a little intimidating, I wouldn't have liked it so much, and the lack of electric light compounded this. That fall, every night at 6:30, just before dinner, we experienced about twenty absolutely nonilluminated minutes: When the darkness fell inside the house, the oil lamps couldn't compete with the glowing sunset. It wasn't until the sun slid behind the trees that the lamps could finally take over.

After dinner, Aaron set a lamp by his side to work on a large bas-relief wood carving, using chisels and a mallet to knock images into a six-foot-wide slab of bowling-alley floor he'd scavenged. Its scene involved intriguing buildings and situations: social clubs whose members had recently taken off, leaving the evidence of their wrongdoing right in the yard; garages with trucks backing out; uprooted trees whose wiry roots formed a madman's hideout; tiny little broken-down fences leading to nowhere. One evening when we had our neighbor George Kueber, the owner of the sawmill, over for dinner, he teased, "Would have to be a pretty skinny rabbit to get through that fence you carved!" The carved slats were as thin as flat toothpicks, and the varnished, painted edges were soft and rounded, as if overfondled by generations.

I tried to be similarly creative and junked around with a letterpress set I'd found at a garage sale. But not having a crafty bone in my body, mostly I read, to my total saturation; there was nothing else for me to do. I sat at a table covered with cookbooks, books of essays, the Becker County historical records of Two Inlets Township. In this I read of people who shot ducks and nailed them to the outside of their cabins to age, judging them ready when their bodies fell from the necks; of times when porcupines were protected, even if they did strip and kill trees, because they were so slow and could always be caught if a person was hungry; of the Widow Knapp, one of the first settlers in Two Inlets Township, who lost her husband soon after she moved out into the forest, but at the end of her hardscrabble life "drank her cup and murmured not, happy now in her old age to think she won the fight, and is honored by all who know her." I was particularly drawn to the farm women's journals, to stories of women who made complex impractical pastries in rudimentary kitchens, who wrote of making "chicken fixings" in the flush times and suppers of "just flour doings" in the lean.

When I put aside the books and tried to write—something, anything—I was totally stumped for subject. The idea of writing fiction, of making things up out of the ether, terrified me. Instead, rambling paragraphs destined for essays came out, nothing more than quotable fragments. Finally, after much sighing over the legal pad, I reached a conclusion: I didn't have anything to write about. It was with pure, hedonistic glee that I realized this and capitulated to my real obsession: reading cookbooks. I treated this infatuation like it was a job and gave it all of my time.

One night Aaron's sister, Sarah, came out for dinner, and afterward she and I sat at the table—me with my cookbooks and some hot-off-the-letterpress canning labels, her with her knitting—while Aaron knocked away at his carving in the studio, a few feet away, the whacks of the mallet echoing off the tall log walls. He was playing an old scratchy classical record on his hand-cranked 78 player, and every ten minutes he stopped to flip it over.

"So is this what you guys are doing out here?" she asked bluntly, but without judgment. She was getting ready to leave for the Peace Corps in Latvia, to enter her own rural stopped time. Like us, she was deep into the cultural pastimes of two or three generations previous.

I looked at the table covered with opened books scratched up with notes and the labels I'd painstakingly stamped out for my latest batch of blueberry jam, all six precious half-pints of it.

"This is pretty much it," I admitted, suddenly feeling like I should have been doing something even marginally as ambitious as she was.

"No, no, no!" she backpedaled. "It's nice. Kinda feels 'cultural' out here."

"Cities," Aaron said, ashing off his cigar, "collect culture, but it all begins in the country."

We laughed out loud because we all knew that he was full of shit, including him, and topped off our shot glasses of sherry, because for a few blooming seconds we wanted to believe it.

I MIGHT HAVE FANCIED MYSELF A RURAL ADVOCATE, but I soon learned that early American homestead cooking was not for the weak. I'd read that before electric mixers came along, meringues were whipped to a froth, then to shiny peaks, on a shallow platter with a kitchen fork. I used a whisk, but still: None of these recipe writers thought to mention how much it hurts. The physicality of early American cooking— the dough beating, the heavy pot-hauling, the picking of leaves and stems from an entire bushel of chokecherries—called up energy from a part of me I hadn't known I had. The part, it turned out, that got a kick out of monotonous hand labor.

Toward the end of one afternoon's nonelectric flourless-chocolate-cake production, my whisk hurling into egg whites that were finally firming up like cement compound in sand, my arm began to throw fire and burn high up on the deltoid. I listened to the birds arguing and the swans squawking and the squirrels chittering over select bits from our compost pile, and then I let out a screaming chorus into the wilderness, happy to be making cake by hand and to be almost done with it. I hoped my brother Marc would appreciate it.

Like homing pigeons, two out of us three kids had returned to Park Rapids, Marc to live with Dad for his last few years of high school. I felt a need to take care of him, the baby brother so far from the mother nest, and did so in the only way I knew how, by leaving phone messages with the night's menu on his answering machine. He expertly played baby-of-the-family aloofness and accepted only reluctantly, if and when the menu sounded good enough, usually on my second or third offer. But I knew that our house was to him what it was to me: within driving distance of childhood but thankfully outside its borders.

I stuck a corsage of fragrant pot marigolds into the mirrored ganache top of the chocolate cake, slid the braised chicken in wine sauce into the stove's tiny firebox to bake slowly into itself, and retired to the porch, where Aaron and I both liked to have our predinner smokes—a stanky Camel for me and an odiferous pipe for him. The porch was still in process at that point, just raw boards laid on square pilings, like a boardwalk hastily assembled for the set of a Western movie. What happened next could have been written in the script.

Sitting in our lawn chairs, I noticed something diving in and out of the corner of my eye. A rabbit. It sat on drummie haunches at the edge of the woods, perfectly still but for a slow tic in its nose, the luxury of its silky gray fur standing out like a foreign object against the brittle underbrush. I was getting good at spotting incongruent textures amid the foliage—the moist skin of the wild mushrooms, the velvety fur of this rabbit. Proudly, without saying a word to Aaron, I squinted, lifted a stiff arm, pointed straight at the rabbit, and froze, as if I were a pointer dog.

He crept to get his shotgun, came back, and shot the rabbit in the gut. It screamed. He shot it twice more. Three times in total before its chest stopped swelling.

I was accustomed to Aaron taking out the garden marauders—the brazen woodchucks that mercilessly mowed our bean rows at dusk, the porcupines we'd find by the light of the flashlight gnawing flat-faced into the wooden siding of the shed—and didn't feel any shame about it. They were so guilty. Just a few days previously Aaron had woken me up in the middle of the night and hissed at me to come down from the loft. I stumbled down the ladder in the dark, put on the sweater hanging by the door, and took his outstretched flashlight.

Before we'd officially cleared out a place in it, the forest fluttered dangerously close to the edges of the house. It quivered with creature movement. Our woods didn't have the stately self-assurance of a graybeard old-growth forest, but instead the scrappy, taunting nature of the truly wild. Skinny poplars swayed perilously in the wind. Branchy, bent-up jack pines leaned on one another for support like old drunks, sometimes for years, before eventually crashing to the dirty forest floor. Our night yard was not necessarily inhospitable to us, but indifferent. I shivered, not from cold, but from ruffled nerves. I felt more unprotected than I ever had. When I shone my light beam onto the compost pile I saw them: two surprised raccoons, their bright eyes glowing in the moonlit food dump, looking as if they'd just been caught shagging. Being half-asleep didn't make killing raccoons any less disturbing, but I forced myself to buck up. Everyone said that raccoons would find a way into your house if you let them. They had wiggled into our friend Bob's remote writer's hermitage while he was away and partied there for months, snacking through his pantry and pissing on every piece of paper and every book they could balance on. Protecting our house and garden like true pioneers was what I thought we were supposed to do.

But now, face-to-face with a rabbit by the light of day, what was supposed to be a simpler task—bagging dinner—was anything but.

"Did you get him?" I whispered.

"I should think so." We walked over to where the rabbit was lying. It looked so much scrawnier without its twitch. Aaron opened his buck knife. I visualized peeling its fur off at the ankles, as I would turn a sock inside out, and reached out to tug at the fringed tufts near the top of its paws. The toe bones were like hard marbles in a plush case. I

recoiled my hand and watched the first of what would be many com-
plications to my throwback fantasy blow away with the breeze.

As we stood there looking at the rabbit's downy belly hair, I knew
I just couldn't do it, couldn't skin and gut this creature. The truth felt
heavy and inevitable. I was going to *waste* it. I know what Grandma
Dion, and her mom, Great-Grandma Hesch, would have done: They
would have jerked the rabbit's fur down past its furry little head, slit it
to reveal its soft innards, let them tumble out and flop onto the ground
at the edge of the woods, and cooked the damn thing.

I knew what my brother Marc would say. "Jesus Christ!" he'd blow
incredulously. "A venison backstrap, I'd like that, but a *jackrabbit*? Hang
it a day or two for me at least!" Marc, whose palate was as discriminat-
ing as mine, wasn't wrong. Even if I'd had the balls to properly finish
the rabbit off, cooking it fresh wouldn't have been doing it justice.

My experiment in taking my place in a long line of fearless Midwestern women cooks who were possessed of sharp knives, sprawling
cut-flower gardens, and big opinions about food was to be a little
harder than just knocking off a rabbit. I had the flowers and the big
opinions down but hadn't quite mastered the knife.

13

IF YOU DON'T LOOK YOU DON'T SEE

A THING ABOUT AARON: When he walks into a room, he will choose a hard-backed chair over a cushy upholstered one. He prefers scratchy wool over cotton, even in a robe. He'd take 30 below over 90 degrees above, any day. When he dreams of places he'd like to visit, he doesn't think of sandy beaches, a hot book, and a cold *cerveza* with lime. No— even though he lives in rural Minnesota, in the coldest place in the continental United States—he wants to go north. Karelia, Finland. The Kenai Peninsula of Alaska. Northern Canada.

In the summer of 1997, the state of Minnesota gave Aaron an artist's travel grant for three thousand dollars and the encouragement to indulge in his uncommon kinship with severe northern places. So that August we took off on a road trip straight up into the arterial passageways of rural Saskatchewan. His stated purpose was to take photographs for his carvings and "to drive as far north as was possible." Mine, less official, was to catalog the local food. Still fascinated with American pioneer women's diaries, I wondered what regional holdouts I'd find from Canada's rural immigrant and native groups. We packed a sketchbook each, two suitcases, Aaron's guitar, and a cooler for road food into his tiny gas-efficient Subaru Justy and drove for hours through what seemed to be the same landscape: the endless plains, flat as a bath mat. During the first two days, I'm afraid I didn't share his fascination. Trying to disguise my boredom, I stared at the huge map on my lap, studiously doing my job to keep us on course. In about seventy-five miles, I figured, we'd have to make a turn.

"Look out the window!" Aaron pleaded, frustrated that I wasn't sharing his excitement for the emptiness. "If you don't look, you won't see anything."

As we drove, the pine trees, shaped at first like perfect cones, gradually grew thinner until they were sharpened to bare twigs with round, wiry tufts on top, until they looked like skinny bottle brushes—fancy ones, for the narrowest of glassware. As the trees narrowed, so did the roads.

According to Aaron's plan, we took roads along the old railroad routes, hitting every little pinprick of a town. Following the main street to the grain elevator to the river, he'd scan the banks for old factory buildings, looking for evidence of the main economic thrust of the place. "See—there are a bunch of town lots there, you can see their square shapes all the way to the end of the block," he'd say, his finger tracing a sidewalk until the end frayed into a heaved-up pile of bent earth and cement, like a crooked string of teeth after a lifetime of chewing.

Turning the car off the main road toward an abandoned railroad station, he'd clutch the wheel and sit up straighter. "And there's the mill. Oh, man, at one point this was a *big town* . . . Any one of these towns could have become the dominant town, the county seat," he said, stretching up to see over the bridge we were passing, like a beaver popping its head high out of the water to scout downstream. Then, looking crushed, he said, "They didn't all make it."

In addition to invisible lots, old buildings really stoked him up. Crumbling town halls. Main Street storefronts with false facades.

Houses with curious additions. Stone-stacked fire halls that had since morphed into cafés. Mason halls, Odd Fellows halls, and Rebekah, the female Odd Fellows halls. These towns looked just like the ones in his carvings, like they'd been booming until some cataclysmic event caused the entire society to take off in an instant, leaving garage doors stuck halfway open and pots of stew steaming on stovetops. It dawned on me that the diluted dream was what he was looking for.

When we passed rare newly built Lions Clubs halls, housed in long khaki-colored sheet-metal buildings with tiny windowless doors, they weren't beautifully decrepit like the rest, but somehow their bleakness won us over, too. With all that stoic we-don't-give-a-shit siding (surely lined with git-r-done drywall), they reminded us of the sheet-metal explosion in our own town. Even here, on the prairie that rode up into Canada, we found our unsentimental Midwest. Looking through Aaron's staunchly optimistic, contrarian viewfinder, I found myself falling deeply in love with what he saw: the grandiose, the downtrodden, and the cheaply built alike.

Like in the rural Midwest, pickings were slim for food in the public sphere. Most of it was indistinguishable from what we ate in the Sysco-fed restaurants back home. We found multiple Chinese restaurants, though, and cafés devoted to Native American food, and Ukrainian restaurants. When I peered down into my shallow bowl of pelmeni, shiny and full-bellied and bobbing in butter, they looked like little clams and tasted just as slippery and sweet.

After each town, we reentered the rural countryside. Soon enough, there weren't two people to rub together, but we talked to nearly everyone we met. The first was Rene Doucette. We were driving into a gray area on the map called the Carrot Valley, and when I looked up, the color in the air was the same as the shading on the map: cement-gray and foggy, even at midmorning. A man was standing next to a horse at his front fence when we pulled up. Only halfway lost, Aaron stuck an arm out of his window.

"Are we on the road to Flin Flon?"

Within minutes of trading weather and geographical banter with Rene, Aaron was exiting the car and following him to his enormous garden. The size of a city lot, Rene's garden seemed to me to contain a lot more food than a single guy could ever eat. In late August, even with a summer with more daylight hours than ours, his tomato plants were starting to wilt, as if they'd already been threatened with real frost. It looked like he'd already dug all of his potatoes. Rene asked us, "You guys ready for a beer?"

What the hell. We were on vacation (weren't we?) and also curious to see the interior of one of these houses we were forever passing. So it was that we found ourselves at 10:30 in the morning sitting at Rene Doucette's kitchen table, drinking tall, watery cans of Canadian beer. It was what skinny, lonely guys like him call their morning coffee.

Hanging above the phone was a shop-equipment-sponsored nudie calendar. The girl's shiny ass pointed straight into the room, providing its only decoration and giving me the feeling that Rene's bachelordom had been a longtime situation. He'd originally raised hundreds of heads of cattle, he told us, and the crops to feed them there in the Carrot Valley, the northernmost farming area in all of Saskatchewan. Past that, the taiga—the northern frozen bog, its soil too acidic to grow anything—began in earnest. Rene shrugged as he revealed the real reason for his many rows of vegetables: his was a free community garden. All summer, anyone who wanted to come out could pick. He sent bags of beans and potatoes and squash back with low-income families who drove out from The Pas.

"Those kids do a good job picking those vegetables," he said, tipping back his can.

Suddenly the phone jangled at top volume, a big black shop model hanging right in front of us on the wall. He looked at us, wide-eyed, and then grabbed it, shouting, "Hello!" He listened for less than two seconds before yelling, "Wrong guy!" and slamming the phone back onto its metal stirrup. It whimpered a final feeble jingle.

"No one ever calls *me!*" he said, as if it were a threat rather than a statement of fact. Clearly, his solitude had been disturbed. As if he was waking up from a dream in which he'd invited two strangers into his house for a morning beer, he looked at us blankly. I was instantly grateful for having been given the chance to hop into his story. And so our peaceful morning coffee with the crabby, kindhearted, dirty-minded bachelor farmer ended. With handshakes and a salute to him from the car, we were back on the road.

WE'D JUST PASSED A SIGN for a town called Love, in northwestern Saskatchewan, when the Justy stopped making its usual car noises. It took about a mile for it to wind down like a toy. "I don't know what's going on," Aaron said. "We're losing power." He steered it to the side of the road, and we sat for a few minutes, trying to figure out what to do. Aaron got out and lifted the hood, but there was no smoke, no smell, no indication of trouble. The engine, which we'd discover later was fitted with an experimental "brush transmission" of the kind used in motorcycles, suddenly looked very tiny.

We could see a town on the horizon, so we walked the half mile to its main street and found an open café. It was midafternoon and we ordered pie and coffee. I chose raisin. Not the sour cream raisin pie I knew so well, the custard the color of a muddy river floating with cinnamon, this was just plain raisin. When it came, the filling was bruisy-purple, suspended in tart, shiny juice. The toffee-colored crust was stamped with dime-size holes, revealing blistered raisin skins bobbing to the surface. As I ate, pastry flakes fell onto the plate. I paused our current distress to momentarily take note: real pie.

Two weeks into our trip, this full stop was jarring, especially since we had been considering not stopping at all. Our return route had morphed into a vague plan to keep driving to the west into Alberta, and if we made good time, maybe even all the way to San Francisco, just in time for a friend's wedding. We had a mutual creeping feeling that our cash reserve was dwindling but—as would become a hallmark of our romantic-financial partnership—neither of us could force ourselves to look at the balance.

We batted around the idea of calling our parents but doubted any of them would drive 776 miles up into Saskatchewan to fetch us and then drive the same distance back.

No, we were going to have to try to fix it. We trudged back. The Justy was parked next to a mailbox, and when we reached it, we saw a compact lady with a head of metallic curls standing in her driveway, holding a pitchfork.

"You folks need some help?" she asked, looking at us with a mixture of warmth and reserve.

We stammered out our story, about the car inexplicably dying and how we'd driven from Minnesota up to Flin Flon. We didn't tell her the reason for our trip through the filament-thin roads of northern Saskatchewan, afraid that an artist's grant wouldn't seem very solid to her. An explanation turned out not to be necessary.

"Can we camp here?" asked Aaron, touching the cigar in his pocket, imagining relaxing around our hobo campfire.

She handed me her pitchfork and said, "You two can sleep in the house if you want to help us get this hay back in the barn," then turned around and started trucking back to the barnyard. The farm's pettibone had dropped a bale, spilling hay all over the yard, and over the noise of the machinery she pointed to where Aaron could find another pitchfork. With that, we had a place for the night—and, it turned out, for the next ten days.

Ruth Ivanenko (not her real name) operated a three-thousand-acre grain farm, the biggest one run by a woman in all of Saskatchewan. We would soon learn that the minute and a half that she stopped to question us was about as long as she could stand in one spot. She speed-walked all over the farmyard as if motorized, tossing out orders to her hired man, Lee, and to her son, Richard. If we were willing to work, our timing suited her. It was the height of harvest time, when their combine tractors combed the fields all day long and into the night.

That night at the dinner table she cheerfully announced, "The last person who broke down here was Red Skelton, and that was almost twenty years ago! He was just as funny in person." She said this casually, as if she were about due for a new lonesome traveler.

Good news or bad news—Ruth didn't linger long on either. Her fork worked her plate with a steady rhythm, and she didn't look up from it. Her Velcro work shoes, which she briskly ripped off before entering her house, were indicative of her high personal RPM. Over the course of dinner we learned the reason for her efficiency: She'd been running this place for years. Not a month after she and her husband had bought the farm, they learned that her husband had MS.

"He walked across these fields only once, just that first time. After that, he was in a wheelchair. Every morning, until he got too sick, we lifted him into the hay wagon so he could come with us." Her eyes flashed, shiny, while she smiled flatly at me and passed me the bowl of potatoes. After he passed away, Ruth began to buy more land, until she'd expanded to farm all the way to the horizon, and then way beyond.

Her son and Lee were essential to her, of course, but I swallowed thickly to think of the sheer volume, the height of the mountain of work, that she had amassed behind her. On the way inside, I'd noticed the vines of scarlet runner beans contorting around the railings of her porch—a variety known more for being decorative than edible. I pictured her as a younger woman, keeping the garden, raising their kids, doing all the canning, all the cooking, all the farming, and still managing to keep a cut-flower garden and plant decorative beans, just for eye candy. It was a reminder that daily beauty is part of what a farm yields. I felt suddenly lazy, guilty for all the times I slept late in our loft bedroom back home, not inspired enough by the chirping of birds going about the main thrust of their day to get up and begin my own.

By supper's end Ruth and Lee decided that they'd load the Justy onto a trailer and hook it up to their new work truck, and in the morning Aaron and I would drive it into Prince Albert, forty miles away, to the nearest repair shop. We protested, reluctant to accept that level of generosity. Our hesitation introduced an element of mistrust, and felt more rude than polite, but they understood. It was decided that Aaron and Lee would ride together into Prince Albert in the morning, and Ruth laid out the rest of the terms: We would sleep in her guest bedroom. I would cook the meals while I was there, and when Aaron got back, he would help Richard and a tall Swedish guy named Dean insulate their new potato barn.

The next day when I walked to the barn to deliver the afternoon cake, the three of them were standing up high on twenty-foot scaffolding near the airless ceiling of the hot barn. Aaron's arms that night were sticky, the insulation particles clinging to his arm hair like dust to a fly leg. Seemed I had drawn the better chore stick.

There were five daily meals on the farm: breakfast, morning coffee and cake, noon dinner, afternoon coffee and cake, and supper. Everything was homemade, nothing store-bought. But when Ruth made the rolls, she used instant yeast, and they rose so fast sitting on the warm woodstove that you could almost watch them inflate. She didn't cook in her squat central woodstove anymore—she used her electric range—but she did use it for burning her small batches of daily paper garbage, which we fed into the stove by lifting a flat burner with a hooked iron rod.

"Twice a week," she informed me, "Richard's wife, Linda, brings the lunches and field snacks." Richard and Linda and their two boys lived on the adjoining eighty acres, in a white rambler nearly identical to Ruth's. Already loyal to our benefactress, I thought to myself that with Ruth running the farm, maybe her daughter-in-law should have been taking on more of the cooking.

The first day I put on one of her aprons and opened every cupboard and drawer, and then opened them all again, thinking that if I was to be as efficient as Ruth, I should try to memorize the lay of the land. I set about making myself useful.

I fried the breakfast sausage in her electric skillet set up on the flat cast-iron surface of the woodstove, as Ruth did, and then fried the sliced potatoes in the grease until they were brown and crispy. I made the toast, stuck a spoon into the jar of her homemade strawberry freezer jam, and set it all on the table. Then I made the rolls and a gingerbread sheet cake for the morning snack and poured two pots of coffee into her large metal thermos. Lunch, what they called dinner, was more elaborate: one day, thin pork chops, from their neighbor's hog, dusted with flour and quickly fried to crackling brown at the edges, the next day chicken and dumplings, and always a side dish or two of plain boiled and buttered vegetables from the garden—beets, beans, zucchini. The food was simple but honest. I gained an appreciation for the natural sweetness of carrots, dug from the garden, scrubbed but not peeled, sliced into coins, boiled in water, and heavily buttered. I learned to give my meal a sweet takeaway, as farmers did, a slice of homemade bread thickly iced with butter and jam to taste like cake.

The strange paradox of farming dictates that the people whose lives revolve around the production of food don't always have time to linger with it on their own tables—they had no time to idolize it. Like the cycles of growing, the table here spun its revolutions, but at a higher speed.

After I finished the lunch dishes, Ruth would pick me up at the porch and take me with her on her chores. I sat behind her on the four-wheeler as she raced like a teenager over the rutted fields, looking for mounds into which she could inject an enormous plunger of mole poison. She took me with her to the grocery store, where she introduced me to others as part of a duo who had "broken down in my yard, but are staying awhile." I sat next to her in the enclosed cab of the two-story tractor, harrowing the fields, which looked like dragging a wide rake over the tops of the rows as far as I could tell. Sitting next to her in the quiet cab, she asked me when Aaron and I had gotten married.

When I told her we weren't, I knew she was thinking of our cohabitation in her guest room, but she just looked to the horizon and said, "You will."

The days were swollen with work, which oddly made the evenings more buoyant. I shuffled around her living room's linoleum floor in borrowed crocheted slippers, fell into the deep sofa, and felt as at-home as I would at a family holiday. A tall bouquet of yellow wheat sat on top of her wood-consoled TV, its dried-out strands reminding me of the husks of palm sprays my grandma kept on her living room wall. Aaron was deeply immersed in the hardbound history of the township, and he kept Ruth talking long past her usual bedtime, trying to get to the nut of what powered the people of this community to settle there, way up north in the flatlands of Saskatchewan. In the book she found a picture of their first house, a primitive-looking straight-log cabin, and told us how in the early days of their marriage she scrubbed the rough wood floorboards with a brush until they shone. I thought of the rough-hewn floorboards in our own house and momentarily flirted with the idea of getting down on my hands and knees to scour them. I imagined doing this in the winter, as she had, with the heat from the woodstove toasting the tops of the boards and the thick arctic humors floating up from the cracks between them.

Toward the end of the week, Richard came over for dinner at Ruth's with his two kids, but without Linda. As I cleared away the table, Richard pulled a fiddle out of its case and Aaron took out his small traveling guitar. The kitchen band struck it up, the sound pinging cleanly off all the hard surfaces—the linoleum counters and floors, the flat top of the woodstove, the paneled walls. Aaron sang, *"She had golden memories of home . . . of her grandfather's ooooold homestead . . . she went all the way to Ponsford on the prairie . . . cause that's where her grandfather lived . . ."* The sound had the telltale metallic echo of the 1400 AM radio station, both faraway and really close at the same time, acoustics that only a cavernous farm kitchen can create. Ruth sat at her kitchen table in a zip-up robe, tapping her soft slipper against the linoleum, cutting coupons out of the local paper with a pair of heavy silver scissors.

By THE NINTH DAY, we felt the need to make a move—or just move in with Ruth permanently. The Justy was a lost cause. Its experimental brush transmission hadn't been up to a three-thousand-mile jaunt into Canada. We gave the car to Lee for parts. I called up my brother Bob, who was working for a car rental company down in Minneapolis, and he was able to pull some strings to allow us to rent a car in Canada, which, because we lacked a major credit card between us, we'd previously been unable to do. We posed for photos in front of the rental truck and then we took the main roads straight down to Winnipeg, this time not stopping at any off-highway towns, running over the details of our unexpected adventure the whole way home.

A few minutes after arriving in Two Inlets, I dialed Ruth's number back in Saskatchewan. It was six-thirty. She would be in for supper by then.

"Ruth!" I said breathlessly, when she answered. "It's Amy! We made it home!"

"Oh?" she replied. I thought she would be thrilled to hear from us, but her flat voice didn't return my fondness. I pictured her standing up next to the phone. "I'm happy to hear it. Say, you didn't take my sewing scissors, did you?"

I had, accidentally. I'd found them in my quilting bag.

"Please send those back as soon as you can. Those are my best scissors." What was I being so emotional about? her tone seemed to say.

As we said good-bye, I got the feeling that she was leaning into her next thing, as if I could almost hear the Velcro on her shoes ripping. We were eight hundred miles away, and our chance meeting clearly wasn't the divine intervention, the wrinkle in rural time, that it was to me. It was just over.

———

BACK HOME, I was still thinking of Ruth's physicality. The way she jumped out of her shoes at the door and pounced on the business of dinner. The way she snapped green beans two-handed so as to get through them faster. The punishing way she drove over the corrugated field's ruts, her four-wheeler bouncing, as if it was a race against time to poison moles. The way she methodically cut coupons and organized them in piles.

Thousands of acres of wheat or a kitchen garden a quarter mile long . . . whichever, she treated them the same. The act of raising food no longer seemed to me just a choice; it was *just what you do*. Long lines of my family had been steeped in this notion, and yet it took driving hundreds of miles north toward the Arctic Circle, and back, for it to come to rest in me. Ruth's ambition was contagious.

We'd traveled farther north and further back in time in search of the roots of our unlikely attraction to our homestead in the woods, and we'd found them. Our place could yield as much beauty as Ruth's if I just put my belief, and my back, into it.

Luckily, when we returned home in mid-September, the garden hadn't yet frosted over as usual and looked to be waiting for us. The frost had come to bite, but just lightly, and all of my tomatoes were hanging ripe on the vines. We harvested two boxes of squash. And then we decided to dig out a much larger garden, carving out a fifty-foot rectangle where the hill teemed with native hazelbrush vines. Our new garden would have two entrances and terraces cut into the hill, and we'd surround it with a seven-foot-high fence that the deer couldn't jump.

My dream of pioneer cooking renewed, I started cooking our morning oatmeal overnight in the tiny oven set into the woodstove. It was kind of a crapshoot, but if I added enough water to steel-cut oats and wild rice, the banked fire plumped them perfectly by morning. With this dish I fell in love with inexactitude, with making things that rely less on precision and more on one's inner knack. We topped it with butter and maple syrup and toasted almonds, good ballast for working outside.

I put on my best Canadian thrift-store finds—a roomy, stiff pair of men's leather work boots with laces that ran clear down to the toe, just like the boots Dean had worn, and a thick hooded woolen sweatshirt encircled with Inuit hunters—and buttoned my hunting-orange vest tightly over that. We had a pulaski axe and a shovel, and we took turns chopping and pulling out the hazelbrush roots. I swung the pulaski into the dirt, hooked the blade under a big one, and then, with my new boots as leverage, leaned back on the pole until the root stretched and snapped. After shaking the roots free of as much coffee-colored dirt as we could, we tossed the mangled rhizomes into a pile for burning. Unlike the rich dirt in northern Saskatchewan, our woodland topsoil only measured about four inches deep, nothing more than a thin layer of chocolate icing on a thick yellow-colored cake of sand, and the garden needed every bit of it. After a week of working in the cool fall air, we decided that if we were going to keep living in this place—and, freshly invigorated after our trip, it seemed we would—we should give it a proper homestead name. We'd call it Hazelbrush, to remind us of the effort we put into it. The nut's hard-shelled, hard-won edibility seemed to fit.

14

CIRCUS OF THE RIDICULOUS

So BEGAN A THREE-YEAR-LONG MIGRATORY PATTERN. We lived up north for the entire gardening season—May to September—and moved down to Minneapolis in the winter, where we would take jobs in order to save up three or four thousand dollars to fund our nonelectric (e.g., cheap) life during the summer. We considered ourselves snowbirds on short leashes, shuttling between the northern and southern poles of the state. This was our plan, when I believed in it.

Like a mother who doesn't remember the pain of childbirth, I somehow forgot the agony of moving that descended on me like an absolute palsy each fall and spring. Every time we had to move—to pack and clean and organize—I collapsed into a chair and threatened never to leave it. Aaron ignored me and pushed ahead. With his charming—borderline annoying—habit of making loony ideas sound perfectly sane, he framed it in a romantic light: "If we're going to do this, we need to be pragmatic. You have to be especially pragmatic about your dreams." Once we were on the road, I quickly recovered and realized I'd been acting like a major pain in the ass. Eventually my constant grousing irritated even me.

That fall of 1997 we harvested the garden, then watched the frost kill the garden plants one by one. I was amazed to find out which plants were fragile—tomatoes, peppers, eggplants, and basil—and which ones had the chops to hold on into the fall. (The beets, the cabbages, and the sage, that's what.) The frost stung the Swiss chard three times before it finally capitulated, and only then, after I shuddered my way through my last freezing-cold outdoor shower (the shortest of my young life), we packed it in for the year. I filled boxes with jars of my canning—apple butter, plum tomatoes in sauce, bread-and-butter pickles, fermented dills, pickled green tomatoes—loaded the back of the truck with flats of blushing not-quite-ripe tomatoes, and then we set off in a two-truck caravan to Minneapolis. My dad, whose generosity was judicious but always well-timed, had surprised me with the gift of a vehicle—not just a loaner, but one with an actual title. It came from the unpaved back row of the lot, the part they called "the dirt," and was what the salesmen colloquially called a "five-dollar car," a junker they'd try to sell for a few thousand bucks. My GMC Sierra pickup truck had wide orange racing stripes down the sides with the words HEAVY HALF scrolled over the wheel wells and was a 1975, the year of my birth, which I took as a sign. I couldn't imagine driving a vehicle that better described my new country lifestyle—and it was free! Thank God for Randy, the parts manager, who had had the foresight to install a power-steering mechanism from a local junkyard, because I could barely turn the wheel without it.

We moved into the studio space Aaron shared with Rob in Lighthouse Bay, a nine-story concrete warehouse off the railroad tracks in the Midway, the corridor between Minneapolis and St. Paul. The dimly lit first floor was taken up with Joe the landlord's spice business. It was a shadowy operation. Open barrels of powdered cumin, coriander seed, cinnamon sticks, and red pepper flakes lined the walls. Slow-moving rivulets of water spread out like a creek bed in the center and rodents bumped along the dark perimeter. The freight elevator rarely worked.

I was glad that Aaron's space was on the third floor of a possible nine and thankful for the overwhelming sting of cinnamon oil in the air, masking odors that would likely have been much worse. (It also taught me to buy spices only from reputable sources. Stapled-over bulk packs still give me the willies.)

Despite the building's grunge, we loved our little corner of it. Through the squint of youth, we had the ability to smudge out all the unsavory details and see just the brilliant shine coming off the nugget of the central idea of it—in this case, the enormous space. Our corner unit measured about three thousand square feet, had walls of grimy marble, and was full of light. Aaron and Rob each commandeered a big studio space, Aaron working on his wood carvings in the front room, and Rob welding his tall steel sculptures in the middle. In the back, they partitioned off a small living space, whose walls they painted barn red and covered with their collected paintings and dusty thrift-store finds.

For artists, it was a coveted live/work situation. On par with those, the living part of the equation wasn't legally sanctioned, although Joe the spice magnate never cared.

In fact, he loved to hang out with his tribe of tenants, often inviting us into his seedy back office to shoot the breeze. Standing on the worn red carpeting and leaning against the front corner of his desk, papers sliding loosely on top, he'd say, "Want some lunch?" If we shook our heads in dissent, he'd look at us incredulously and say, "You sure you don't want some noodles?" as he sprayed butter from a can onto a paper plate of microwaved pasta and dressed it with a few shakes of canister Parmesan. The nine floors of Lighthouse Bay were filled with artists and street punks and, come evening, homeless guys who wandered in to sleep in their favorite crannies in the dark corners. The backyard was usually occupied by an encampment of hardcore kids, heavily inked-up and metal-punched, who stayed in a bus with the words CIRCUS OF THE RIDICULOUS painted on the side. They traveled the country hopping trains and survived by Dumpster diving for food and materials. Some of them made zines, some of them supported themselves by fire-dancing or riding comically tall bicycles in their circus. Even though I learned to say "No thanks" to their proffered dumpster produce after using a batch of "perfectly good" rotten onions, they were affable and interesting warehouse-mates. When it got cold that fall, a bunch of these kids and their trusty canine side-kicks moved into spaces in the building, some into the studio directly above us, where they set up shop fixing motorcycles and illegally tat-tooing faces.

Joe seemed to love the madhouse aspect and wielded his power via his henchmen, a band of young Mexican guys. Some of these workmen possessed advanced college degrees earned back in Mexico, in fields like engineering, but they set their gazes out far ahead of them as they hustled around doing Joe's bidding in exchange for his inflated Ameri-can cash. "Calling all Mexicans! Calling all Mexicans!" he'd broadcast over the loudspeakers. He was king of the whole shithole kingdom.

The bathrooms were few and far between. There was one on the sixth floor and one on the fourth floor, but the latter was so bad, so terrifically foul, that it had a nickname: Little Bosnia. I will spare you the graphic details, but in short it was at Lighthouse Bay that I culti-vated the ability to hover for any length of time over any toilet seat. It made me wonder if warehouses like ours (not free to us in particular, but free to some of us) weren't called squats for another reason.

Aaron and I spent our time much as we had up north, except that most mornings he went to work as an assistant to a stonemason. He was also working on a number of large pieces for his first real gallery show, so he was fairly solvent and hopeful, but I spent most of my days sitting on the couch, knitting, waiting for a potential employer to call. Easily, this was the nadir of our brokeness. When running errands, I didn't have enough money to go out to lunch, so I would go home and cook up a batch of white beans with a ham bone, my bangs dragging in my eyes. That I couldn't afford a haircut or buy a pound of good coffee beans or fill up the truck with gas without feeling a bolt of anxiety never occurred to me to be the reason for my general distress. Broke was so quickly my baseline.

I made dinner in the evenings and afterward Aaron worked on his sculptures while I read books and underlined the passages I liked. When he knocked off work around 11, we'd sit in the cowhide-covered chairs in the glow of the warm light from the floor lamps (with Aaron, the lighting is always good), and our talk would balloon. We'd get excited about our future, the drives we would take, the places we could go, the ways we would improve our place up north . . . and then we'd sometimes sip straight Jim Beam from little shot glasses to calm ourselves down, sitting among the thrift-store finds that grew more precious to us by the blooming minute. On the weekends we listened to public radio—*Bluegrass Saturday Morning*—and I made some half-hearted attempts at sewing a patchwork quilt, gently pumping on the small treadle sewing machine Aaron had dragged in for me. In February, we planted our seeds for the next year's garden, stringing up grow lights suspended just above the sprouts. It was a big space and cold. I piled on thick wool socks and sweaters and timed my phone calls around the heater: when the industrial blower hanging in the corner intermittently came to life, its flames glowed through the grille menacingly, like dragon teeth, and its fan bellowed so loudly that it drowned out all conversation.

The hot plate Rob had been using wasn't going to suffice now that I was there, needing to cook to keep sane, so Aaron brought in a used avocado-green electric stove, which his friend Steve, a hobbyist electrician, hooked up live to the building's main power source. We watched him disable the main circuitry for the building, which was in our bedroom, and reattach it, and then like idiots we returned our bed to its nook in front of the electrical circuit board. It hummed behind us, gently microwaving our cerebellums, rocking us to sleep.

I cooked nearly every meal on that electric stove—just as my mom had on hers. When I made a beef stew, at the point when the onions were caramelizing and it was time to add the tomato, I peeled it using one of her tricks: I cranked the heat on the biggest burner and watched as its bright red coils turned from red to chalky-gray, then stuck a fork in the stem end of a beefsteak tomato and held it just above the coil until the skin blistered and popped open and I could quickly peel it away. But a lot of what I made fell flat. I learned the hard way that you shouldn't make tomato sauce in cast iron because it turns sweet-metallic; it chills the tongue. Twisted up the rest of that evening, I couldn't stop thinking about how I could get that so egregiously wrong.

Finally, one day, my call came in: a freelance job at a custom publishing company in Minneapolis that came courtesy of Rob's girlfriend, Pilar. I started getting up early every day to go to work. After pissing in a widemouthed quart jar—trial and error led me to embrace a widemouthed opening over the regular size—I threw it out the window to avoid making any more trips upstairs to the fourth-floor bathroom than absolutely necessary, always looking to make sure that the Circus of the Ridiculous bus wasn't parked below us. This was all going swimmingly until one bitterly cold day in February when I dropped the heavy window instead of guiding it down, sending half of the pane to the floor. Aaron and Rob both howled at me when the subzero air came pouring in, and for the rest of the winter it wore a bandage of duct tape.

Then I would dress up in business-type attire and drive the Heavy Half to downtown Minneapolis. By every definition of the word, it was a plum job. I knew nothing of publishing but had a recent graduate's false confidence and enough of a grasp of grammar that I could do the bones of the editing work Pilar needed and write copy when required. For this she paid me well, more than I would make for many, many years afterward. I could make my rent with a few days' work, and she had me coming in every day. This meant that together with Aaron's cash from doing stonemasonry, we were able to bank a lot toward our simple-life summer.

ONE DAY, Pilar took me to lunch at Café Brenda, an upscale vegetarian place near our office. We sat by the window and watched the lunch crowd passing by on the street. A slow-moving guy ambled in front of us, bulked up with layers, and when his eyes met mine, I recognized him. I'd talked to him the night before in Lighthouse Bay, when he'd been standing in front of my door, disoriented, staring at the nook beneath the stairs.

"Where did I sleep last night?" he mumbled.

"I think you usually sleep under the second-floor stairwell," I said, pointing down the stairs. He looked at me blankly, the buzz in his head almost audible. "Down one floor!" I shouted cheerfully, as if I were in a mall giving directions to a turned-around elder.

Now on the street, he raised his hand and nodded respectfully at me, and I raised mine back.

"Who's that?" Pilar asked.

"Oh, just a guy from the building," I said. She laughed because she knew. She sort of lived there, too.

But at work I couldn't shake the sinking feeling that I should have been enjoying myself more. Real-life editing and writing of corporate material? Swerving between cubicles, my skirt swishing? Going out to lunch in trendy restaurants? This was what I had dreamed of.

At night I let loose large, room-filling sighs of boredom. The technical writing we practiced, while as vibrant as the form could possibly get, felt like an internment in the dullery. Rearranging the English language to inject excitement into boring events felt dishonest to me—a near sin in my authenticity-seeking youth. Worse, I acted childishly at the office, ducking away from the boss whenever I came back after a particularly long lunch, even though I was being paid by the hour.

At one point we were working a lot of overtime, and Pilar asked me to let out one of her coworkers and lock the big main door behind her. I let her out of the thick glass door and dropped the bottom metal pins into the slots to bolt it shut. The woman, middle-aged, with a neat gray-blond bob, smiled politely and looked away. Unlike me, she was at ease with professional distance. Unsure if I should wait with her or go, I chose to wait. The round seconds trundled by. Suddenly I held my arms high above my head and started shaking my body against the glass door in rolling waves, doing a pantomime of a monkey rattling the bars of its cage, mouthing the words, "Get me out of here!" I smiled, expecting her to laugh at my joke.

Her expression froze up to her raised brows, and she escaped into the elevator. I walked back stiffly to the office where Pilar was pouring small glasses of expensive scotch in the conference room, kicking off our late-night editing drive.

"Did you meet Susan, our CEO?" she said, nodding encouragement.

That's when I knew: Maybe the office life wasn't gonna be for me.

15

GOOD NEIGHBORS

WHAT I AM FINDING OUT ABOUT MYSELF is that I have a decent ability to adapt to austere circumstances. I'd grown up in a suburban house so warm, so thickly carpeted, that my brothers and I wore shorts on deep-winter −30-degree Saturday afternoons and rolled around on our bellies in front of the enormous television screen like tropical fish in a tank. My parents liked to keep the thermostat strictly unseasonal—75 in the winter and 65 in the summer—and the windows shut year-round. But somehow I have just spent the cold months living in a nine-story cement building with a belching dragon for a space heater. I've become very attached to my winter hat, wearing it inside, even in bed.

Now in the country, I experience a newfound love for summer breezes coming in the window. I walk by myself to the outhouse at night. When we're outside and I'm too lazy even for that, I can piss on a tree in the pitch-black dark, holding myself at such an angle that the stream flows around stones like the early meandering part of the Mississippi River and always misses my shoes. I can drive Aaron's old stick-shift truck fast through the oily spring mud of our road and make it, sliding widely, all the way to the end. I cut my own hair. (Not always well.)

Certain parts of our back-to-the-land lifestyle come to me more naturally than others. For example, I enjoyed picking wild berries. It was just the sharp saber nails of the wild raspberry canes, the yellow pine pollen sticking to my sweaty arms, the spring-action brush, the incessant cloud of soul-pricking deer flies—those were the only parts that bothered me. I discovered that nature doesn't coddle, that branches ricochet back in your face just because they can.

I hadn't grown up foraging for delicacies. My all-capable mother had always taken care of the hunting and gathering, mostly at the Red Owl. She'd grown up weeding Grandma's half-acre farm garden in their backyard, picking thorny cucumbers from between the razored vines; she liked to shop at the store.

But these painstakingly picked wild raspberries, they were so sweet and so tart that even a ladybug-size one could make your mouth run with desire for more. I learned that washing them turned them into sweet red mush, so I spent nearly an hour picking through my haul spread out onto a wide platter, sifting through each one with my fingers, pinching out aphids and flicking out leaves. That night we sat on the candlelit porch and spooned up these meticulously clean unwashed berries beneath a drift of whipped sabayon—positively stinging with the whiskey I had naively subbed for the marsala wine I didn't have—and yet the flavor of the berries still triumphed. They were that strong.

I didn't work in the traditional sense that summer but instead coasted on our collected savings. My ambitions were funneled into making our life more delicious, and we both considered our chores to count toward the business of living.

Aaron, powered by an incessant drive to finish projects around the homestead, was stomping the steep slant up the hill from the garden all day long, digging new holes, and dry-stacking heavy stones to create landscaping barriers. He was sweating. And me? Lady of leisure, waking up well after the hot sun had burned off all the dew and started to turn the ground to dry, fragrant toast, I made breakfast, shoved the dishes behind the curtained shelf, then walked down to the garden, picked some vegetables, and walked up the hill to start making lunch.

It was all I could do to hustle three hot-cooked meals into the waking hours of my day.

I quickly learned that cooking with limitations is what breeds invention. The broccoli rabe grew like a weed, so I threw it indiscriminately into everything until I discovered that wet heat accentuated its bitterness but that dry-cooking in oil or butter calmed its bristles and turned it sweeter.

But I also discovered that I couldn't cook meat as well as my mom did. My chicken breasts came out tough (overcooked), my chicken thighs wiry (undercooked). Cooking meat clearly involved something more than just following directions. A beef roast doesn't surrender its tenderness to you just because you can read. Each chunk comes with its own idiosyncrasies. You have to imagine the protein's inner architecture, the layout of its fibers, its juice pathways; you have to find a darkened side door into which you can slip inside; you have to put your thumb on its needs.

Increasingly, I stuck to the vegetables. The night Aaron's friends Bruce and Cheryl first came to dinner, I was nervous. Aaron had been friends with Bruce—a silver-bearded, ageless Vietnam vet with dry comic timing and a well-articulated sense of political outrage—since he was a teenager. He joked that Bruce was one of his best high school friends. Bruce had moved out to the Smoky Hills in the early 1980s during the back-to-the-land exodus, and he and Cheryl lived in an underground house of his own design just a few miles away. Their place was off the grid and a paragon of modern counter-culture architecture. It was outfitted to the hilt with natural luxuries—an outdoor solar shower, a living roof covered with squash vines, paths lined with clover for barefoot after-lunch walks. Inside the house, a sauna was tucked right behind their central woodstove so that in the winter they could heat up canners of water in the chimney's leftover heat and, via a submersible 10-volt pump, shower in the sauna. (I tried it once: rainforest-soft.) They had just recently built a studio out of stacked straw bales for Cheryl's massage-therapy practice. Their indoor root cellar was stocked with Cheryl's impressive store of canning. They knew how to build, they knew how to live, and they knew how to eat in August—from the garden. The minute they walked in the door, they handed off a jar of Cheryl's pickled asparagus, which I took as a hint to whip up a batch of Bloody Marys in which to sink them. Our friendship was instant.

In retrospect, the dinner I made that night was nothing remarkable, but it was full of the latest discoveries from my Alice Waters–Edna Lewis–Deborah Madison phase. I can't pick up one of their books without being overwhelmed with warm thoughts of meals made from those pages. The scribbled margins contain the blush of first-taste love that my future professional-cooking self would strive to recapture. My first caramelized onions. My first corn pudding. My first roasted heads of garlic.

Aaron lit the oil lamp in the center of the table and I set down the pizza, a whole wheat version topped with wilted blossoms of garden spinach, thin orbs of my family's sausage, and pads of mozzarella cheese—the last contraband from the store. With it we ate cubes of sautéed zucchini and a simple salad of spiky arugula from the garden, dressed with a thin layer of garlicky, lemony cream. Good-tasting olive oil was hard to come by in town, so I made dressings out of various dilutions of heavy cream and buttermilk flavored with garlic, ginger, lemon, rosemary, or anchovy—not realizing until later that cream dressing was an old Midwestern farmhouse staple.

As Bruce and Cheryl got up to leave, they both hugged me with force, my nose diving deep into Cheryl's reassuring mane of essential-oil-scented hair. Bruce slapped Aaron on the shoulder and said, "Well, it looks like you've found yourself a homestead honey!"

The words slapped my cheeks to a red blush. While this was a comment that likely played fine back at the height of the hippie movement, when Bruce was our age, the part of me that had minored in women's studies did not take it very well. And she was not too happy with my pioneer-cook counterpart, either, the one who couldn't suppress the hot tinge of pride in being authenticated as a homesteader.

It came off a little sexist, but I knew what Bruce meant. His point was that Aaron had found himself a girl, and one who cooked. Backwoods homesteads wither away without the cooking. This little cabin, with the soaring, rusty ceiling, the walls cluttered with paintings, the Swede saws hanging over the window, and the deer pelt draped over the railing, was—with the addition of food to the mix—becoming a home.

AARON LOVES TO DIG. ("If I could make a living doing it, I'd be happy.") Digging turns the human back into a nodding oil rig, as if hinged in two pieces; it renders a person automatic. I think he likes it because it's full of simple purpose—just one scoop after another, nothing much to think about but progress made real. I feel the same satisfaction in the minutiae of kitchen labor. Whenever Aaron seems crabby, I'm tempted to hand him a shovel; and when I get surly, he wants to set me in front of a bushel of shell peas.

That summer, he shoveled out the hole where the porch would sit and a wide moat around the house in which we could plant flowers, holding back the dirt with lanes of dry-stacked fieldstones. It took just a single summer for the long prairie grass to grow in nets around the rocks and hold them in permanent suspension.

Then we set out to plant everything we'd need for the long term, the yard crops that turn a country place into a homestead. We got some horseradish roots from Aaron's dad and planted them near the rock flower beds (a rookie mistake, for the spreading horseradish taproots would colonize my flower beds for years to come). I planted chive and tarragon, herbs that would return naturally every year, the chive so early that their moist green spires rise through the clear sponge holes of the melting snow. We planted rhubarb and crab apple trees and lilacs, the classic triumvirate of the Midwestern farmyard. On our

walks through the woods, we always knew we'd found an old farmstead when we came upon any of these planted at the edge of a clearing. Lilacs outlasted generations; ours would probably outlast us.

We were still hauling our water that summer, and every couple of
days we would go to George and Marie Kueber's place down the road to
fill up our five-gallon plastic tanks. I was well into the groove with the
oil lamps, and the water kettle, and with splashing my face with cold
water each night from the enameled basin. But even with four five-
gallon jugs in our possession, we could hardly haul enough water to
suppress the hoarding feeling. As the summer progressed, I began to
catalog my peeves: how quickly the dirty dishes stacked into mountains,
how impossible it was to rinse oily crud from your hands with cold
water, how greasy and dark my bangs looked on the third day . . . the
mosquitoes, which clamped onto my ankles when I was digging potatoes with such herd force that I feared I'd stepped on a hill of fire ants.

And the outdoor camp showers we took were a little cold. As I stood
on a mere square of stone, the wind ravaged my naked body as a ribbon
of warm water trickled through my foaming, shampooed head.

I began to long for the old days, when the power companies ran
free electric lines to coerce rural people into getting hooked up to the
grid. George and Marie had told us such a thing had happened to them
in the 1950s, so I knew it was true. But in 1998 the power companies
didn't need any new customers. In fact, they didn't give a crap if we
hooked up or not. They let us know the terms and conditions: about
ten thousand dollars, due to the length they'd have to run cable to us
from the nearest box two miles away, a sum we could not afford.

But my cooking habit was thirsty. It needed more water. The garden agreed. That long dry summer, we babied the plants the best we
could. After weeding, mostly we cheered them on. When it got really
dry, we poured some of our precious hauled water into metal watering
cans and stood by each plant for long moments with the heavy can
levered from our hips. Anyone could see that this sustainable lifestyle
was about as unsustainable as it gets.

"Aaron," I said, growing gradually hysterical, "we need WA-TER. I am not coming back here next year without water, and I mean the kind that runs! From a real faucet!"

The next morning I contritely rephrased it. "It would be really cool if you could rig up something else."

What we needed was our own well. Bruce came over to dowse for water—otherwise known as witching—and his out-held willow branch dipped at the bottom of the hill. It would be a trek, pumping the water there and hauling it up to the house, but we had no choice.

Aaron went to town to rent a well-pounder. I expected him to return with some kind of automated machine, but he came back lugging a heavy iron cylinder, which was open on one end. It looked like a giant hollow bullet with handles. Apparently we'd be pounding this thing by hand.

Everyone else who came over to help, friends Dave and Steph and Chris, knew what we were in for, all of them having known the joys of pounding a sand point at their own rustic places.

Taking turns heaving the pounder, we loaded five lengths of pipe, until when at about fifteen feet down, we hit hardpan.

Dave, a self-made expert in the engineering of homemade systems, looked down into the hole and said, "You're getting close to a depth that will require a stand pump, not a hand pump." We took turns again pounding through the hardpan, and an hour later, when the string finally came up wet, meaning we were in the vein, we were at about thirty-four feet. Dave said, "And . . . now we're in stand-pump territory."

Aaron's junk pile in the yard actually contained a rusty old stand pump, but it was missing a few parts. We got into the truck and drove to visit the only person Aaron thought might have them, Leo Kueber—George Kueber's younger brother. His tan house, the Kueber family homestead, stood tall on the only hill in sight, the road in front winding close to it, as it does in children's books. At one time the house had anchored a small community called Goldenrod and Leo's front parlor had been the town post office. Now a chair sat in front of an open window on the porch, a rifle sticking out through the screen.

"That's my perch for eyeing wolves!" Leo cackled. "The cattle farmers around here—and that means me—appreciate that." Shooting wolves wasn't normally a position I took, but on him the lawlessness was charming.

He gave us a tour. At the center of his sprawling farmhouse kitchen stood an enormous cast-iron woodstove, its flat cook-top stretching six feet across. On the front sat a pot of Leo's famous perpetual stew. It brewed all day, he ate some of it for dinner, let it cool overnight, and then added to it the next day. It was a woodstove thing.

Surprising to me, food was everywhere. Buckets of onions he'd grown. Two-gallon jars of mayo from the commercial aisle at the store. A gallon of peanut butter. Strings of peppers. A bushel of apples. It seemed that Leo the bachelor was quite the entertainer. Deer camp at Leo's was legendary. Upstairs in the communal sleeping room, a toilet sat in the middle of the room, cordoned off by a calico curtain, a convenience installed to accommodate a room that came to life during deer-hunting season. The entire place was a nesting doll into the past, a journey of retrofitting through the eras.

We walked down the front steps toward the shed. Beaver carcasses littered the yard, tossed there for the dogs. The skulls had been lovingly licked clean, as white as if they'd been boiled. Some . . . not so clean yet.

"Doesn't quite smell spring," Leo said, by way of explanation for the brain-fogging stench and beckoned us into the shed. Of course he had the pump parts. He was an old-ways angel.

The next day Dave came back to commune with us around the hole. He and Aaron repaired the stand pump with Leo's parts and tried it out. It didn't work. For hours it didn't work.

"Cripes, we know there's water there," Dave said. "You're just going to have to try to dig down to it. I don't think you have a choice."

So Aaron, who could dig, dug. Four feet down, then six, until the top of his head lined up with the grass. Standing way down in the hole, he screwed the pump onto the pipe and tried it again. It worked. We took turns pumping. It was nearly too stiff for me to pump—*How convenient,* I thought, *Aaron will have to pump it all*—and then I filled up a quart jar to taste.

"Pipe dope!" Aaron spat. It tasted like chemicals and clay, worse than the adhesive at the dentist. Once it ran clear it tasted delicious, though, and we eventually had it tested: about 99.5 percent pure, with a touch of added calcium. As close to perfect as it gets, and as cold as water floating with a disk of melted ice.

Aaron lined the pump hole with stones that he'd picked up from a neighbor's field pile and finished the steps with flat stones. He pumped up two five-gallon plastic jugs and lugged them up the hill, as he would every day afterward.

The first time the water came rushing out, rock-cold and forceful, I felt more rooted than I had in years. This one small improvement to our simple water-and-power situation made it feel like we had entered yet another new era. Without the constant sense of a diminishing water supply, our days lost some of their anxiety and began to feel more comfortable. I could now cook, and wash dishes, to my complete saturation.

Before I could give that a spin, we scrubbed up at the wash basin because it was time for Bruce and Cheryl's party.

PRIOR TO MY ENTRANCE INTO HIS LIFE, Aaron prided himself on his ability to smoothly, strategically, stop by other people's houses at happy hour. If he was lucky, as he often was, a drink slid into a dinner invitation. At Bruce and Cheryl's, if they were feeling devout and healthy, the drinks offered were milk-thistle tea or freshly extracted beet-carrot juice, all from their garden. There were homemade pickles to start and soba noodles for dinner.

If the collective hungers were up, they served gin and tonics floating with precious ice and slow-grilled pork ribs. As the fire jumped up and down in the pit, guitars were pulled out.

This was a party of the latter variety, a feasting time. Bruce made pulled bison barbacoa in the solar oven, monitoring it all day while they worked outside in the yard, and he'd called potluck for the rest.

I crawled sideways out of our low-riding Buick holding a covered dish that contained my most recent crush—buttery fried corn, browned in a cast-iron pan until it tasted like the sun had roasted the sweet kernels on a twirling spit. I kicked the Buick's heavy door shut. Outside, it was what you'd call authentically dark.

The night air, without any electric light around to dilute it, thickened into a material substance. The dark vibrated fondly around me like an invisible swarm—either gnats or a force field, it was always hard to tell. As usual, neither Aaron nor I carried a flashlight, even though we'd been negotiating similarly blind pathways all summer long at our own place. With the insouciance of twentysomethings, we felt freer without a flashlight, like it deepened our trust. It was kind of like a woods version of going without underwear.

We walked blindly down the sandy path, like bugs drawn to the warm flames of the campfire, our pace keeping time with the conga drums. The compiled effect of the darkness, the zippered beats of the drums, and the distant sound of party voices made me feel like we were entering some kind of womb. *Why must the woods settlers of the '60s' back-to-the-land movement be reduced to the word* hippie? I thought. It puts such a negative spin on the contagious generosity, the backwoods magnificence, of that cultural moment in perfect action.

On the potluck table where I set my corn, a full landscape quickly sprouted: there was falafel; tangy, fermented tomato salsa; black threads of a hijiki-carrot salad; Dutch-oven potatoes; and three bowls of cucumber salad, two creamy, one vinegary. (It was the week for cucumbers.) A whole slew of open quart jars lined the middle space, all of them stuck with forks: dill pickles, sweet bread and butters; pickled asparagus; sweet spiced beets; mixed hot vegetable pickles; dilly beans.

Cheryl walked up from the house carrying an earthen pot of black beans. Small-boned, barefoot, olive-skinned, with long brown curls falling down her back, she wore a large scarf twisted up behind her neck to make a tropical halter dress. They were calling this their Shangri-La party, and she was dressed for it.

After dinner, sitting with Cheryl in the dark screen house, I heard about her own transition to the woods, nearly fifteen years previous. When she arrived with her long nails and city clothes, all of Bruce's friends nicknamed her Barbie.

"As in *Barbie doll*," she said, shaking her head and pulling on her beer. "They thought I'd never make it out here, with no power and no shower. I was like Ha! Bruce, just show me which ones are the weeds and which are the baby plants, that's all I need to know." She smiled, having long since become the woman who gingerly relocated wildflowers with the tip of her spade, who spent her days weeding their walking paths.

"That first year Bruce told me to give away my city clothes, including all of my heels and my collection of lingerie—*vintage lingerie*—and trade them in for Birkenstocks and cargo pants."

Now, proudly braless, her transformation from city sexpot to hippie princess complete, Bruce was now asking why she'd thrown away all of her nighties.

"Good riddance to the heels, but I wish I'd kept those corsets with the covered buttons!" she pealed. "Gorgeous little satin buttons, and all to Goodwill!"

"Wah, wah, poor Bruce!" I replied, wearing my own woods uniform, a matronly calico button-up and baggy olive-green military pants hitched up with a sturdy belt. We clinked our longnecks in solidarity.

My sexless garb hardly made a case for the romance of dressing the rural part, but I failed to see it, for back then I rarely looked in our single foggy antique mirror. As if proof of the fact that illumination was not a given in those days, I have loads of memories but very little photographic evidence of this time. It comes as no big surprise that the girl who didn't carry a flashlight also didn't take any pictures. I have a mere handful, and whenever I look at them, it's a stare-down.

To the girl standing next to the enormous log on the Hanna Ore forest road I want to say: *Get yourself a real haircut! Good Lord, at least a decent bra! You look like a schlumpf!*—the sloppy state of dress my grandma Dion had cautioned me against. But the look in the girl's eyes goads the camera to a challenge, staring my future self down with a distressing amount of haughtiness, clearly high on newfound self-sufficiency.

Suddenly, the rain started to pound down and people streamed into the screen house, crowding in on me and Cheryl. A bunch of people were still outside, some huddled under the umbrella over the table, some dancing out in the rain. Everyone was excited because the rain was filling up their rain barrels. Aaron and I joined them, because we possessed rain barrels, too, but were delighted with the irony of not needing them today or the next day. With the hand-pumped well, we finally had a backup water source. Truly, when it rains, it pours.

16

CHEF SALAD, NO EGGS

ANOTHER WINTER SPENT DOWN IN MINNEAPOLIS, another summer up north at the house in Two Inlets—our third. The sun had been hitting my face in our loft bedroom for hours already. The birds had been awake forever and were already on to lunch.

Thud . . . thud, thud.

I registered the sound before I saw the clock: 9:00. I was really late for work.

But what the hell was that? Was someone at our door?

It could be. Around Two Inlets, and especially before we had a phone, visitors would just show up unannounced at ungodly early hours. Our neighbors got a kick out of our throwback lifestyle and loved to pop in on us in our little cabin out in the woods—like people used to in the old days.

I looked out the kitchen window and didn't see anyone in front of the door. A closer look revealed that a massive snapping turtle had crawled up out of the creek and ass-planted itself in my flower bed next to the door and was now whapping its prehistoric tail against the wood. With eyes like shiny coffee beans, he glared menacingly at me. His knobby, vicious head was not tucked inside his shell; it was definitely out.

"Don't open the door, he could bite your arm off," Aaron shouted down from the loft. "We're going to have to get a stick, or an oar, for him to clamp onto so we can lead him away."

Whoom, whoom. The thumping was like a vise tightening on my cranium. Wickedly hungover, glowing from the inside out, I was thankful to have an excuse—even an absurd one—for being late for work. I called Jorg, my boss at the Schwarzwald Inn on Main Street in Park Rapids, mumbling about a snapping turtle at my door and not being able to leave my house.

"What?" he shouted, as if he couldn't hear me. "What? What turtle? What the hell are you talking about?"

Finally I started whining. "Jorg, I can't come to work today. I'm sick. I am *so* hungover. I'm sorry, I just can't function."

He paused for a second and then yelled into the phone slowly and distinctly: "WE ARE ALL HUNGOVER HERE! GET YOUR ASS TO WORK!" He hung up.

The previous summer I had worked a couple of days a week at the Schwarzwald Inn, the German-American diner on Main Street, mostly just showing up to make some pies and prep some carrots and onions for the soups. Jorg paid me five dollars an hour, hardly worth the price of the gas to get there. When I walked into the restaurant this summer, now on the short-cooking schedule for three-day weeks, I saw an unfamiliar head of spiked platinum-blond hair on the line. When she came around the corner, she was flustered, her words coming out in spits and stops.

"Hey, I am Tonya!" she said, pronouncing it Tone-ya. "From Mallorca." We pumped hands. Fashionably lanky, she had what some locals would call an out-of-town figure.

"And that is Klaus," she said, tipping her head to the hot line. Her boyfriend Klaus, tall and dark with curls that licked the collar of his chef shirt, had grown up in Germany with Jorg, and he and Tonya had met while both were cooking in her native Spain. Why they decided to work that summer in Park Rapids I never did understand. Tonya and I struggled to talk, but we shared the international languages of cooking and fashion. I introduced her to all my favorite permanent garage sales in town, where she found tons of perfectly outrageous vintage outfits for her drag-queen friends back home. Straight from Dolores Nepsund's garage to a nightclub in the Balearic Islands—it was a clothes pipeline that I treasured, and figured had to be a first.

"Amy," I told her, "from Park Rapids."

"*Estoy crudo,*" she said, sticking out her tongue to loll at one side of her mouth. "*Cru-do.*"

Crudo. I didn't know a lick of Spanish. She made a quick sketch in her kitchen notebook and then I guessed it: "Hungover! You're hungover!"

"Yes! Yes!" she replied, hopping and doing a tiny clap, totally delighted.

I guessed she had heard about the turtle.

"Amy!" Jorg bellowed. We quickly scattered—her to the back prep, me to the grill. We could hear the little bell on the front door dinging away. We served nearly a thousand hungry tourists on busy weekends, most of them queuing up for Schwarzwald's famous smorgasbord and the rest ordering hot short-order plates. I tied on a white apron and threw a sausage patty for myself on the grill. Troy read out a table: "Two stuffed hash browns, a pork chop breakfast, and a kid pancake." Troy, a chesty guy with permanently wet-looking curls, was surprisingly graceful. He spun around to the grill. "And a solo schnitzel."

Jorg smiled theatrically at me and said, "Oh, look who showed up for the battle!," which was how he referred to the Sunday brunch service. And then he snarled, "I want you to show up on time! And I want you fed!"

"Okay, okay," I said. Maybe it was time to reel things in a bit.

He glanced out the peephole kitchen window to see who had ordered the schnitzel. It was a big guy, patiently waiting with his legs planted wide at 10 and 2. Jorg dipped into the reach-in cooler, grabbed a second piece of tenderized, paprika-dusted pork, and threw it into my working breading bowl, which was circled with planetary rings of dried-on egg wash. "Better do two." Damned if they were truly ravenous, but the skinny ladies only got one. At the Schwarzwald we cooked not only to order but also to size.

WHEN JORG BOUGHT THE RESTAURANT that his parents had established, he inherited Arlys. And, unfortunately, she did not do hash browns.

When I first met Arlys she must have been tipping eighty years old, the last twenty of which she'd spent in the back prep area. She had a frizzy mess of hair like a woolly pad and shuffled around the kitchen stooped into the shape of a lowercase f, slinging five-gallon buckets of fodder vegetables as if she were working a farmstead instead of a kitchen.

I worked the grill with Klaus and Jorg, and sometimes Troy. Tonya took to the back, helping Arlys, whose job it was to peel all the vegetables: countless five-gallon buckets of russet potatoes, onions, and twenty-five-pound bags of food-service carrots so fat you couldn't get your fingers around them. Arlys's duties included grinding the ham for the ham salad, making the house cinnamon rolls, and washing the dishes. For a long time she didn't so much as speak to me as growl. "Move it. Hands out of my dishwater," she'd say when I hopped in to work on the backlog. A human routine, she wasn't looking to hand off any of her daily tasks. Soon I came to understand her loyalty to the dish circuit when I watched her openly scarf uneaten food off the plates.

I knew we had come to a meeting of the minds, though, when one day she came in with a jar of pickled tomatoes, tiny pear-shaped yellow ones she had grown herself, and shoved it toward me. "For you," she said, her rheumy eyes sparkling. The ring was caked with rust, throwing my trust for their food safety into doubt, but I had to admit, they were lovely and exactly my kind of thing.

On Fridays Arlys started her main vocation, which was making the dozen or so salads for the Sunday smorgasbord. In addition to the most obvious things, like an Italian-ish pasta salad with black olives and mini pepperoni slices, she also made a classic German salad of ham, cheese, and pickles that didn't quite translate without good German ham; a herring salad with apples and Miracle Whip; a crushed ramen-noodle-fake-crab-almond thing with sweet sesame dressing, so addictive it was like the opiate of Midwestern salads; a greasy little turkey giblet mixture, nearly cleansed with a strong dose of vinegar (when I asked about the contents of that one, she always just cackled); serviceable deviled eggs, chilled to cadaver stiffness; a few varieties of Jell-O, usually orange chiffon or something with suspended cubes of canned fruit cocktail and miniature marshmallows; and chocolate pudding, which in some way had slipped into the "salad" bar—perhaps through the gate the Jell-O left wide open. Proper Midwestern salad buffets such as this one ensure that your meal is properly bookended in sugar, so that everything you eat before the meat main course is sweet, including the so-called savory salads, right up to the desserts that follow.

And we were constantly replenishing the salad bar. Arlys would toddle out there to check the lineup, her nude pantyhose drooping down to puddle around her ankles like excess skin, while one of the lowly kitchen assistants trailed quietly behind her holding a plastic bowl of luminous, unbroken Jell-O.

Jorg always had a new five-dollar-an-hour summer hire, usually a teenage boy, to dice the carrots, onions, and celery for the soups and of course to shred the potatoes for the hash browns. During the height of the tourist season the restaurant would sometimes serve over four hundred people a day, and as a great percentage of them ordered breakfast at any hour, we easily went through three large plastic bus tubs of shredded potatoes daily.

Jorg made hash browns as his mother, Gisela, had, beginning with a stockpot of russets. He covered the potatoes with water and when the

water came to a boil he turned off the heat, let them sit for five minutes, drained them, and shredded each potato by hand. If they'd been
fried in real butter instead of the mysterious semiliquid orange grease
we squirted on them, they would have been phenomenal, but they
were still easily the best hash browns around.

That summer I shredded my share, running the cold half-cooked
russets against the sharp face of the box grinder, trying to imagine my
arm as a pumping gear. When I was called away to work the grill, Jorg
would stand at the prep table and furiously shred them himself, visibly
fighting off childhood memories.

Jorg was loyal to his mother's recipes, pounding out the schnitzels
and sprinkling them with red paprika salt; boiling whole peeled carrots until they were as soft as putty and cutting them with a crinkle
cutter; adding fresh grated nutmeg to the chicken noodle soup. Half
of the cooking there was beautifully old-school and half was straight
off the truck. He'd bring in a hog that he'd raised on the family farm,
toting it over his shoulder, and we'd spend the morning running the
slices through the tenderizer (which looked like an old-fashioned
mangle iron) and freezing them in packages. His German noodles
were particularly firm and chewy when fresh, and had he warmed
them up in a pan with a little brown butter, they would have rivaled
my mother's. But out of habit he refrigerated them and then re-
warmed them in a sieve set into simmering murky water until they
were hot and overblown—at which point we plopped them onto the
plate unadorned. The rye bread, moist with added mashed potatoes
and thick buttermilk, was too soft and heavenly on its first day to go
through the slicer, so he waited up to a day or two until it hardened to
slice and serve it.

The lesser items of the book-length menu traveled a straight path
from the freezer to the deep-fryer: fish patties, slipped between two
butter-toasted halves of a confectionery bun; chicken-fried steak,
squiggled with tan gravy base; breaded shrimp, fried into tight fists
and sent off with a twisted lemon slice. The freezer also contained the

sea sticks—fake crab. For chef salad orders, we thawed one out in the microwave, letting it ride in there until we could smell its peculiar crustaceous funk, deep but not offensive. A typical lunch special was a grilled ham and cheese with a cup of soup for $4.25.

One Saturday, the kitchen gears halted. A waitress didn't show up, leaving the one whom Jorg accused of stealing from the till to work alone. Everyone was ordering smoked pork chop breakfasts, and we had to cut more chops on the saw. It was then that the five-dollar teenager dropped a tub of hash browns on the floor in a puddle of water. Jorg yelled at the kid with such force that he seemed to blow backward, his white apron a sail. Within seconds he bolted out the side door. We were down a kid and a tub of browns and the little bell on the front door was going crazy. People were just gushing in.

"Arlys!" Jorg bellowed. "Put on more potatoes!"

A food-service delivery guy showed up in the back hallway and called out, "Hey, Jorg!" Jorg spun around and then walked slowly to the back, reeling in his fury as if it were a loose rope. He spilled the entirety of his terrible morning, all the way up to the dumped hash browns, to the Sysco guy. The guy said, "Don't you have a Hobart?" and pointed to the enormous standing mixer across the kitchen. It was an animal, six feet tall, with beefy steel arms.

Jorg nodded. "Ja."

"Why don't you use the Hobart shredder attachment to shred your potatoes?"

Jorg stiffened and his eyes drifted slowly across the room. "Ja . . . I could do that."

Within a few minutes he had the machine going and was pushing potatoes through the top, eyes gleaming, laughing and carrying on like he had just struck water. Arlys stood on the sidelines, a carrot in one hand and a swivel peeler in the other, too shocked by the change to speak. In a voice about as joyful as I'd ever heard him, Jorg said, "We got six tubs of hash browns, you guys!" and whacked the walk-in door shut with his heel.

———

THERE WAS RARELY A MOMENT when I didn't love that job, when I didn't leave sweaty, with swirls of pancake batter splattered on my bare arms, totally content. Especially in late August after the tourists had left and my garden at home was finally ripening, all at once. Each day after coming home from work at four o'clock and pumping myself a full quart jar of bedrock-chilled water to drink, I filled the giant enamelware boiling water canner and the big water kettle, then brought them up the hill. My tomatoes were ripening rapid-fire and I was loving canning them, standing in front of my butcher block, leaning hard on one hip, blanching and peeling my heirloom romas. One year I grew San Marzanos, the next Amish Paste, but this year the best yet, Opalka. They grew huge and heavy. Eastern European tomatoes liked our climate. I concentrated on boiling them just enough—not too much, not too little—so that the thin outer epidermis of the tomato peeled off in one great whispery translucent sheet, leaving the smooth, basal tomato sublayer behind. Thus peeled, the tomatoes were comically slippery, almost impossible to hold, and were, I was sure of it, more flavorful than the carelessly blanched.

For weeks during the late-summer harvest, this was my routine. The needs of our place were beautifully predictable. But personally, down in my subconscious, my own needs were starting to fog up. I realized that my inner clock was ticking too slowly; real time was passing me by.

One day at the Schwarzwald I saw my dad's order on the check wheel—chef salad, no eggs—and put his salad in the window, then padded out to the dining room with a cup of coffee and sat down at his table.

"So what are you doing now?" he asked me, making it sound official.

"I guess I'm having a cup of coffee with you. It's slow. I can take a break."

"No." He leaned forward. "I mean, what are you doing with your life?"

This was the guy who, when pop-quizzed, never knew my college major, which hadn't ever changed. (It was English.) He'd been coming in for lunch, eating the best chef salad I could make out of the scraps we had in the kitchen, and had never hinted that he expected something else from me. His complete lack of criticism was generally welcome—but his uncanny gift for suspending all judgment about his kids also sometimes left us without much guidance. At this moment, "What are you doing with your life?" was a question I was actually relieved to hear him ask. Out poured my idea, which I'd only just floated with Aaron a few nights before.

"I was kind of thinking of going to cooking school. In New York City. To become a chef."

To my surprise, not only was my dad fully supportive, he was a cheerleader. "Then *do* it!" he said, raising a fist in the air. ("Do anything!" was probably more what he meant.)

It took me about three days to convince Aaron to move to New York. Ruralness was a part of his ethic, his story, his belief system. But his friends Rob and Sara and some others from Minneapolis were moving there to make art, and New York was doubtlessly the center of both the art world he needed and the cooking world I needed. The move seemed suddenly obvious.

I found a cooking school in the back of my latest *Saveur* magazine. It was in Manhattan's Flatiron district, cost two-thirds less than the famous Culinary Institute of America in upstate New York, and would only take five months of my time. Aaron overcame his reticence by coming up with a plan: his brother, Matt, was a pilot who flew planes carrying checks regularly out of Washington, D.C., and whenever he wanted to get back home Aaron could simply take the train down to D.C. and hop the plane home with Matt. His exit strategy figured out, Aaron agreed: New York City it would be. Our plan was to live there six months of the year and then move back home to Two Inlets in the summers to garden. It would be like moving to Minneapolis for the winter, but just a little farther. Or so we thought.

I flew out, solo, three weeks ahead of our move to find us an apartment. I walked the streets in Brooklyn, idiotically carrying my backpack on my front as had been advised, looking for addresses of apartments I'd found on Craigslist. After seeing a bunch of completely unsuitable dives, I finally handed my money over to a guy who was subletting his one-room studio with a sleeping loft in the on-the-cusp-of-gentrifying neighborhood of Fort Greene. He cautioned me, as he slid my three months' rent, a thick pile of bills, into his coat pocket, that the landlord didn't allow sublets. If he saw us, we'd be thrown out on our asses. If I had only known then that he planned to take our monthly rent and not pay the landlord . . . It was to be a newcomer's storybook welcome to the intoxicating bedlam that is New York City.

Back at the house in Two Inlets, we got ready to move. We packed up a few things—our clothes, our tools, our freshly harvested wild rice, my canned pickles and tomatoes and preserves—all of which fit into the back of a twelve-foot U-Haul truck, and planned to set out the next day for Brooklyn.

Now that we had a secondhand solar panel from Dave, and the car battery to power it from Bruce, we were inching our way toward modern living out at Hazelbrush. On our last night there, as we walked back from the outhouse, our new solar-powered electric life glared out of the windows. We felt a little embarrassed about it, as if we'd somehow made a devil's bargain. With the new overhead fixture illuminating the room to the corners, my evening reading lost all of its shadow-weight and felt about sixty percent less compelling. Compared to our formerly oil-lamp-lit house whose blurred edges faded into the black night, whose dim orange windows promised secret historical-society contents, this new brightness shot from the windows up to the house's roofline so that we could see it for what it really was: a sturdy wooden pole shed dwarfed by swaying trees, with two sharp windows cut for eyes. Before, it had felt so monumental, so towering. Now it looked small, like a house in one of those decorative Christmas villages.

Like it wasn't even real.

17

POUNDS AND PENNIES

AFTER SEVEN YEARS OF COOKING IN NEW YORK CITY, I arrived at the moment that I can now pinpoint as the end of the end: I was sitting on my haunches behind the pastry counter in the basement of Cru, scarfing a hot duck meatball on a roll, trying to erase the sour taste of discontent in my mouth, plotting my defection. It was the tipping point. My future in restaurants was in peril.

Aaron was faring better. He had quit carpentry to make art full-time. Not only that, he was selling every piece he made, putting us, for the first time in our life together, into the financial black. His career as an artist outweighed mine for both primacy and drama, a shift in focus for which I was thankful—but that meant that it was time for us to have *the talk*.

Aaron and I both knew that someday we would return to our house in the woods to sit on the porch and grow old, but for now our loyalties were evenly split between the city and the country. We thought of both places as equally dramatic: the country for its stunning remoteness, the city for its relentless density.

Like classic expatriates, we were a little addicted to the outsider feeling that accompanied every return, and our imaginations were always attuned to the place where we weren't. We basically lived in each place with one foot in the other. In Brooklyn, we thought of ourselves as rural people on a long sojourn, listened to a steady diet of old country music, and bemoaned the loss of our multigenerational social circle back home. (*Where are all the older people?*) When we went home for the summer, we felt like visiting New Yorkers, seemed not to need Waylon or Willie, and missed New York's creative culture, its museums, its restaurants, its fellow artists and cooks.

But nine years into our relationship, the same split loyalty to both country and city that had originally kept us teeter-tottering between homes began to dip to one side—at least it did for me. Our youth was waning; at some point we'd have to make a choice on which side to land. At the present moment it looked like Brooklyn, where we could each make a living in our respective careers, was the more responsible choice.

Sitting at our tiny dining-room table facing the windows that overlooked congested Atlantic Avenue, Aaron plumbed the depths of his algae-green spinach soup, his spoon clinking, telegraphing to me his wish for a little texture. He's not a puree guy. Not even for one as thin and elegant as this one, spiked with both truffle oil and melted clouds of Taleggio cheese—an aphrodisiac double-down.

No amount of seduction could stop him from saying what I knew was coming. The ghost in the room—a black-and-white photo of our house in the woods—hung on the wall like one of our ancestors. It was spring, that time of year. I knew what he was thinking. The road less traveled begins to disappear, and I had to admit that it was true: Our dirt driveway back home had started to blur at the edges with brush. The forest was starting to reclaim it.

"I think we should take the money I've made this year to pay for a new studio building back home," he said, testing the waters. "Eventually, I'm going to need a place to work back there, and now's the time. I've already called Vern and he can do it."

"You've already called Vern?" I put down my spoon. He meant Vern Schultz, a carpenter neighbor whose skills were in high demand.

I was not game for spending our precious surplus cash on our impractical place back home. No. I was settled here. I was hoping we could use that money to buy a place in Brooklyn, or at the very least burrow into a better rental and hold on to it as prices rose, because they always rose. I cursed the intrusion of our original plan. It was getting inconvenient.

He continued. "And then we're just going to have to hook up to the grid."

"What?" I said, shocked to realize that the power lust with which I'd previously struggled could be so easily bought. We could now afford to run the power line two miles down our driveway to the house—if we chose to.

"Running power back there will give us the thing we need more of, and that's time," he ramped up, having obviously prepared his argument. "You can't spend all your time heating up water for dishes and I can't spend all my time lugging it. And I'm going to need to run power tools in my studio."

My first thought was, *Then I'm getting a stand mixer.* Instead I challenged him: "Don't you need to stay here, where the art world is?"

"Don't you always say you want to cook out of the garden?" he shot back. "I need to be wherever I can make the most work. There, we'll both have more time and more space."

He was making it sound logical, even audacious, to ply our crafts at our home in the middle of nowhere, he with his Japanese chisels, me with my Japanese knives.

"Besides," Aaron said, inverting the cheesiest of New York clichés with a maddening grin, "if you can make it in Minnesota, you can make it anywhere." He rested his case.

Paradoxically, the minute we had enough money to relieve the constant stress of trying to make it in New York, I felt my claws for staying in the city retract. For years I'd let Aaron carry the heavy weight of pining for home, but in truth Two Inlets had its hooks in me—even more so if it had electricity. He might have built the house, but we built the *place* together. Between the creek full of wild rice, our garden, the orchard, and the trails that cut through acres of wild raspberries, we had built an edible kingdom. It was a cook's paradise.

And it was becoming increasingly obvious to me that place of origin was the primary tool in any chef's toolbox. Dishes that leaned too hard on culinary trends felt slightly derivative, no matter how technically perfect they were. The most powerful cooking I'd ever tasted—Michel Bras's Trout with Milk Skin that mimicked the clotted top of his mother's cream; Bouley's Scallop with Ocean Herbal that was thick with the pulpy vegetables his grandmother had cooked in the brushfire coals; Shea's Tomato-Sauced Ricotta Cavatelli that pulled hard on his Italian-American upbringing—had sprung organically from taste memories. The link to the past was what made these dishes contemporary and what made them original. Even if I wouldn't be cooking professionally in Two Inlets, I knew that it was time for me to play around with the ingredients I had access to there. I was a proud Midwesterner, and yet here I was, making purees instead of stews; I never made anything that called up my personal history. I closed my eyes. It was either a bad game of Monopoly or the story of my life or—just maybe—my fate: in order to move forward, I had to move a few steps back.

Aaron knew me too well. I hadn't helped him plant those cherry trees or dig out that garden by hand for nothing. I gave him, and Vern, the green light to build the studio. The next day Aaron called the power company and sent the check that would hook our place up to the twenty-first century.

A FEW WEEKS LATER I gave Shea my notice at Cru. We sublet our Brooklyn apartment and moved back home to our house for a three-month summer, which we hadn't done since our wedding in 2002. We immediately planted the garden. I carefully unpacked my Japanese knives in my incongruously rustic kitchen—the propane stove, the water jugs above the sink, the buckets below. The new electric line powered a few more lights, but we didn't have the money to go all the way and plumb the house for running water. Not having a job, and not seeing a way to get one, I concentrated on our daily three squares. I picked vegetables from the garden, brought them up the hill, cooked them, and then we ate them. The amount of cooking that would have taken me just an hour or two back in a restaurant kitchen now filled an entire day. Within weeks of arriving from New York, my internal clock had slowed to a calming tick.

Just like before, we drove around a lot, Aaron taking photos of abandoned buildings to hang up on his studio walls. We still received our mail at the Osage post office, about eight miles to the southwest, and every few days we drove there to retrieve it, sometimes going the long way to stop at the cemetery where Aaron's brother, Matt, was buried. We never went anywhere without throwing our garbage into the back of the truck to dispose of at the Osage dump.

Maynard, the suspendered dump attendant, sat in a building not much larger than a phone booth, just big enough to hold a chair and a small wooden desk with a pad of paper on it. He heaved his round belly out of the doorway to get a better look at the contents of our truck bed before assigning some odd value to its disposal. A bag of garbage and an old broken nightstand might cost us "A dollar sixty-three." Four bags and two grocery bags of recycling: "Three eighty-eight." It was random like that, as if he were using some sort of complicated penny-calculation system to keep his mind sharp. More likely it was to allay his boredom, although his delivery was perfectly deadpan. The ease with which he kept up his ongoing joke seemed to me like country-living candy, our weekly treat.

After grabbing our mail, we hit the Osage grocery, attached to the post office. The store wasn't much—good for basics like sugar and butter and second-rate VHS videos—but it had a decent selection of meat. With or without a stop there, getting the mail always had a way of eating up an afternoon.

I held a piece of scrap paper on which I'd sketched a plan for the next two days' cooking, but nothing was set in stone. I loitered at the meat counter just as my mother had done before me, considering the heavy question of dinner. Steak on the grill? Rubbed with anchovy and rosemary? Or should I make teriyaki chicken legs, glazed with mirin and soy? A woman in a long plaid shirt next to me was doing the same thing, holding a pack of thin pork steaks in a loose grip but still peering into the shiny, plastic-wrapped abyss. Pork butt was on sale, ninety-eight cents a pound. We glanced at each other's hands and silently agreed: It didn't get much cheaper than that. Standing there, marinating in the salty brine of my childhood, I remembered how it felt to be a side-child, an accomplice to my mother's indecision. Now I was the unsure lady of my own house. The plaid stranger and I stood there like players in a reconstructed grocery-store drama, making me think that the whole town was doing this, and had always been doing this, calculating pounds and pennies.

On the way home, as the bag of groceries with the pork butt in it rolled around the back of the truck, we saw something in the distance in the middle of the road. It was an animal. No, a kid. Finally we drove close enough to make out an elderly lady crouched on the asphalt, digging in a hole in the middle of the dotted line.

Before we had even fully pulled our truck onto the shoulder she stood up and shouted, gesticulating toward Aaron, "Young man! Young man, you can help me pull this up!"

When we got out, we could see that the hole's bottom was deep and black. She puffed out the words: "We've got . . . to get . . . this thing up! Just . . . you try it." She sat back with a huff and handed him a pair of pliers.

"That's my house over there," she said, pointing to a white one-story across the road. Two of the biggest apple trees I'd ever seen stood like bulldogs in the front yard.

"I've lived there all my life. I know my borders. And now that guy"—she pointed her elbow toward a beige new construction—"is circulating a different story."

Her feistiness clued me in to who she was. This lady, wearing a trim pair of pedal pushers and a doughnut-size bun, had to be the one who wrote long letters of great opinion to the Park Rapids newspaper, signing them "Margaret Sexton—Osage."

Eventually we understood the problem: Margaret was trying to pull up a buried property stake and move it a few feet up the road. Turned out that every few hundred feet there was a buried metal property stake dividing the imposition of the road's footage fairly between owners. Like invisible buttons connecting one piece of property to the other. The stake seemed pretty permanent to me, but Aaron was now embroiled in her mission, his body curving back over his heels, all of his weight pulling on the pliers. He caved forward.

"This stake isn't going anywhere." He looked behind him to see if any cars were coming, but I'd been keeping watch. There'd been no movement in either direction for the past five minutes.

"No!" Margaret howled. "The stake has to come up and then it needs to go back down right here!" She scooted eight feet up the road and slapped her blue Keds sneaker on the hot tar.

A semitruck approached and we slid to opposite sides of the road. When it left, we crossed and I held out my hand to shake good-bye.

"I'm sorry we couldn't help you," I said.

The high rounds of her cheeks drooped suddenly and the lines in her face deepened into pleats. She looked into my eyes and said, "Now you need to come to my house for some pie."

I had a strong feeling that she made very good pie, probably from strong-smelling apples she gathered up from the ground, pared by hand into small, worried c's, and then cut crosswise into sunlight-yellow triangles. Old-school ladies like her made pie from what they could find around them; they didn't buy fruit for it. Not just because store-bought fruit was contrary to their thrift, but because they knew that commercial fruit had long since been bred to be sweet and complicit. Compared to the homegrown, store fruit had lost much of its essential fire, its acidity, and its attitude—all of which Margaret had in spades.

"Just some pie and a cup of coffee. I have apple pie. And wild blueberry," she pleaded. "I make the pies two at a time and freeze them and it would take just half an hour to thaw one in the oven."

My eyes locked with Aaron's. As much as I wanted to sit at her kitchen table among the paraphernalia of her life, and as much as I loved to let a day unspool loosely into the evening, Aaron and I simultaneously decided against hanging around to wait for a pie to thaw.

"Another time," I said, sincerely regretful, shaking both of her hands, light and downy like little animals. We turned toward our truck.

I spun back around after she started yelling.

"You need to come for pie! I mean it! You come back!" She stood in the middle of the road, one foot on either side of the line, bent forward with red-hot hospitality.

In the way that you never claim your rain checks like you should, we never did stop that summer and ring her doorbell for pie and coffee. Not long after that we saw her obituary in the paper. Sadly, we failed to make the time, on even the blankest of days, to enter her world.

As I stood in my cool, dim kitchen after lunch I let the dawning truth of my continual, confusing attraction to this place wash over me. The rural life was bossy, like Margaret, in a way that I craved. There were real food limits here. Seasonal deprivations. Provisions you had to go after yourself. You need water? Pound down into the ground for it. Hungry? Go down to the garden and pick it. Need heat? Make a fire in your woodstove. And heat was heat. If the stove was already going, you might as well use it to dry out apple slices, or herbs, or tomatoes. The full sheet pan of cherry tomatoes I set on top of the woodstove, mooning about in a bath of oil, garlic, and herbs, took about eight hours to shrink into powerful nuggets the size of cranberries and barely filled a pint. I thought of them as summer's gold coins in a jar, and for weeks afterward I spent them carefully: a few dropped into my chicken salad, a few more spooned out over sautéed blue gills.

In the dark of the afternoon, I whipped together a pie from my own limited resources: the first crab apples that had grown on our tree. I was coming off a five-year standoff with pie. My crusts, which had turned out for me since I was in my teens, had grown tough, as I'd discovered with the twenty-five Thanksgiving pies I'd made at Cru. It was the revenge of beginner's luck.

So I returned to not measuring anything, just as Grandma Dion had taught me. I cubed coolish butter and added a pawed-out scoop of Crisco for good measure—Crisco being my inaugural piecrust fat. I mixed some sugar with small, fragrant chunks of crab apple, peels and all, until they tasted sweet enough, then added enough flour to make a milky fluid that I hoped would bind in the oven.

When I pulled out the pie, the nut-brown crust swelled with thickened juice, and its crimped edge felt as sturdy/delicate as wet beach sand. After it had cooled, I transferred the first slice to a plate and sucked in my breath until it made it there in one fragile, perfect piece. The crab apples, whose skins had dissolved, leaving a deep coral-pink fruit with a flowery fragrance, were a dead ringer for baked quince.

The gaps in my Midwestern culinary education were as obvious to me at that moment as Margaret Sexton's gaping pothole in the middle of the road—which, the last time we drove by, was still open to the problem stake. Headcheese, rendered lard, homemade cottage cheese, I had yet to make any of these things my grandma had so rapturously described, the rural recipes that had originally drawn me to this place. I wanted to try them all. Maybe if I pushed my brain out of the way, as I had with the pie, my hands would know just what to do.

18

MORBID SUGAR

ONE MORNING toward the end of that summer in Two Inlets, I walked to the outhouse hiding a suspicious bump in my robe and took a pregnancy test: the pink plus sign in the white window glowed a hallucinatory neon against the rough wooden floor.

True to form, neither Aaron nor I could see how having a child would change our grand master plan. As we walked down our driveway on a cloud, trading potential names, we also discussed our new future, agreeing that we'd stay in Brooklyn while our kid was young, summer in Two Inlets whenever we could swing it, and move back home for good eventually.

"Maybe we'll move back when he or she goes to school," I speculated, because even the childless had heard stories of the epic hassles involved in finding a home for your kid in the New York public school system.

My career was a little more in doubt, but after Cru I'd turned the lock on the fine-dining brigade. I was at a crossroads. I couldn't see too far past my belly to think ahead, anyway.

Yet our next move virtually cemented our future in the country: We called our neighbor Ron Schultz, Vern's brother, who came over and poured an enormous silver pad of concrete next to our one-room house for a future addition. When it dried, we walked around it eagerly, marveling at its size. It would make our house twice as big as our Brooklyn apartment. Using a two-by-four board like a giant ruler, we plotted out the rooms and marked them in weatherproof construction pencil, moving walls and doorways and going from room to imaginary room until the flow felt natural.

"This second bedroom is huge!" I said, viewing the modest ten-by-fourteen space with eyes accustomed to Brooklyn small-scale. "If we someday have two kids, we can just divide it in half."

"Totally!" Aaron agreed.

"You're sure we don't need an architect?" I frowned, suddenly doubtful that the pencil lines would remain over the harsh winter.

"Nah," Aaron said as he measured out five windows in our bedroom and rubbed their specs onto the cement. "Vern's as good as any architect. In the spring, he'll just follow these lines." (Remarkably, that's just what he did.)

When we finished sketching out the addition, Aaron unfolded two lawn chairs in our future bathroom. After years of trekking out to the outhouse, I'd decided to make it huge, and Aaron insisted on putting three windows around the tub so that we could open them to the summer breeze, out of fondness for the years we showered outside.

"Maybe we'll stay until middle school," Aaron said.

"What are you talking about now?" I replied.

"Maybe we can stay in Brooklyn until our kid reaches middle school. I'm sure the elementary schools are fine, some of them probably better than the one in Park Rapids."

I cocked my head and murmured assent. I was no longer surprised by the guy who sat in the shadow of his new construction and talked about leaving it. He was a hardened dreamer. He really believed that we could go back and forth forever.

This time when we moved back to Brooklyn we avoided the quicker straight-shot, Interstate 80/90, and took the same slow route we'd taken the first time, the high road that snaked through Michigan's

Upper Peninsula, into Canada, then by ferry across Lake Erie to Tober-
mory, and then to New York, leisurely stopping to eat fried perch at
small cafés the whole way.

As we drove the curving ribbon of midnight-blue tar from upstate
New York toward the city, our truck slurping up the yellow middle lines
like someone mindlessly mawing fries, I calmly faced facts: My cooking career as I knew it was probably over. Well aware of what kind of a
cook I was—a complete control fiend—I realized that my conception
of cooking and motherhood were totally incompatible. Other women
chefs did it, and I admired them for it, but I knew I wouldn't want to
work the eighty hours a week, or even fifty, that my brand of cooking
required. I wanted to be present for my baby's first year—at least. I
swallowed a small pill of regret: My perfectionism had done me in. I'd
chosen to keep my head down in fine-dining brigades, at hedonistic
close range, for too long, past the point when I should have been scanning the horizon for opportunities to helm my own kitchen. Before I'd
left New York the last time, I dreamed of doing just that, of finding a
chef job in a small place, maybe somewhere in Brooklyn, where restaurants were sprouting up like mushrooms and were in search of
chefs with résumés like mine. But now I couldn't see it. I couldn't
imagine not being pregnant; my devotion to our baby was instant and
fierce. Indulging myself in a moment of mourning, I conceded that I
might never hold the title *chef* that I'd worked so long to earn.

Back in our Brooklyn apartment, I searched my computer for catering jobs, temporary test-kitchen jobs in food magazines, anything
temporary, with growing despondency. I had worked so long with outrageous, blunt, bawdy restaurant people, in restaurants that pulsed
with electric energy; restaurants were my home. Two weeks later, like
the homing pigeon I am, I beat my familiar footpath to Cru and asked
Shea for a job.

In the Cru office, I informed him of my new condition. He looked
shocked, as if I weren't a woman of childbearing age, and said the first
thing that popped into his head: "You *look* pregnant."

I wished I'd replied "Are you going to throw me a baby shower, Chef?" but I wasn't quick enough. I mumbled, "Thanks," and looked down at my small paunch, hardly visible.

I wanted to cook for the next five months, but I didn't want to work nights. Being that Cru was closed for lunch, I put the pressure on him to take me on as an extra cook—on what the guys and I referred to as "special teams." Remembering my time working on the Danube cookbook, Shea hired me to spend my days in R and D, cataloging the recipes for both the VIP tasting menu and a future cookbook of his own. We met daily in the dining room and he filled my prep list with ideas swirling in his head: a bunch of different pickles, flavored butters, a new sauce for the scallop crudo, methods of cooking vegetables he'd never had the time to try himself. Without the pressure of an impending dinner service, and with my creativity on a long leash, I'd never been happier in the kitchen.

That first week back, my pregnancy shocked the crew, as if I'd crossed some invisible line that changed my species. When I walked in that day, exaggerating my small belly with a slight pregnant waddle, the guys on the line remembered that I was in fact female. The Spanish-speaking porters smiled and all ceremoniously offered to carry my full bus tubs up the stairs. "Oh, mami, mami, please let me do that for you." Their kindness was touching, but as the weeks passed, it proved unsustainable. My trips were just too frequent. They looked over at me with sympathy as I softly trudged my tubs up the stairs, trying not to rest the bottoms on my growing gut.

Setting up my work area on the wide marble-countered wine station, I let my freak flag fly. I cooked dishes that straddled the line of too-caramelized or too-incongruous until one or two toppled over the peak of weirdness into originality. I fried hen-of-the-woods mushrooms in garlicky oil past the point of reason, until they were like mushroom jerky, and then crumbled them over roasted scallops. Shea liked them. "Toss these with torn mint," he said, "and make me a batch for tonight's VIP menu." Emboldened, I ran my workstation like a communal experimental space for the line cooks to swoop by and drop commentary. Walking past, they pinched clumps of dandelion greens that I'd braised and topped with an anchovy Caesar-style dressing, to mixed reaction.

"Cooked dandelion gets way too bitter," Todd commented.

Peter, the meat entremet, agreed. "But it's an addictive bitter. Feels so good when it stops it makes you want more."

They were unanimous about my milk chocolate pine-nut financier, though, lobbing chunks of it into their mouths until the batch was reduced to crumbs.

"Fucking good." Rich looked at me incredulously. "Why didn't you make that when you were in pastry?"

As MY BABY GREW from a normal-size squash into a prizewinning pumpkin, the divide between me and the other line cooks grew, as did their curiosity. At a time when most pregnant women are conspiratorially sharing their baby names with their girlfriends, I was throwing mine by this crew.

"How about Sven for a boy?" I said. "Sven Spangler."

"Sounds like a Norwegian bachelor farmer," said Todd, who was from Minnesota. "Too *Prairie Home Companion.*"

"Vote for Sven. Sven rocks!" Jason called out from the crudo line where he was blowtorching a kombu-wrapped yellowtail loin.

"Okay, what do you guys think of Adeline for a girl?" I said as I poured a curried carrot-juice reduction into a pan of steaming mussels. I wondered, *Should it have both dill and cilantro on the finish, or just dill?* "I like it on a little girl, but when she grows up . . . I mean, is Adeline sexy enough? A twenty-five-year-old Adeline? Or an Addie?"

There was a long pause. "I'd take a twenty-five-year-old Adeline to bed," Jason said, grinning.

"Oh, yeah," the others confirmed. "For sure."

As I ushered the clattering mussel shells into a serving plate, I looked over at Kyle, the one who had guessed my predilection for Heart, the one who had marked our quart of communal sugar with a satanic symbol and the words MORBID SUGAR and who was now labeling a container of braised baby romaine BABY REMAINS. That was one of his darker quips, but nonetheless consistent with his death-metal takeover of our kitchen. "Ky-o," I called. "That's so not funny, man. Do you see what I'm carrying here? You ever cook with a pregnant lady before?"

He swooped his head deferentially toward me. "Can't say that I have, ma'am."

"It's mami, my friend."

"Okay, Mommy," he mocked. "You know what, when you go back to Minnesota you should make a really good version of sloppy joes, and you should call them 'Morbid Joes.' "

"Do you know what some people in northern Minnesota call sloppy joes?" I paused dramatically. "Barbecues. Plural."

A chorus of booing rang out in the kitchen, and Kyle grinned. "That's truly messed up, dude. I've never heard of something so wrong."

I turned away to hide my smile, because there was nowhere I'd rather spend my pregnancy than here, where I could be referred to as both *mommy* and *dude* in the space of a minute.

BY MY SEVENTH MONTH OF PREGNANCY I could not walk. Not because I was so huge, but because after even three blocks of pavement a thick pain settled deep into my left side. My midwife group, the most laissez-faire bunch of birth professionals in the city, dismissed these as harmless Braxton Hicks contractions and alternately told me to take a chill pill, to try to ignore them, or just to walk less. I was already like a frail one-hundred-year-old lady, plotting whether or not I could make it the four blocks from the subway to my intended destination; in New York City it was pretty hard to walk any less.

One day in March I woke up, felt worse than ever, grabbed the phone to call Shea, and told him without preamble, "I'm sorry, I'm done." I hung up and considered our next move. I was due June 1. When I weighed the prospect of staying in New York and spending the first relatively housebound month with a newborn in our apartment above a grease-belching deli, amid the clattering of the metal scrappers and the coffee klatch of methadone users who assembled every morning to gab around the piss tree, versus having our baby at the hospital back home and cuddling with him on our screened porch in the warm summer breeze, there was no contest. Besides, while I waited around for my baby to be born, I could begin diving into old Midwestern recipes. I could drive down the road to the dairy farm for unpasteurized cream and make naturally soured cottage cheese. I could spend his first few nap-filled newborn weeks making pickles and jam.

Within weeks we'd found a subletter to rent our apartment and Aaron's studio and started packing. As usual our seasonal haul was significant. It included, in addition to clothes, all of my kitchen equipment, dry goods, all of my home-canned pickles and jams from last year that we hadn't yet eaten, four boxes of my favorite cookbooks for reference and inspiration, plus the entirety of Aaron's studio, his many chisels, art books, and three half-finished sculptures. One of them, seven feet tall, filled a third of our ten-foot box trailer.

We set out westward, on superhighway 94, and on the second day decided to make a detour to Bloomington, Indiana, to pay a visit to Aaron's sister, Sarah, who had just the day before given birth to baby Irene. His parents, Maurice and Carolyn, were already there. We would surprise them all.

Driving through the mountains of West Virginia during an uncharacteristic cold snap, at seven o'clock in the evening, we hit a patch of ice on a bridge. The heavy trailer we were carrying turned into a pendulous weight, swinging our car in three circles, as if it were the ball at the end of a hammer throw. The last thing I remember seeing before closing my eyes were the lights of the big rigs behind us, boring straight at us. Our trailer flopped over in the ditch, stopping our motion and raising our back end, leaving our tires to spin in the air. On the other side of the road was a deep ravine. The accident made the local nightly news, but miraculously, no one was hurt. Our trailer was totaled, but the contents inside were all salvageable, except for my jars of fermented pickles, which had broken and covered everything with garlicky brine. It was April 5, seven years to the day of Aaron's brother Matt's death. And though I am generally not one to talk about signs or angels, as I stood in our hotel room that night, I leaned into Aaron and choked out sobs. I think we both felt the full weight of our baby's determination to be here. The words flew between us: *We can't raise this kid in New York—we can stay while he's a baby—until he goes to school—but then we have to take him back home, near his grandparents— all of them—I want him to grow up playing in the same lakes, knowing the same Main Street—the same three stoplights.*

When we reached Bloomington, we were thankfully distracted by the new baby. The only hint of our near-miss showed up later in the photos, in the unmistakable gray cast to our skin. Aaron, Sarah, and I stood in a small clump in the kitchen and talked about the accident in fervent whispers that Carolyn, Aaron's mom, wouldn't overhear. We'd been warned over the phone not to bring it up. Aaron's mom, who had lost her son almost exactly seven years to the date that Irene was born, wore a huge camera on her chest and a resolute smile of family expansion on her face. The minute she saw us, pale but intact—all three of us—she struck the accident from her memory and has never mentioned it since.

19

STALKING THE BEAST
CALLED DINNER

IF I HOPED ON MY RETURN TO THE COUNTRY to dive deep into rural Midwestern food, then I've certainly achieved it. Here I am, three weeks away from my due date, full up to the lungs with my little fateful lump, squatting in our front yard, heaving a forty-pound hog's head from a bucket into a pot. I am so far up the ass of rural and local that I can't see the lighted tunnel out.

Vern, our builder, is banging away on our house addition, and I, with the ever-present dull pain in my side now shooting up into my shoulder, am making headcheese. Aaron and his dad, Maurice, are down the hill inside the rock-lined well hole trying to get the water going again, because our sand point has inconveniently decided to stop running. I only hope it hasn't run dry. With the new addition we'd have real modern plumbing, both hot and cold running water, but I've insisted that we hook up the pipes to the same well we'd pounded ourselves a few years earlier. Filtered through about forty feet of pure sand, that water tastes faintly stony. It's the white Bordeaux of water, and I figure there's no point in living in the country if we have to dig a regulation deep well and risk tapping into sulfuric, brackish water. How would I cook with that hard, acidic water? My beans would never soften.

Despite my present discomfort, I can no longer recognize in myself the girl who spent three years here sleeping in the loft until ten thirty and lazily rising up to go pick zucchini for my breakfast scramble. My years of professional cooking have long since ignited my personal motor. I can't bear to sit and be idle, especially when there's asparagus to pick or black currants waiting to be stripped from their stems. I am a fussbudget. A tinkerer. A woman who not only uncannily resembles her mother but also pads around the perimeter of the kitchen like her, calmly stalking the beast called dinner. Some people might identify the humming I felt in my hands as "nesting." Whatever it's called, my instinctive reaction to my son's impending birth is to stockpile food. Big meaty piles of it.

My current concern is that I don't have a bigger stockpot. As the water around the pig's head comes to a boil, I am distressed to see the snout still poking out above the pot's rim, blowing bubbles at me through its nostrils. I cannot contaminate cooked meat with raw meat. I grab the handles, slide a protective towel over my enormous belly, and jerk the pot outside, where I conveniently spot the thing I need lying in the grass—Aaron's Sawzall. Using two forks like corn handles, I hump the pig's head into a clean roasting pan, grab the Sawzall, buzz through the soft fat and then the hard palate, the reverberations of which I can feel deep in my belly, and cut off the snout. *Damn, I sheared off the tip of the tongue.* But what's done is done. The head returned to the pot and the pot to the stove once more, hot water seethes over the sawed-off nose, to my great relief.

WHEN MY COUSIN MATT ARRIVED early that morning at our neighbor's farm to kill the pig and take it back to the family meat market in Pierz for butchering, he stood in front of the hanging animal and asked me to repeat my requests.

"You sure you want the feet?" he asked, giving my belly a side-long glance.

"Yep, and the liver and the kidneys," I assured him, holding out a clean bucket for transporting them.

He shook his head. His lifelong tenure cutting up farm animals had killed his romance for offal. "You are not going to want to eat the feet. They're going to taste like they've spent their lives marinating in pig shit—because they have."

"I want them!" I insisted. "And I want to make headcheese, so let's leave the head whole."

We both remembered the sturdy headcheese Grandma Dion used to make for Christmas Eve supper. She'd cut hers into neat cubes of translucent aspic, arranged them in two obedient lines on a flowered platter, and served them with a sidecar cruet of white vinegar. The cubes quaked whenever we awkward teenagers knocked our knees against the table. Matt and I shuddered at it while his dad, Uncle Keith, taunted us: Smacking his lips, he reached for more, lewdly consuming cube after gelatinous cube.

I was armed with visions of fancier headcheeses I'd eaten in New York. French tête de porc en gelée. Italian formaggio di testa. Served at room temperature, the testa was a mosaic of bits tugged from the pig's most intimate, cranial spaces, and it was marvelous—more luscious than Grandma's. Mine, I thought, would be on the soft side but still rustic, something like the delicious offspring of Italian testa and Midwestern souse. And while the head simmered, I'd poach the feet, debone them, roll them into roulades like we'd done at Danube, slice and sauté these sticky pucks in a hot pan until the edges browned, and then set them on a pile of steely, mustardy French lentils. I'd julienne the ears and fry them until they were the color of tobacco and as crisp as onion rings and serve those over sweet garden greens.

I frowned at the gray brew of meat in the pot. It didn't look right. Having watched Todd the meat cook make testa in the subterranean

Cru kitchen, I knew I should have cured the head for two days in a plastic bucket of fragrant brine. Two days' cure was the usual—as cooks say—"ride" for headcheese. I had no time for protocols, though. I brined it for three hours.

When the pig's jaw loosened from its carriage, I pulled out all the tender pieces. My hands ran through the pile, feeling out good bits of meat instinctively, blindly, tasting as I went. There were obvious gems—nuggets of dark tender meat at the apples of the cheeks, another nice pocket above the brow, the squidgy-soft tongue, and a triangle-shaped disk of sweet meat along the jowl. Like the middle streak of bacon that's not quite fat and not quite lean, the jowl trembled with its marbling. I threw it intact into the pile. But then there were the hidden parts, the surprises awarded to those who pick from bones: a strip of tender meat hanging in the nape, a pleasing bounciness to the gelatinous snout, a sweet melting quality to the white fat. When I was done, the pile of what I considered usable outweighed my scraps and bones—as it should, I thought. I had watched this poor hog go down this morning; I couldn't bear to waste an inch of it. Showering the contents of my bowl with finely minced garlic, thyme from the herb bed, and tons of chopped parsley, strewn like grass clippings, I delicately packed the headcheese into molds.

I then threw the pig's feet—petunia pink and covered with bristly white hair—into a fresh pot of water and the furred ears into another. When they came to a simmer, a great fog rose toward the rafters into our bedroom above the kitchen, filling every cavity in my head with pigsty earthiness. I realized that I'd failed to take into account the super-nose of pregnancy. Matt was right; the feet reeked. I'd have to blanch them at least three times.

Aaron came into the kitchen looking as if he'd just come back from the mines, in a downpour, through a pack of pawing dogs.

"The pump's not drawing," he said, walking across my kitchen floor in his muddy boots to pour a glass of water from the plastic five-gallon jug.

"Sand point's clogged. It's probably just calcium." Aaron drank the entire pint of water in a single laborious swallow. Gulping for air, he said, "We rented an old well-puller at R and R Rental and now we're dragging the pipe lengths up with a lever. Fucking brutal. We're doing nineteenth-century work here." His dad followed him, eyes wide to the floor, his shirt dirt-streaked, and finished matter-of-factly, "And then when we get all the pipe pulled up, we're going to repound another sand point."

"Today?" I asked. They looked spent.

"Definitely." Maurice laughed. "We will not be returning to this job tomorrow."

The lack of a water source was making this entire pioneer day a lot more historically accurate.

"That smell is vicious!" Aaron gasped, following the sight of the fumes billowing up into our bedroom. He shot me an incredulous look, pivoted around me to the stove where the feet and ears were simmering, stacked the ear-blanching pot on top of the foot-blanching pot, and promptly took the stinking mess outside. A few moments later I heard it softly flop at the edge of the woods.

Half of my butchering-day projects were in those pots, but I didn't say a word. I toddled across the kitchen to my new rocker and sat down heavily. I felt as bulbous and full of juice as a ripe melon. Never in my career as a cook had I been squeamish. I had dealt with my fair share of dead soft-shell crabs and rotten wild mushrooms, had ingested scraps of raw lamb to find out whether or not it was too old to serve. (It was.) I had been caught in a walk-in refrigerator with a tub of steaming tripe whose pastoral pestilence overtook all the good air. I was not afraid of barnyard.

Previously, all my intimate meat moments had taken place in a Manhattan basement kitchen, divorced from the source. This was different. Having seen the pig's blinking eyes in the morning, and still looking at its empty stare seven hours later, I was as close now to real ingredients as I'd ever get. And at such close range the view was a little grisly. But the urgencies were also more natural. My ingredients in Two Inlets would not necessarily arrive in my kitchen in boxes, according to my timeline. The beans I planted in my garden would ripen when they felt like it, and when two bushels of apples, or a pig's head, arrived in my kitchen, it would be my duty to cook them, no matter how busy I was on that given day. Or how pregnant. For better or worse, I was hooked to the seasons.

I fell deeper into the rocker. I knew that I'd finally earned the use of my personal talon—the paring knife that had been like an extension of my mom's hand. And I'd finally gained the family motion, that smooth, vehicular way of moving around a pot. But I had to admit, simmering a pig's head in my awkward physical condition was a day's labor enough for this old girl.

Aaron came trudging through the door, even sweatier than before, his face blown wide with relief.

"We got it going," he said, panting and leaning on the doorframe.

"Really?" I scooped myself up and followed him down the hill to the pump.

I was so excited to taste our rock-chilled water again that I joked, "The joy I feel at this moment is going to eclipse this kid's birth!" and then immediately felt a sharp pang of guilt in my side, because of course that wasn't true.

OUR SON'S BIRTH WAS PERILOUS to say the least.

When I woke up in intensive care, a kind priest with a deep Irish brogue was sitting next to me, his thick white hair glinting in the sunny room. A succession of young nurses with different-colored ponytails had been taking care of me for the past day or however long it had been, gently rolling me this way and that way, changing my bedding, and as they moved my concrete legs I imagined that this was what it felt like to be a baby undergoing a diaper change. I couldn't open my eyes and I didn't know how long I'd been out, but Aaron was feeding our boy, holding him, I knew that. He had probably already given him his name: Hank.

My mother was sitting on the other side of my bed, her wide eyelids at half-mast, her hands clasped. Even in my haze I knew that she was the one who summoned the priest and that his presence at my bedside could mean only one thing: last rites. I was going to die.

"Relax!" My mom shushed me and petted my hand. "You're going to be okay. I found Father in the hallway. He's just going to say the Prayer of the Mothers." As he canted the words, the Catholic rhythm of my childhood came back like a familiar pop song.

Turns out that the easygoing midwives had it all wrong and my side pains indicated that I had a rare pregnancy-related blood disorder, with a touch of liver failure on the side—on my left side, to be specific—called HELLP for short. Their neglect was strangely fortuitous, because the lack of a diagnosis allowed me to ripen Hank up all the way. I was shaken and yellow for a few days, but our baby was perfect, and Aaron was indeed holding him. And that was all that mattered.

A WEEK LATER, when we came home from the hospital, Vern had finished the addition and taken down the partition that divided the old house from the new. The electricity we'd hooked up the previous year now flowed throughout the entire house, powering lights left and right. And water was running, in my kitchen, out of the faucet, like a miracle. Nonchalantly, as if it had always done so.

Hank, my new appendage, was wide-eyed, with a flirtatious smile and a near-constant sigh. Sometimes his sighs sounded like contentment and other times just as if he felt the need to put some sound on the passing moment, to make us aware that he was taking up new space in the world. I woke up every day with the sinking feeling that I had only dreamed his sweet skin, that he didn't really exist after all. I was so relieved when his cries turned out to be real.

After going through our morning routine, I laid the fragile, sleeping Hank in the bassinet for his nap and went to the fridge to find the block of headcheese. The hunger I'd lost in the events of the previous week had returned with a vengeance. The chunks of pork in golden gelatin looked like fossils floating in amber, caught in time. When I tried to carve a thin refined slice, the cake crumbled like a bunch of stacked stones. So I cut a thick slice—a proper Grandma-size hunk—set it on hot toast made from plain supermarket-white, and tasted it. Sadly, it was nowhere near as good as the Italian testa. My aspic was the right strength, but I'd thrown in too much fat. The meat tasted vaguely swinish, and yet curiously still bland. I should not have short-shifted the brining. That two-day salt cure was not optional. I opened my pine cabinet, found the white wine vinegar, plugged the top with my thumb, and sprinkled droplets over the headcheese.

Just like my mother's butter, the salty golden pork juice seeped all the way to the bread's bottom edge. It wasn't perfect. But it was close. Not by degrees, but literally—like a local who'd never left, it was born, raised, and ceremoniously consumed within ten miles of home.

THAT FALL, STICKING TO THE PLAN, we moved back to Brooklyn with Hank. Aaron got to work on finishing the sculptures for his second solo show at his Chelsea gallery.

Brooklyn, with Hank at my side, felt almost unrecognizable. I took Hank with me everywhere, to the large suburban supermarket in Red Hook, to the nearby playground where he clung to the monkey bars like jailbait and shook his diapered booty, to the coffee shop where I checked my empty email in-box. There was not a minute of taking care of him that I begrudged him the brief derailment of my working career. Well before he could speak, his expression conveyed perfect comic timing, and his eyes glimmered with unspoken punch lines to my doofy jokes; he was that delightful of a companion.

But having an infant in New York shows you how inhospitable this city, with its many stairways and rarely working elevators, can feel to the infirm, the elderly, and to those who tote the very young. When I wasn't picking up his stroller like an oversize package and scaling the subway stairs, Hank and I were spending an inordinate amount of time inside our four walls. Staying in, eating in, napping in, playing together on a six-foot-by-six-foot square of rug in our windowless living room. Hank's world in this huge city, I worried, was so interior and so small. It would have been fine if we'd had a nicer place, but when you have to turn on the oven and let the door hang open so the baby doesn't freeze because your landlord insists on turning off the heat during the day, baby's first year in Brooklyn is not so hot. Thankfully, Hank's range of vision was so narrow he never knew it.

In May, after throwing Hank a blow-out first birthday party on our roof deck, we packed up our stuff to return to Park Rapids for the three months of summer, where he could practice taking his first steps in bare feet, on the grass.

20

PRIMARY SOURCES

BACK IN TWO INLETS FOR THE SUMMER OF 2008, Aaron jump-starts his mornings in country fashion, by immediately going outside and hopping onto the tractor to mow the trails, not returning until his eggs have grown ice-cold on the table. He's like Pa from *Little House on the Prairie* (book Pa, not the TV one who's detained indefinitely in Walnut Grove), giddy with outdoorsy possibility. After a full day of making sculptures in his studio, he gets out his chain saw in the evening and cuts down surplus trees—of which we have many—reductively carving out the landscape as if it were a chunk of wood, making more and more of the hillside visible. As scrabbly jack pines thud to the ground and wiry brush meets its maker, he reveals a new yard stuck with multiple bunches of birch clumps. They are a single organism, connected to one another via a mushroomlike network of root mycelium, and seem to hold down the hill. With our new view we can see that the creek doesn't just flow in front of the house but surrounds us on three sides.

From my kitchen, I can hear swans on the creek exchanging hot, guttural words; an annoyed blue heron thunders out for silence from his dock perch. The sun streams through the leaf bunches of the trees and hits the ground in round spotlights that dance with the surging wind, which can't decide its mood today. Despite my amused baby, who's enthralled by everything at his feet from grass to rugs, a garden that's ripening as fast as an oncoming train, and my flowers spilling rambunctiously over their rock barriers, neither can I. Aaron might resemble Pa, but I am not as relentlessly cheerful as Ma—not by half. I am, in fact, a very conflicted homesteader, far less resolute than the girl who pounded a sand point well here just eight years before. Divorced from the world of haute cuisine, but still infatuated with its visuals and high standards, my future in food flickers in the air with uncertainty.

I'm no longer a professional cook, and yet not quite a civilian. My tastes have changed. I've become accustomed to braising chicken with the wrinkled black olives I couldn't hope to ever find here. I've grown a taste for other rarities: bitter endive, raw ocean fish, and ricotta salata. I'm used to shuffling six pots to make a meal—a protein, a starch, a vegetable, a sauce. After years of layering bold, exotic flavors, I've grown insatiable for them. Now I was back to where I'd started, with a basket of zucchini, some dirt-stained potatoes, and a simple plan to make a decent plate of supper. I wonder if and when the convergence of my two worlds—high and low, the clouds and the dirt—will ever take place.

As always, my current mood hinges on the success or failure of my most recent kitchen project. My first stab at making sauerkraut came out smelling like sour wine mixed with barn bedding, like ten full pounds of failure. Hopelessly overfermented. I chucked the entire crock over the compost fence, the slimy strands landing with a resounding slap.

It was the shortest of all recipes, just two ingredients—cabbage and salt—and shouldn't have been that hard. But I'd failed to consider the third ingredient—time, the wild card of all ingredients, the one that requires the real skill.

I dial Grandma Dion for a dose of her blunt, firsthand knowledge but don't reach her. So I call Katie, my neighbor down the road—first for commiseration and second to beg for advice.

She laughs, because preserving failures are like colorful foreign currency around here, more valuable than the silent successes. "You made some cabbage wine, did you?"

"More like cabbage schnapps," I tell her. The odor had been closer to fifty-proof. She tells me to use a cabbage so fresh that water runs like juice out of its cut sides and to check it sooner, after ten days. I cut a fresh cabbage from my garden and this time decide to go for broke: I mix chilies and hot paprika into the cabbage, until it glows orange like kimchi. After shredding and salting and packing, my kitchen floor is covered with hair-thin debris like a cabbage barbershop. I tie a string around the dishtowel covering the crock and vow to coddle it.

Ten days later, I nervously check the kraut. Carefully unwrapping the towel, I pull back the whole leaves lying on top and dip in my fork. It looks right: light and springy, like hay. It tastes right: fizzy, adamant, alive. Not low-down and mushroomy like sake, but as clean and tingly as bone-dry sauvignon blanc.

The chilies make it racy. Just like the fermented pickles I remember from childhood, where the tartness shot straight to my spine and plucked my nerves like guitar strings, where it played me. I remember my mom watching me clink my fork around the cloudy brine in the jar of fermented pickles and, not finding any, tip up the jar for a shot of fizzy juice instead. The acidity shook through my body like a seizure, and when I came up for air she laughed and gave me a knowing smile. Good? The taste fairy had chosen rightly. I was no sweet tooth.

I decide to put a little sauerkraut on Hank's high chair tray to see which of these fairies—sweet or sour—has captured his soul. He wraps a yellow strand around his fat fist and backhands it into his mouth. Then another strand. And another. He gums the spicy kraut, enlisting his few teeth to chew. And then his face flushes and his small body shivers—three small familiar zaps that look like the ignition of a small car twitching to life. Could it be his first spark of fermentation love?

But no, maybe not. He's reaching for it, but he's starting to cry. His mouth is burning. I pick him up but can't hold on to his fitful body. *What was I thinking, giving my baby something spicy?* He twists his torso out of my pretzeled arms, flinging himself into full backbend, his arms trying to reach the tray, the tears on his face now flowing upriver instead of down.

"Moah!" he screams.

He wants more. It's genetic. He's what my mom refers to as "one of ours." A sour tooth.

MY SAUERKRAUT WASN'T JUST SLOW FOOD—though it was—it was stubbornly territorial. If I preserve it in a water bath, I'll kill all its living juices. I can't take it back with us to Brooklyn.

I catalog the few jars in the pantry that will survive the trip back east. Roma tomatoes canned in their thickened juice. Homemade harissa from my sweet, fleshy Alma paprika peppers. Spicy green schug, packed with herbs and hot green chilies. Smooth black currant jam that tastes like grape, but muskier and more interesting.

I look at all the things in my freezer that I'll have to leave here: chive oil, frozen shell beans, smoked eggplant. My eyes canvass the stuff I've made that won't last the week: the pot of cream sitting on my counter solidifying into the pudding of crème fraîche, the homemade cheese in my fridge that I mash and mix with heavy cream for Hank's first cottage cheese. I dip my spoon into the cheese, pull out a divot, and mix it with the harissa: delicious. I pull out another divot and mix it with some black currant jam: another world of good. I spread a heel of bread with jam, then another with cheese, then spicy green schug, and the flavors swirl up and around my head, and I experience the familiar flavor wheel of cooking on the line on a busy night, the endless parade of strong tastes and bright colors.

And finally I know. The dream I have for my cooking life doesn't live and die in the professional kitchen. My affliction belongs here. It lives in both my successes and my mistakes. In the batches of overfermented sauerkraut I've tossed over the fence. The black currant jam that tastes like a feral grape. The thin skins of freshly dug potatoes that pop at the bite. The ripe face of a cut tomato gushing all over my morning toast. All my years of nearsighted devotion to tiny plates culminate in this moment: This is as close range as my cooking bug can get. It was so near to me that I couldn't see that I was standing on top of it. The best food is fleeting, and unlike Aaron and me, it tolerates no wanderlust. Its flavors don't travel.

"HAVE YOU ENROLLED HANK IN PRE-K YET?" my friends in Brooklyn email me to ask.

"No. God. Already?"

When I hesitate to enroll my crawling toddler on a waiting list for his school career, they call it. They've seen it happen before.

"You're not coming back."

I insist to the contrary. When the first frost arrives to kill the tomatoes, the old familiar feeling of seasonal migration returns. As I tug the chilled red tomatoes from the vines to make one final batch of tomato sauce, summer feels over. It's time to go back to New York, our city, to our friends and our work. But when I walk into Aaron's studio to check on his packing progress, I'm doubtful. The nine-foot-tall anchor piece he's making for his winter show in Berlin—an intricately carved wooden sculpture that weighs an actual ton—is really amazing, maybe the best thing he's ever made, and obviously unfinished.

"Are we . . . taking that back?" I ask, vowing then and there not to let myself and Hank ride in the truck that will be pulling that behemoth.

"Actually, I think it's too big." He sighs.

"For the trailer?"

"No. For my Brooklyn studio."

"Oh."

And so, just like that, we decide to stay in Two Inlets for the winter.

It will be a lark, I think, a new unexpected move within a lifetime of unexpected moves that have begun to settle into an all-too-predictable pattern. Ironically, now that we have power at the house, our days in the woods have grown more convenient than our life in Brooklyn with a baby, navigating the inconvenient, dense adult playground that is New York.

Then just when the first chilly fall wind arrives to shake all the dry leaves from the trees, the economy dramatically crashes on the news. It appears that it has taken the luxury market down with it. With growing anxiety we assume that no one will be particularly keen to buy a giant, expensive sculpture right now, and that suddenly, we no longer have an income. Our freeing choice to stay at home in Minnesota becomes instead the—unthinkable—most practical thing to do. Our personal economy has always run on hope, though, and for the first time I trust it and classify this situation as temporary. Nevertheless, the familiar feeling of being broke that I've known in the past settles around me like an old worn afghan—dusty but garishly bright.

I knew we'd one day move back home, but I didn't know it would be so soon. The upside is that we have stopped moving. The downside is that for the first time in recent years, I do not have a job and I am not in a place to get one. Aaron works long days and nights in the studio making his best work to date, for which there are no guaranteed sales. He continues to knock away in the studio, the familiar sound of his carving mallet echoing out over the creek, because that is just what he does.

Over the phone, my mom frets, although she's happy that we've expanded and modernized our place. Even with its original gappy floor—"next, you need to replace that"—our house now registers a full two steps above a hovel. But she worries about my stove. "You can't bake in that old oven," she says, and she is not wrong. So she buys us a new one, a really beautiful stove with a hammered brown-coppery finish and five burners, big enough to fit my canning kettles and side projects at the same time. I no longer have to light my oven through the blowhole with a long match as I did with the Roper. Now I have burners that poof alight with a gentle push and a light reassuring *click-click-click*.

Armed with a proper piece of equipment, I can now do what I do. Only when cooking, when I'm standing in front of the stove skimming the gray scum from a cauldron's worth of shaggy beef bones, do I know that we're not lost. As I ladle the hot broth over bowls of Swiss chard, they wilt and float to the surface, and I know we'll be okay. I'll scrub the rough wooden floorboards until they shine, as Ruth did, and call my kitchen a cooking school. *Cooking at Hazelbrush.* I'll invite people to eat, to drink—and everything will come from the garden. They'll sit around my counter on wooden stools and I'll serve them five courses, with wine pairings, each set with clean silver as is done in fine dining. I don't fret over such technicalities as licensing—it's a cooking class, like my own modern-day forest speakeasy. The money I take in will be like egg money, enough to keep us richly fed. I'll fill the deep freezer with local animals and blanched garden vegetables and the cupboards with pickles and jam and canned tomatoes, and if things get really bad, I'll dig deeper into books of peasant cookery; I'll confit the wild ducks on the creek if I have to.

BEFORE WE KNOW IT, winter comes. I'd forgotten about the winter.

The weather Aaron wished for the entire time we lived in New York arrives in full force, and it's a character. Petulant, beautiful, roaring, and blindingly arctic, winter in Minnesota is the most histrionic of seasons. My friends back in New York wonder how we can do it, how we can live in such a dull place. I try to describe to them how the dramatics are high, but words fail to capture it.

For fun, we search the internet for places that we think might be colder than our own—Minsk, Moscow, Thunder Bay, Ketchikan—and then roll with delight when we beat them out by being lower. We are victorious! We realize that our location, about as far away from any temperate body of water as you can get, right in the bottom nipple of the Alberta Clipper, creates the ideal conditions for epic, record-breaking cold. And this first winter back is a bruiser, one that defies normal thermometers. Our smiles fade when we realize that the number on the thermometer appears to be stuck at −40, because as the night goes on our world surely grows colder.

Despite the arctic winds, people in town still walk around with polite, ten-percent grins. They gently ask us what it is that we *do* back there, way out in the woods, with an unsaid *Don't you people have jobs?* fluttering behind them. I'd forgotten about Minnesota-nice, too, but I come to a theory about it: The frigid winter wind supplies all the honesty and directness the local population can stand. It knocks everyone's sharp observations sideways. The weather is meaner than mean, and after a while, there's nothing you can do but greet it with a shallow smile.

On this wind, childhood memories begin to blow in. In the shine beaming off the bluish snow boulders I see another 25-below day, when my friends and I huddled in the basement of Rocky's Pizza around the new Metallica song on the jukebox, the tingling bass like heartbeats in our heads, pounding relentlessly like our own teenage perseverance.

I see myself waiting for the bus with my brothers and the neighborhood kids, standing on a beaten-down pad of glittering snow sugar, wearing thin canvas shoes. The hair nearest to my head is still damp, my bangs are curled into a frothing surf, and the cold finds the moisture burning at my scalp. The air is sharp and crystalline, minty. The winter light comes at us from every direction, refracted in diamond cut every place it lands, until it appears that we are the lone humans standing in a white landscape and all of the world's spotlights are trained right on us, a stiff clump of kids in the middle of nowhere.

The winter light is that bright, so bright there's no safe place to look.

HERE'S THE FUNNY THING about going back to your hometown. You don't just jump into the same old story. You step back into your shadow, but into a totally new narrative. You fold back the new page until it touches the old one, making a twin out of yourself, and then you have to walk around town like that, the old glued to the new. Mostly you forget about it, but then, every once in a while, you feel something flickering behind you, that jelly feeling of your former self.

I couldn't have predicted it, because on the surface it defied common sense, but moving home had been in the cards for me for a long time—my stubborn nostalgia foreshadowed my path back. (And if Grandma Dion had ever dared to read my palm, she might have spotted it.)

My return has isolated the variables of my life in a valuable, almost scientific way. Standing in the same geographical spot, nearly twenty years later, I look at the landscape with new eyes. Only by freezing myself in place, I think, can I take an accurate measure.

It doesn't escape me that only a native Minnesotan would think this.

I walk around town burrowed into my own head, gathering up memories with increasing affection, like it's a pastime. On my way to the coffee shop, I see my dad driving past me at exactly 10:20, on his way to the post office to get the mail for the dealership, and I wave. He spots me through the windshield—in the way that all small-town residents look past the cars to their drivers—and waves back. I'm inflated with fondness and remind myself that when it comes to family relations, mundaneness is everything. The more insignificant the interaction, the better.

I drive down the wide Main Street, making a dramatic flip at the end of it to cruise back, this time not whipping the wheel like I would have in my youth but pulling out a smooth arc like an old-timer on a

Sunday drive, taking it slow, because now I have a small boy in the backseat. And the boy is very hungry.

I never once thought, all the times when I was pregnant and glanced back at my unhatched imaginary kid in the backseat, that I'd ever drive that child through the fast-food drive-through window for a small order of fries, but now, in times of severe need, this is just what I do. I wryly remind myself that we do live, after all, in the fried-potato headquarters of the nation. French fries are a local food.

Through the haze of these thoughts, I make my way to the grocery store. When I pulled out my last bag of frozen smoked eggplant, I saw my freezer's white bottom—the telltale sign of deep winter. My brother Marc must have liked the latest menu I've dropped on his answering machine—fancy meatloaf, more like pâté, shell beans with chive oil, an undetermined vegetable, and smoked eggplant baba ghanoush to start—because he's left me a voicemail. As with everyone in my family, he and I express our affection through the menus. He's coming to dinner tonight.

I unclick the child car seat harness and pull Hank to my hip. The Red Owl my mom frequented gave way more than ten years ago to a larger chain; the biggest local store is now called J&B Foods (so named after its proprietors, Jeff and Bob) and it is by and large my winter larder. Open twenty-four hours and as large as a suburban big-box store, this grocery store has both the interests of the budget-conscious (baked beans by the gallon) and the cooped-up gourmet cook (Medjool dates) in mind. It has an encyclopedic selection of dry goods like powdered milk and masa and pasta, and plenty of meat, but a pretty hit-or-miss produce department. For example, no bitter greens to speak of—although the green beans look like an embittered bunch. I beg the produce manager to stock shiitake mushrooms, promising to buy all of them if he brings them in.

The produce manager assumes I've imported my pickiness from New York City, but little does he know that it was steeped in me locally. I inherited it from my mom, and she from hers.

At the store I settle Hank into the seat of the grocery cart and roll through the aisles: through the produce where I wish they sold basil in a bouquet as they do in Brooklyn—even in the bodegas!—past the carrots and celery in plastic bags. After a summer of growing my own produce, they look like they're suffocating in there. I dart down the middle aisles, weighing pounds against pennies as if I were living out my childhood dream of training for *The Price Is Right*. Out of gourmet habit, I grab panko ($3.99) instead of finer bread crumbs ($1.99) and bars of chocolate ($4.00 each) instead of semisweet chips ($2.43). I swallow thickly, knowing I should be more frugal, but what can I say? I cook with primary sources.

And yet my cart is nearly bereft of them. I've taken a full trip around the store and precious little has caught my fancy. The limits of food snobbery have been located, and they're just as imperceptible as Margaret Sexton's illusory property line. They lie, winking darkly at me, within my own borders. If I want to survive this winter, I'm going to need to get off my high horse and be a lot more resourceful.

I might as well embrace my Midwestern history full-throttle and adopt Grandma Dion's sense of thrift. I remember the note she scrawled on the recipe card for caramel nut bars—*very good, but expensive*—and see that she's right: whole walnuts are going for $14.99 a pound. I grab the cheaper walnut pieces at $2.99 a bag.

Steering in a wide circle back to the celery, I pick it up. Under the printed plastic, the lime-green stalks glow faintly, like vegetables in the garden do by twilight, cast into darkness but alive. I remember that time in the Cru kitchen when a line cook whined that he couldn't make a vegetable for the family meal because all we had was celery and then had to stand by and watch Omae, the veteran Japanese fish cook, julienne the stalks and toss them with a brilliant, addictive, garlicky sesame dressing. That line cook was now me. I could remember that dressing. I could make that tomorrow. My current deprivation is a gift not to be wasted. I throw the bag onto the cart lattice.

At the meat cooler, I lean in and consider a chuck roast, sitting next to the bulkhead display of shiny, plastic-wrapped red ground beef tiles. I plan to cut the chuck roast into cubes and grind it at home—my meatloaf will be so much lighter with the freshly ground. I'll cover it with an overlapping weave of blanched cabbage leaves. I throw this idea by Hank, who replies with a languorous yawn, and then I think to myself: This is crazy. It's more expensive, takes more time, and this day is already running out. *Jesus Christ, just buy the preground.*

As I drop the square red package in my cart, I can almost hear a crack of lightning sounding in the meat aisle as I am promptly returned back to earth. I have reentered the atmosphere of home cooking.

But I am shocked back into childhood at the exit: the tremulous sound that my full grocery cart makes as I push it across the hard, molded-ice-ribbed parking lot to my car strikes me as powerfully familiar. What strength it took for my mother to propel this thing across the same corduroy ice road! It's like pushing a grocery cart across the surface of Pluto. I look at Hank and he's giving me one of those bottomless baby smiles that seep up from the deep. Sitting in the cart hopper in the burning cold air, his tiny face exposed, he starts to sing. The faster I push my cart, the louder he sings and the harder he laughs, his cheeks high and flaming pink in the icy wind. He opens his mouth wide and allows the corrugated bumps to drag out a low washboard melody, thrilled with our new landscape, our new chores, our new life.

AUTHOR'S NOTE

THIS BOOK IS MEMOIR, meaning that the facts and events stand on the old creaky chair legs of memory. In fact, I'd say that writing this book involved a careful readjustment of every false assumption I held about my own history.

Piecing together my past, especially after Mr. Wanderlust pulled up in his 1973 Buick hardtop, was a job for a historian more skilled than I—and I can't even use old age as an excuse. Aaron and I moved often enough in our early years to make an editor's head spin. Going back to my journals, I discovered that the year 1997 alone seemed to contain eight seasons rather than four, each with its own adventures, some of which—including the time I almost started a restaurant with a hippie couple from Park Rapids—were cut because they clogged up the greater narrative flow.

I compressed a couple of summer gardening seasons into one, mostly out of concern for the reader's patience for consecutive dim nights of non-electric living. I changed a few names out of respect for individuals' privacy. I reconstructed dialogue, but only when I remembered complete phrases with total clarity and when the entire full-bloom conversation felt true to its real-life characters.

Those creative licenses aside, this account of my life is as true as I remember it—which is to say, a lot more loyal to time and fact than my old prememoir memory would have had it.

ACKNOWLEDGMENTS

Endless gratitude goes to Janis Donnaud, the fiercest, warmest, and most diligent agent around, for envisioning this book before I did, and for caring enough about it—and me—to push-prod it onward.

Thanks to Peter Gethers, whose sharp mind helped me wrangle my life story into a tangible shape, and whose optimism gave me courage.

Thanks to Chelsey Johnson, my first best friend, who has read my stories since the third grade and read this one tirelessly, with great care, thoughout its many versions . . . I'm grateful for her writing mentorship and thank her for her consistently fine cheerleading. (Go, PR.)

Enormous thanks to my editor, Rica Allannic, for her astute observations, shrewd sentence-whipping, and generous extensions. Special thanks to everyone at Clarkson Potter for their continued faith in this book, especially Doris Cooper, Erica Gelbard, Stephanie Huntwork, Phillip Leung, Christine Tanigawa, Jennifer Wang, and Stephanie Davis.

Thanks to Sara Woster, Mimi Lipson, Julie Caniglia, and Eric Thomason for reading early drafts.

Thanks to Bruce Brummitt and Cheryl Valois for letting me write in their idyllic forest hut, where I could pump water by hand again.

Thanks to my family: to my mom, Karen, for forever standing at the stove and telling me the stories, and then later lending me her vacated house in which to write them down; to my dad, Ted, and his wife, Mary, for their never-ending support; to my brothers, for agreeing to be in this book and for trusting me with our shared history; to the Spanglers, for giving me a second home.

Many thanks to Aaron, the hardened dreamer with the soft heart and the liquid voice, for building us a life, and for keeping the fires going.

Finally, thanks to Hank for teaching me that one's appetite can be insatiable and picky at the same time . . . if I could bronze your discerning little palate along with your baby shoes, I would.

INDEX